Danube Bike Trail

From Passau to Vienna

An original *cycline* guide

Esterbauer

cycline® Danube bike Trail

A-3751 Rodingersdorf, Hauptstr. 31
Tel.: ++43/2983/28982-0, Fax: -500
E-Mail: cycline@esterbauer.com
www.esterbauer.com
1st edition 2003

ISBN 3-85000-160-1

Please quote edition and ISBN number in all correspondence.

We wish to thank all the people who contributed to the production of this book.
The *cycline*-Team: Birgit Albrecht, Beatrix Bauer, Grischa Begaß, Karin Brunner, Anita Daffert, Michaela Derferd, Roland Esterbauer, Jutta Gröschel, Dagmar Güldenpfennig, Carmen Hager, Karl Heinzel, Martina Kreindl, Veronika Loidolt, Michael Manowarda, Mirijana Nakic, Maria Pfaunz, Jutta A. Ott, Petra Riss, Tobias Sauer, Gaby Sipöcz, Matthias Thal.
Translated from German by Otto Mayr.
Photo credits: Marktgemeindeamt Ottensheim: 28; Archiv: 38, 70, 84, 92, 96, 97, 99,100, 102, 103, 106, 120, 124, 134, 136, 142; Donauregion: 42, 58; Brigitte Dieplinger: 58; Fremdenverkehrsverein Mitterkirchen: 60; Donaukraft: 62; Klemens Fellner: 64; Niederösterreich Werbung, Simoner: 68; Tourismusverband Enns: 76; Gemeinde Wallsee: 82; Fremdenverkehrsamt Pöchlarn, Alfred Pech: 88; Marktgemeinde Schönbühel-Aggsbach: 95, 117; WTV, Gredler-Oxenbauer: 138; Österreich Werbung, Bohnacker: 140.

What is cycline?

We're a young team of active cyclists who started making cycling maps and books in 1987. Today we're a highly successful publisher and have published both bikeline® and cycline® books in four languages in many European countries.

We need your help to keep our books up-to-date. Please write to us if you find errors or changes. We would also be grateful for experiences and impressions from your own cycling tours.
We look forward to your letters.

Your cycline team

Preface

The Danube bicycle route between Passau and Vienna ranks as Europe's best-known and most-loved bike route – and for good reason. No other section of the river offers as diverse a range of landscapes and cultures or as many historical sites. Tranquil valleys, fertile plains, and steep vineyards line the banks of one of Europe's great rivers, where pretty farms and glorious abbeys stand side-by-side. The loop of the Danube at Schlögen, the abbey at Melk, and the romantic Wachau wine-producing area are just some of the highlights along the 350 kilometer route.

This bicycle touring atlas includes detailed maps of the countryside and of many cities and towns, precise route descriptions, information about historic and cultural sites as well as background information and a comprehensive list of overnight accommodations. The one thing this atlas cannot provide is fine cycling weather, but we hope you encounter nothing but sunshine and gentle tailwinds.

Map legend

(The following colour coding is used:

- main cycle route
- cycle path / main cycle route without motor traffic
- excursion or alternative route
- planned cycle path

The surface is indicated by broken lines:

- paved road
- unpaved road

Routes with vehicular traffic are indicated by dotted lines:

- cycle route with moderate motor traffic
- cycle route with heavy motor traffic
- cycle lane
- road with heavy motor traffic

- steep gradient, uphill
- light gradient
- 3 distance in km
- cycle route direction

Scale 1 : 50.000

1 cm ≙ 500 m   1 km ≙ 2 cm

0 1 2 3 4 5 6 7 8 9 10 km

- Schönern picturesque town
- ( ) facilities available
- hotel, guesthouse; youth hostel
- camping site; simple tent site
- tourist information; shopping facilities
- restaurant; resting place
- outdoor swimming pool; indoor swimming pool
- buildings of interest
- Mill other place of interest
- museum; theatre; excavation
- zoo; nature reserve
- panoramic view
- parking lot; garage
- boat landing; ferry
- bike workshop; bike rental
- covered ~; lockable bike stands

- church; chapel; monastery
- castle; ruins
- tower; TV/radio tower
- power station; transformer
- windmill; windturbine
- wayside cross; peak
- mine
- monument
- sports field
- airport, airfield
- natural spring; waste water treatment plant

- dangerous section; read text carefully
- stairs; narrow pass, bottleneck
- X X X road closed to cyclists

in city maps:

- post office; pharmacy
- fire-brigade; hospital

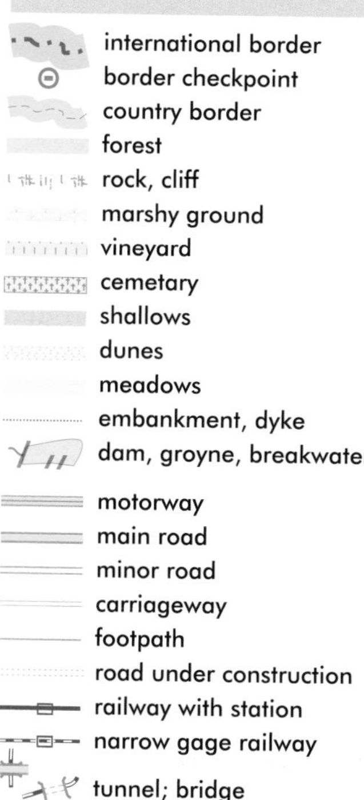
international border
border checkpoint
country border
forest
rock, cliff
marshy ground
vineyard
cemetary
shallows
dunes
meadows
embankment, dyke
dam, groyne, breakwater
motorway
main road
minor road
carriageway
footpath
road under construction
railway with station
narrow gage railway
tunnel; bridge

Contents

Danube Bike Trail

In the last ten years the Danube bike Route has emerged as Europe's most important long-distance bicycle touring route. Its popularity is due primarily to the Danube's natural beauty and the wealth of cultural and historical sites that line its banks. But the large numbers of bicycle tourists visiting the Danube would not be possible without a well-developed infrastructure and services. The Danube bike route has benefited from well-built posted bike trails and an extensive network of services oriented to meeting the needs of bicycle tourists. The following pages provide a few practical notes about how to use the book, and some tips on getting ready for the tour.

The Route

Length

The total distance from the start in Passau to the final destination, Vienna, is 350 kilometers. This figure does not include possible side-trips and alternative routes.

Surface quality and traffic

The Danube bicycle route is very comfortable to ride. Virtually the entire distance follows paved bicycle trails or lightly traveled public roads. For most of the distance, a bicycle route is present on both sides of the river.

Signage

The Danube Bicycle Route is thoroughly posted with signs that show the way. However, it does occasionally happen that signs are missing or turned in the wrong direction. In Austria, rectangular green signs are posted along the route and in most places the route is clearly named the "Donau-Radweg." Other regional bicycle trails branch off from the main route. Excursions and alternative routes often follow their own signs, and are also described in this book.

Planning a tour

The descriptions of the 350-kilometer tour follow the river downstream, from west to east. This allows cyclists to take advantage of the prevailing winds and the river's downward slope (minimal though it may be).

The Danube usually has bicycle trails on both sides of the river. All of these trails are marked as parts of the Danube bicycle route. This book describes the routes on both sides of the river: the route on the northern, or left, bank is described first, followed by the route on the southern, or right bank. The entire tour is divided into three sections: Passau to Linz, Linz to Melk, and Melk to Vienna.

The two sides of the river are identified as the left and the right sides, as seen when looking downstream. Unlike other major rivers, the Danube's kilometers, however, are counted from its mouth in the Black Sea. To simplify orientation, towns and cities are given with their kilometer number on the Danube (ex. Passau ≈km **2226** or Vienna ≈km **1929**) and the side of the river they occupy (**L** or **R**). The Danube's kilometers are also shown in the maps (|1925).

The division of the tour into six sections is intended to aid tourists' general orientation and does not necessarily suggest one-day stages. If you intend to include museum visits and swimming pauses along the way, we recommend planning at least a week for the entire distance. The book also includes descriptions of short side-trips which offer riders opportunities to expand the ride according to their desires.

If the tour turns out to take longer than expected, there are along the first stage taxi companies that will transport bicycles if the need arises. The telephone numbers of these companies are listed in the information about individual towns. Rail lines also run along much of the Danube, giving riders the option of boarding a train to complete a stretch.

Information

Additional information is available from regional tourism offices:

Oberösterreich (Upper Austria) Touristik GmbH, 4040 Linz, ✆ 0732/6630240, Fax: 0732/663025

Email: info@touristik.at, www.touristik.at

Tourismuswerbegemeinschaft (Tourism promotion association) Oberes Donautal (upper Danube valley), Engelhartszell, ✆ 07717/805511

Landesverband für Tourismus in Oberösterreich (Upper Austria state tourism association), 4020 Linz, ✆ 0732/600221242

Werbegemeinschaft (marketing association) Donau Oberösterreich, Hopfeng. 3, 4020 Linz

✆ 0732/772545, Fax: 0732/7725454

Email: info.donau@netwav.at

www.tiscover.com/donau.ooe

Mühlviertel tourism region, A-4020 Linz, ✆ 0732/735020

Werbegemeinschaft Donauland-Strudengau, Grein, ✆ 07268/7290

Tourism association Tullner Donauraum, Tulln, ✆ 02272/65836

Lower Austria Information, Heidenschuss 2, 1014 Vienna, ✆ 01/536106200

Tourist Information Vienna, Obere Augartenstr. 40, 1020 Vienna, ✆ 01/211140

International telephone codes:

Germany 0049

Austria 0043

Arrival & departure

By rail:

Information:

Österreichische Bundesbahnen (Austrian Rail): ✆ 01/51717

Bicycle Hotline Germany:

✆ 01805/151415 (Open: March-Nov, Mon-Fri 8-18, Sat 8-12), www.bahn.de

Schedules and fares: ✆ 01815/996633

The main train stations in Passau and Vienna offer good connections to many European destinations. Trains also run along the Danube between Linz and Melk as well as between Tulln and Vienna. Trains from Passau to Linz do not travel along the Danube valley, and therefore do not provide alternative transportation for bicyclists along this stretch of the river.

Bike and ride

Public bicycle parking facilities at all important transport hubs, especially U-bahn (subway) stations, have capacity for about 14,000 bicycles, and make it easy to transfer to public transportation. There is no charge for parking a bicycle at these facilities, though bicycles should be securely locked to deter thieves.

Bicycle transport

Bicycles on trains/as baggage: Hermes Versand (shipping) will deliver a bicycle door to door. The charge is € 23.50 for the first bicycle, and € 18.40 for each additional bicycle. Delivery takes two workdays. Opening times for delivery or pickup are Mon-Fri 9-17. The Kurier-Gepäck-Ticket (courier-baggage ticket) can be purchased directly with your BahnCard or through Hermes Versand, ✆ 01805/4884.

Note that this service is only for door to door. The service will not hold a bicycle at a train station for pickup by the customer. If you wish to name a train station as the delivery address, you must be present to receive delivery of the bicycle.

Furthermore, when shipping a bicycle it must be completely packed. Shipping pouches can be borrowed or purchased from the Bahn AG (German rail). Further information is available from Mon-Fri at ✆ 01805/4884.

To ship a bicycle by rail in Austria, one delivers the bicycle to the train station and picks the bicycle up from the destination train station 24 hours later. The fee is € 6.54. If you have a valid Umweltticket (rail pass) or Fahrradmitnahmekarte (bicycle pass), the fee is reduced by half.

Shipping a bicycle across national borders costs € 8.18 or € 10.17.

Rail passengers in Austria and Germany may bring bicycles on board only those trains that are marked with the 🚲 symbol in the train schedule, and only if they have a valid bicycle ticket and there is sufficient space on the train. It is therefore a good idea to reserve a place in advance. The price for all distances in Germany is € 6.00, or € 3.00 for regional trains and distances up to 100 kilometers. Bicycle ticket prices on Austrian trains are as follow:

One-day bike ticket:	€ 2.18
One-week bike ticket:	€ 6.54
One-month bike ticket:	€ 19.62
One-year bike ticket:	€ 156.97

Bike & train

Rad-Tramper: A special train with bicycle racks in modified wagons, run by ÖBB (Austrian Rail). Travels from Vienna/Franz-Josefs-Bahnhof (departure time: 920) to Passau (arrival 1510) over St. Pölten, Linz and Wels (Fri, Sat, Sun only, between 29 May to 19 June and from 9 Sept to 25 Sept. Daily between 24 June and 4 Sept).

There is also a train that stops in Krems a. d. Donau, and which has a wagon for bicycles. Passengers change trains in St. Valentin to continue to Passau; the bicycle wagon is hitched from one train to the other.

It is a good precaution to purchase train tickets for the return trip from Vienna one day in advance. The "Rad-Tramper" also stops in Klosterneuburg, and makes it possible for tourists to avoid Vienna city traffic.

Bicycle rentals: Train stations along the Danube bicycle route that have bicycles for rent are listed below.

To rent a bicycle in Austria, it is necessary to show an identification card with photo. The rental costs € 6.54 per day (or € 3.63 if you arrive by train). For longer tours the ÖBB offers a cheaper "5-Tage-Pauschale" (5-day flat rate). We recommend reserving a bicycle in advance by telephone.

In Germany, one should always obtain information about bicycle rental prices and opening times in advance. To rent a bicycle, it is necessary to show identification with photo, and pay a € 127.82 deposit. Rental fees can vary between € 3.07 and € 12.78 per day.

A rented bicycle may be returned at any staffed ÖBB train station in Austria. That means, it is possible to rent a bicycle in Passau and return it in Vienna. Austria also has mobile bicycle rentals that can be ordered in advance to meet groups at any train station. It is not possible to rent bicycle panniers.

Passau, ✆ 0851/5304397

Linz Hauptbahnhof, ✆ 0732/1700 or 56411-3459

Mühlkreisbahnhof Linz-Urfahr, ✆ 0732/56411-5010

Mauthausen, ✆ 07238/2207

Enns, ✆ 07223/2133

Grein/Bad-Kreuzen, ✆ 07268/334

Ybbs/Donau, ✆ 07412/2600

Pöchlarn, ✆ 02757/7301-385

Melk, ✆ 02752/2321

Spitz ✆ 02713/2220

Krems ✆ 02732/82536-357

Stockerau ✆ 02266/62721-0

Korneuburg ✆ 02262/72467

Klosterneuburg-Weidling, ✆ 02243/2073

Vienna Westbahnhof ✆ 01/5800-32985

Vienna Südbahnhof ✆ 01/5800-35886

Bike & ship

Traveling by ship can make a charming addition to a tour along the Danube. Passenger ships run by the Wurm + Köck line travel between Passau-Engelhartszell-Brandstatt-Linz and back, and from Passau to Vienna: **Wurm + Köck**, Höllg. 26, ✆ 0851/929292, Fax 35518, Email:

wurm-koeck@t-online.de, internet: www.donauschifffahrt.com. Schedules: Passau-Linz-Passau, April-Oct, Mon-Sun; Passau-Obernzell-Passau April-Oct, Mon-Sun; Passau-Engelhartszell-Passau, April-late Oct, Mon-Sun.

Passau-Linz-Vienna takes two days. Voyages Linz-Vienna-Linz (Passau-Linz see above) on 9 dates between April and Oct, with departure on Saturdays and return on Sunday.

Donauschifffahrt Ardagger runs ships between Linz and Krems from May to Sept, departing Linz Sun, Tues, and Thurs; return from Krems Mon, Weds, and Fri. Information: ✆ 07479/64640

Blue Danube Schifffahrt GmbH serves the stretch between Krems (or Dürnstein) to Vienna from March to October on Saturdays and Sundays. Information: ✆ 01/727500

Additional information about seeing the Danube from ship and about local passenger ship lines can be found in individual town descriptions in this book.

Bike & bus

Austrian Bundesbus lines will accept bicycles on the following routes: Line 2006 Passau-Linz, Line 2146 Aschach-Linz, Line 2202 Grein-Perg, Line 2216 Grein-Amstetten.

In general, the buses can carry 5 to 7 bicycles. Larger groups can call in advance to request a special bicycle trailer (up to 20 bicycles). Information: Linz, ✆ 0732/1671

Bike & info

Special information facilities have been installed along the Danube bike route especially for bicycle tourists. These provide information about available tourism services and landmarks in the region, and can help arrange overnight accommodations. At present such bike stations are located in Passau (Hauptbahnhof), Engelhartszell (Marktgemeindeamt), Kramesau, Aschach, Mauthausen and Mitterkirchen.

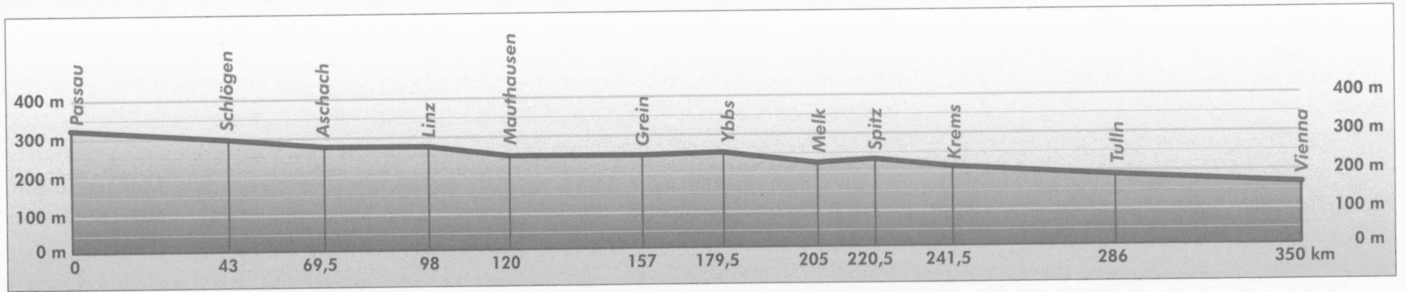

Overnight accommodations

Because the Danube River and adjacent regions are so popular with (bicycle) tourists, inns and hotels may not always have rooms available during the peak season. This is especially true for the relatively sparsely populated stretch between Passau and Aschach. For this reason some hotels that are not directly on the Danube, and in the Nibelungengau between Ypps and Melk, have set up shuttles that pick up bicycle tourists from the trail. Accommodations may also be hard to find between Tulln and Vienna. It is always a good idea to reserve rooms in advance.

In general, during the peak season we recommend reserving rooms one to two days in advance. A comprehensive list of overnight accommodations is provided at the end of this book.

Seasons

The Danube bicycle route's popularity means large numbers of bicycle tourists fill the trails, especially in the peak summer season.

Weather in the Danube river valley is influenced primarily by the systems moving into the continent from the Atlantic Ocean. One result is that the prevailing winds generally blow from west to east, and can be strengthened by the river valley's west-east orientation. Bicycle tourists starting in Passau can generally expect pleasant tailwinds, though the winds can occasionally turn and come from the east. Further east, the weather is increasingly affected by the continental climate, which can bring longer periods of stable good weather.

The **Wetterdienst** der Zentralanstalt für Meteorologie (weather service at the office of meteorology) in Vienna (✆ 01/3656702310) can provide long-range weather forecasts.

Bicycle tours with children

One of the Danube bicycle route's great advantages is that almost its entire length follows paved trails with virtually no inclines. Furthermore, the main route described in this book takes bicycle trails and lightly traveled public roads that children over the age of 8 can safely use with supervision. Only rarely does the route share the road with heavier traffic, and in most such cases there is an alternative route or the option of taking a train. Those sections are in the Strudengau, between Wallsee and Ardagger-Markt (public road), Wachau (narrow two-way bicycle trail along the main road).

A rule of thumb: Do not overestimate a child's stamina, and keep open options like taking a train or ship for some section of the trip. Depending on physical condition, most children can easily manage distances of 30 to 50 kilometers in a day. But remember that most children will not ride safely and with full concentration for hours on end. Choose bicycle trails whenever possible, or lightly traveled minor roads. Finally, no child will enjoy the ride if his or her bicycle is heavy and poorly equipped for long distances.

The right bicycle

The Danube route can be ridden on just about any functioning bicycle. The entire route follows paved smooth trails and roads, and there are virtually no hills. Gears are necessary only for several of the excursions that lead upward out of the Danube valley. Touring and trekking bikes ideally combine comfort with sturdiness and enable most riders to enjoy hours of riding.

Bicycling in Vienna

The bicycle trails and lanes in Vienna have their peculiarities, as you will see. Here are some of the most important rules:

Bicyclists must yield the right of way at the end of the bicycle trail, or when leaving any bicycling facility (bicycle path, bicycle lane, multi-purpose lane or bicycle crossing)! At bicycle crossings (marked on the pavement), the bicyclist has the right of way but may not ride faster than 10 km/h! On one-way streets (Einbahnstrasse), bicyclists may ride against the flow only where this is explicitly permitted. In Vienna's pedestrian zones (Fussgängerzone), bicyclists must dismount and push their vehicle.

Bicycles in public transportation

U-Bahn: Mon-Fri 9-15 and after 18:30, Sun/Hol all day. On the U6 line, bicycles may be transported only in the special low-floor wagons, and may be entered only at doors marked with the bicycle symbol. Half-price ticket: € 0.80.

Schnellbahn (commuter trains): Bicycles may be transported at all times only on trains shown with the bicycle symbol on posted train schedules. One-day tickets cost € 2.90.

About this book

This cycling guide contains all the information you need for your cycling vacation along the Danube from Passau to Vienna: Precise maps, a detailed description of the route, a comprehensive list of overnight accommodations, numerous detail maps of cities and towns, and information about the most significant sights.

And all that information comes with our cycline pledge: Every meter of the route described in this book has been tested and evaluated in person by one of our editors!

The maps

The inside of the guide's front cover shows an overview of the geographic location area covered by the guide. It also depicts the area covered by each of the detail maps inside the guide, and the detail map's number. These detail maps are produced in a scale of 1:50,000 (1 centimetre = 500 metres). In addition to exactly describing the route, these maps also provide information about roadway quality (paved or

unpaved), climbs (gentle or steep), distances, as well as available cultural and culinary highlights.

Even with the most precise map, consulting the written description of the route may be necessary at times. Locations where the route is difficult to follow are shown by the ⚠ symbol on the maps; the same symbol can then be found in the written description where the route is explained in detail.

Note that the recommended main route is always shown in red; alternative and excursion routes in orange. The individual symbols used in the maps are described in the legend on page 4.

Route altitude profile

The route altitude profile provides a graphic depiction of elevations along the route, the total length, and the location of larger towns and cities along the way. It does not show every individual small hill and dip, but only the major changes in elevation. On the detail maps smaller gradients are shown by arrows that point uphill.

The text

The maps are supplemented by a written text that describes the route starting in Passau and proceeding down the Danube to Vienna. Key phrases about the route description are indicated with the ~ symbol.

The description of the main route is also interrupted by passages describing alternative and excursion routes. These are printed on a light orange background.

Furthermore, the names of **important villages,** towns and cities are printed in **bold** type. If a location or community has important points of interest, addresses, telephone numbers and opening times are listed under the headline with the name of the place. The two sides of the river are identified as the left and the right sides, as seen when looking downstream. An L or R after a town's name indicates which side of the river it occupies.

Descriptions of the larger towns and cities, as well as historic, cultural and natural landmarks help round out the travel experience. These paragraphs are printed in italics to distinguish them from the route description.

You will also find paragraphs printed in purple or orange ink to help draw attention to special features.

Text printed in purple indicates that you must make a decision about how your tour shall continue. For instance, there may be an alternative route that is not included in the tour description, or a turn-off to another location.

Orange text suggests possible excursions to points of interest or recreational facilities that do not lie directly on the cycling route.

The ⚠ symbol indicates difficult locations, for instance where a sign is missing or the course of the route is not obvious. The same symbol is then given in that part of the written text which describes the route.

List of overnight accommodations

The last pages of this cycling guide provide a list of convenient hotels and guest houses in virtually every village or town along the route. This list also includes youth hostels and campgrounds. For more detail, please refer to page 146.

Passau to Linz, left bank

98 km

Departing the three-rivers city Passau, the Danube flows through the densely-wooded slopes of the narrow valley between the Bavarian Wald (forest) and the Sauwald until it reaches the Danube's loop at Schlögen. Here the river does something unexpected: Blocked by a granite mountain, the Danube does a U-turn around a sharp curve and flows back towards the west in the first part of a tight S-curve. The valley begins to widen at Aschach as the Danube enters the fertile plains of the Eferdinger Basin. Our destination for this stage is the steel-making city of Linz, with cultural offerings that belie the city's industrial reputation.

The route along the left bank from Passau to Linz is almost completely marked with signs. It follows bicycle trails and paths as well as minor public roads. There are no significant inclines. From Schlögen to Inzell the route is present only on the right bank.

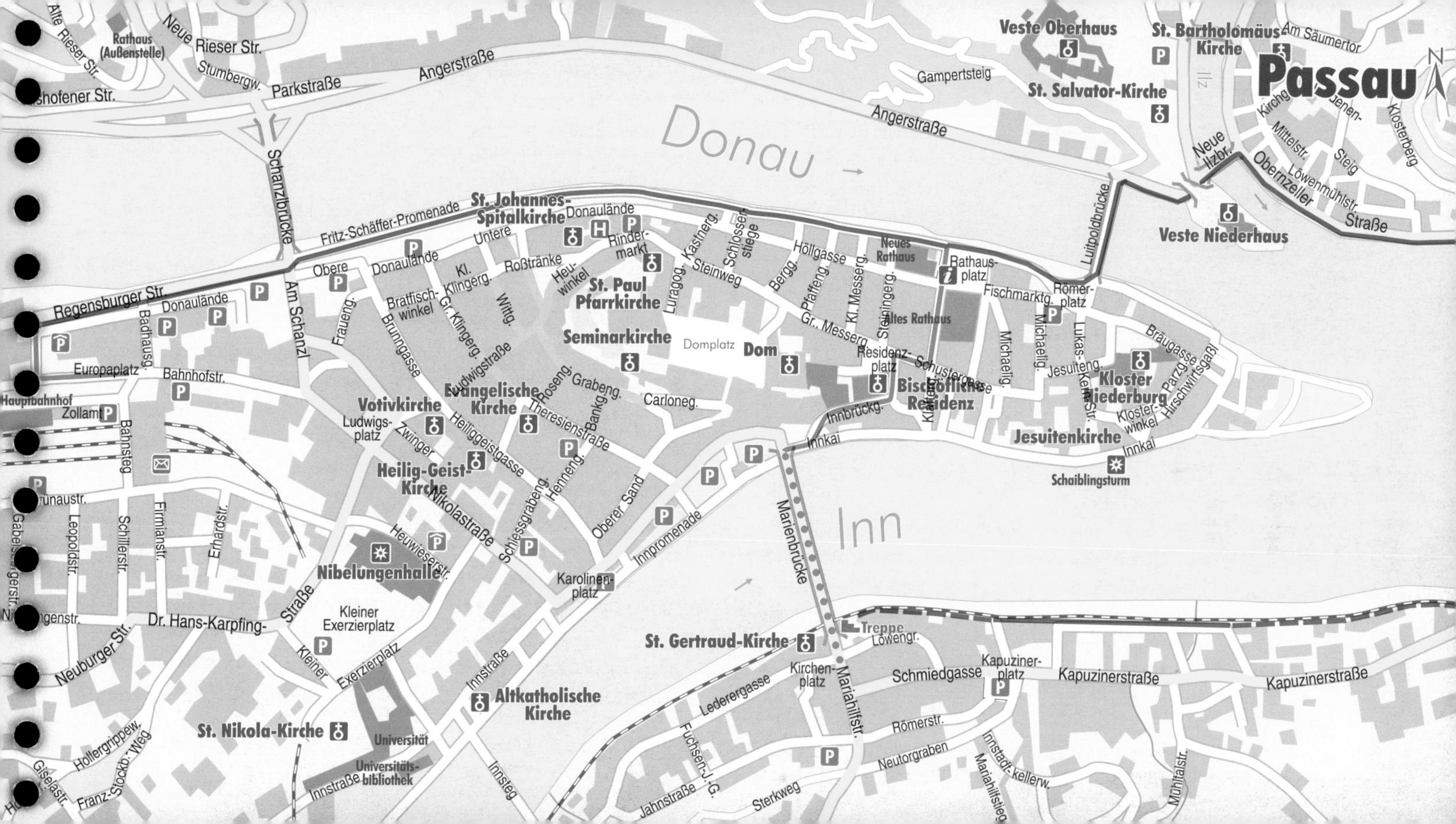

Passau
Donau
Inn
Veste Oberhaus
St. Bartholomäus-Kirche
St. Salvator-Kirche
Veste Niederhaus
Am Säumertor
Gampertsteig
Angerstraße
Parkstraße
Stumbergw.
Neue Rieser Str.
Alte Rieser Str.
Rathaus (Außenstelle)
Schanzlbrücke
Ilz
Neue Ilzbr.
Obernzeller Straße
Kirchg.
Ilzer Mittelstr.
Jenen-Steig
Löwenmühlstr.
Klosterberg
Luitpoldbrücke
St. Johannes-Spitalkirche
Fritz-Schäffer-Promenade
Donaulände
Untere Donaulände
Obere Donaulände
Regensburger Str.
Am Schanzl
Rindermarkt
Roßtränke
Heuwinkel
Kl. Klingerg.
Gr. Klingerg.
Bratfischwinkel
Wittg.
Frauenq.
Brunngasse
Ludwigstraße
Luragog.
Kastnerg.
Schlossersteige
Steinweg
Höllgasse
Bergg.
Pfaffeng.
Kl. Messerg.
Gr. Messerg.
Steiningerg.
Neues Rathaus
Rathausplatz
Altes Rathaus
Fischmarktg.
Römerplatz
Michaelig.
Lukas-Kern-Str.
Jesuiteng.
Bräugasse
Parzg.
Hirschwirtsgaßl
Klosterwinkel
Kloster Niederburg
St. Paul Pfarrkirche
Seminarkirche
Domplatz
Dom
Residenzplatz
Schusterg.
Bischöfliche Residenz
Innbrückg.
Innkai
Jesuitenkirche
Schaiblingsturm
Badhausg.
Europaplatz
Bahnhofstr.
Hauptbahnhof
Zollamt
Bahnsteig
Roseng.
Grabeng.
Carloneg.
Evangelische Kirche
Votivkirche
Ludwigsplatz
Zwinger
Heiliggeistgasse
Theresienstraße
Bankg.
Henneng.
Heilig-Geist-Kirche
Nikolastraße
Schiessgrabeng.
Oberer Sand
Innpromenade
Karolinenplatz
Leopoldstr.
Schillerstr.
Firmianstr.
Erhardstr.
Heuwieserstr.
Nibelungenhalle
Dr. Hans-Karpfing-Straße
Kleiner Exerzierplatz
Neuburger Str.
Kleiner Exerzierplatz
Innstraße
Altkatholische Kirche
St. Nikola-Kirche
Universität
Universitätsbibliothek
Innsteg
Hollergrippew.
Franz-Stockb.-Weg
Giselastr.
Marienbrücke
Treppe
Löwengr.
St. Gertraud-Kirche
Kirchenplatz
Ledererqasse
Mariahilfstr.
Schmiedgasse
Kapuzinerplatz
Kapuzinerstraße
Römerstr.
Neutorgraben
Fuchsen-J.-G.
Jahnstraße
Sterkweg
Innstadt-kellerw.
Mariahilfsteig
Mühltalstr.

Passau

The tour begins at the Passau Hauptbahnhof. The train station has a bicycle information station for Passau and Upper Austria.

From the train station proceed right, and then immediately turn left into the **Parkgasse** or the **Badhausgasse** ~ at the **Donaulände** (riverfront) turn right. After 50 meters, at the parking lot, go onto the river promenade.

Tip: If you are interested in the Danube River upstream from Passau, get a copy of the *bikeline* bicycle guide "Donau-Radweg, Teil 1: Donaueschingen-Passau" (available in German).

Ride along the river until you reach the city center with its many cafés and souvenir stores.

Tip: In front of the Renaissance Rathaus (town hall), a sightseeing route through the city branches off from the promenade. It also leads to the alternative Danube bicycle route down the right, or southern, bank. Tourist information is available on the corner.

The left bank route continues straight to the next bridge, the **Luitpoldbrücke**, where it crosses the Danube.

Passau (D) ≈km **2226 R**

Postal code: 94032; Telephone area code: 0851

Tourist information, Bahnhofstr. 36, ✆ 955980

Tourist information, Rathauspl. 3, ✆ 955980

Donauschifffahrt Wurm + Köck, Höllg. 26, ✆ 929292. Three-rivers tour from March-Oct, daily scheduled service to Engelhartszell, Schlögen and Linz from April-Oct. No charge for bicycles.

Inn Schifffahrt Schärding, ✆ 07712-3231. Daily scheduled service from 1 April-26 Oct to Wernstein-Neuburg, Ingling and Schärding.

Museum in der Veste Oberhaus, ✆ 396-312. Open: Mid March-late Oct, Mon-Fri 9-17, Sat/Sun/Hol 10-18. Historical city museum with exhibitions on city history, Böhmerwald museum and Neue Galerie der Stadt. Viewing tower. Shuttle bus from April to late Oct departs from the Rathaus every 30 minutes between 11:30-17.

Cathedral museum, entrance through the cathedral, ✆ 393374. Open: 2 April-31 Oct, Mon-Sat 10-16. History and artifacts from what was once the largest bishopric in the Holy Roman Empire.

Kastell Boiotro Roman Museum, Innstadt, Lederg. 43, ✆ 34769. Open: March-Nov, Tues-Sun 10-12 and 14-16, June-Aug, Tues-Sun 10-12 and 13-16. Exhibits include the excavated foundations of the Roman fort and archaeological discoveries from Passau and surrounding areas.

Passau glass museum, in "Wilden Mann," Rathausplatz, ✆ 35071. Open: Mon-Sun 10-16, off-season from 13-16. Collection of 30,000 objects documents the world famous "Bohemian glass" through Biedermeier to art nouveau to art deco.

Museum Moderne Kunst (modern art), Stiftung Wörlen, Altstadt, Bräug. 17. Open: Tues-Sun 10-18. Alternating international exhibitions on 20th century art presented in one of the most handsome old buildings in Passau.

St. Stephan. The original church was destroyed in 977. Construction on a late-Gothic cathedral began in 1407. Destroyed in the fire of 1662, it was replaced by the current cathedral, which is regarded as the largest religious baroque building north of the Alps. Especially noteworthy are the stucco decorations, the frescos, the world's largest organ and the imposing marble altars. Organ concerts: May-Oct, Mon-Sat 12-12:30 except holidays.

Rathaus, Rathausplatz. Open (main chamber): Easter-Oct, 10-16. Especially noteworthy is the great chamber (from 1405) with its outsized history paintings by Ferdinand Wagner (19th century). Rathaus tower glockenspiel plays Mon-Sun

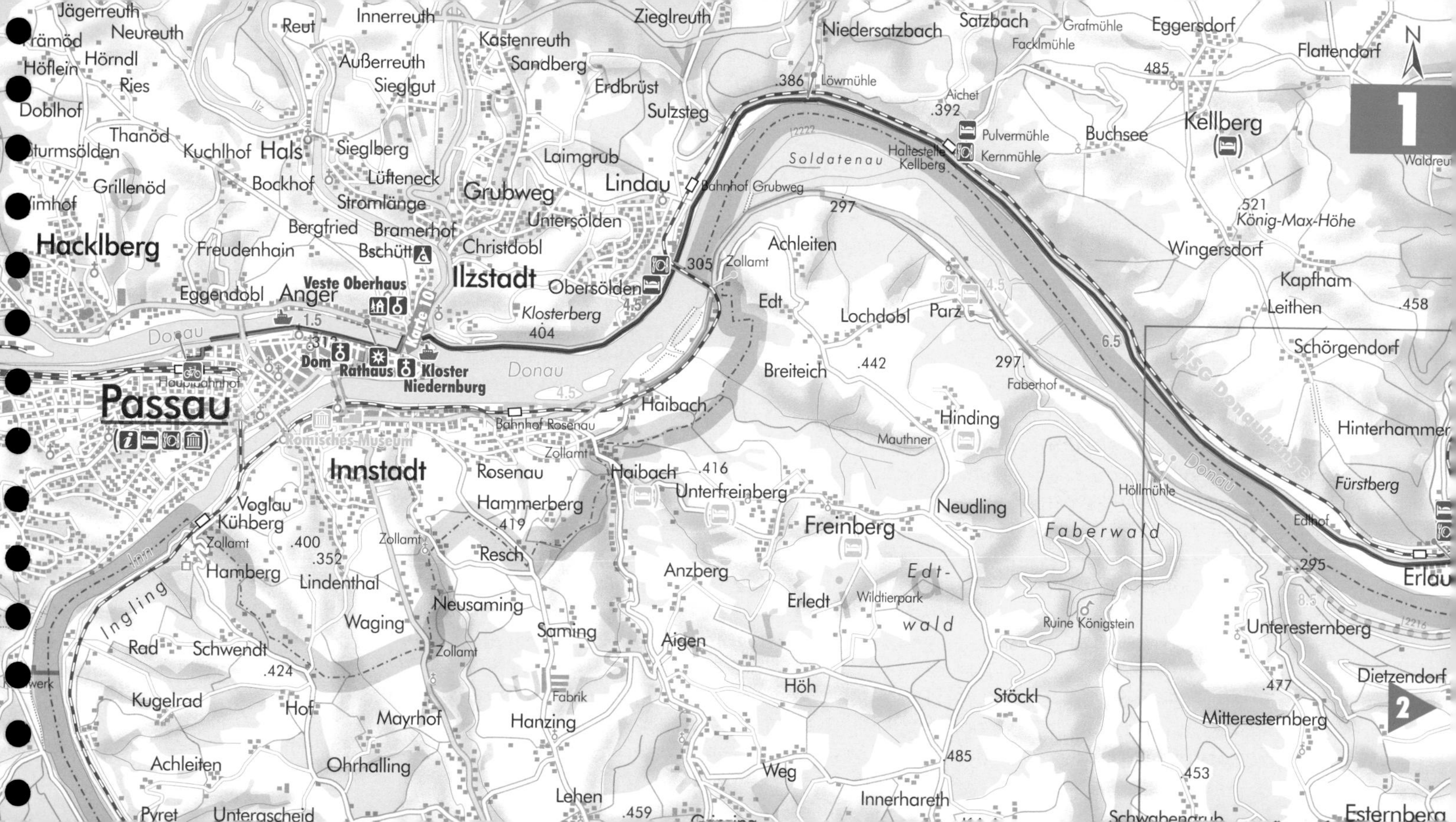

Passau
Hacklberg
Ilzstadt
Innstadt
Grubweg
Lindau
Hals
Anger
Veste Oberhaus
Dom
Rathaus
Kloster Niederburg
Hauptbahnhof
Römisches Museum
Bahnhof Rosenau
Bahnhof Grubweg
Haltestelle Kellberg
Donau
Inn
Ilz
Karte 10
Kellberg
Freinberg
Haibach
Achleiten
Edt
Lochdobl
Parz
Breiteich
Hinding
Neudling
Faberwald
Edt-wald
Wildtierpark
Ruine Königstein
Höllmühle
Erlau
Unteresternberg
Mitteresternberg
Dietzendorf
Esternberg
Soldatenau
NSG Donauhänge
König-Max-Höhe
Pulvermühle
Kernmühle
Löwmühle
Zollamt
1
2

10:30, 14 and 19:25, Sat also 15:30.

Neue Residenz, Residenzplatz. Built in the early 18th century according to the prince-bishop's taste, on the site of the early-medieval royal court. The simple facade is an important example of Viennese early-classicism in Passau.

Nibelungenhalle, Kleiner Exerzierplatz. Built in 1935, the hall is the traditional venue of "European Weeks," an annual demonstration of west-occidental culture that was started in 1952 and originally aimed at the Iron Curtain. Since the political shifts of 1989, a festival held in lower Bavaria, upper Austria, Böhmen and Passau.

Stadttheater (city theater), Innbrücke. The former prince-bishop's opera house was built in 1783 and is Bavaria's only surviving early-classical theatre.

Veste Oberhaus, Georgsberg. One of the three major structures that dominate the cityscape, along with the cathedral and the pilgrimage church Mariahilf. Construction of the mighty complex began as the bishopric's defenses against a popular revolt in 1219, and continued to completion of the fortifications in the 19th century.

Veste Niederhaus, over the mouth of the Ilz River. Probably built in the 14th century, at the foot of the Oberhaus. In the 17th century it served as a prison, later as a factory, today privately owned.

St. Severin, near the Inn landing. The church dates back to the 5th century and contains chambers once used by St. Severin.

Niedernburg Monastery, on the eastern tip of the city. Niedernburg is one of Bavaria's oldest monasteries in continuous use. Its grounds include the graves of Gisela, the beatified queen and wife to the Hungarian King Stephan.

__Passau__, the City of Three Rivers, has long been regarded as one of the most beautiful cities in Germany. The confluence of the Danube and the Inn rivers, plus the waters of the Ilz river from the north, created optimal conditions for the growth of the city. Its rich history as bishopric and one of the centers of power of Roman Catholicism gave Passau great cultural wealth. In the year 460 St. Severin established a monastery at the confluence. Three centuries later it became a bishopric. Pilgrim von Pöchlarn, Passau's first great bishop, is believed to have commissioned the Nibelungenlied. He was also a successful missionary in the Danube region, spreading Christianity as far as Hungary. Vienna's St. Stephan's Cathedral was established by clergy from Passau.

The Passau of today still reflects the one-time importance of the bishopric, despite the fact that much of the city was destroyed in the great fire of 1662. After the fire, the Gothic ruins served as the foundation for a new Passau, which was built in the style of the Italian baroque to symbolize the city's power and influence.

Passau to Engelhartszell 26.5 km

The route along the left bank of the Danube crosses the river on the Luitpoldbrücke beneath the Veste Oberhaus (the castle on the left bank) ~ then turn right, ride through the tunnel and cross the Ilz.

Tip: To reach the Veste Oberhaus, turn left after crossing the Ilz and proceed up the river. Cross it again on the next bridge, and then turn right to climb the mountain.

To continue down the Danube, stay right on the **bicycle/pedestrian path** next to the main road towards Obernzell ~ proceed under the **railroad bridge** at Lindau, pass the Löwmühle and **Kernmühle** mills and continue towards Erlau.

Erlau

The __Donauleiten nature preserve__ stretches along the left bank of the Danube from Passau to the Austrian border at Jochenstein. Its six segments, with names like Fuchsberg, Fürstberg or Jochenstein together comprise 405 hectares. The steeply-rising slopes form the southern edge of the Bavarian Wald. Over the eons the Danube has cut a path that is up to 300 meters deep through the mountain ridge, which is called

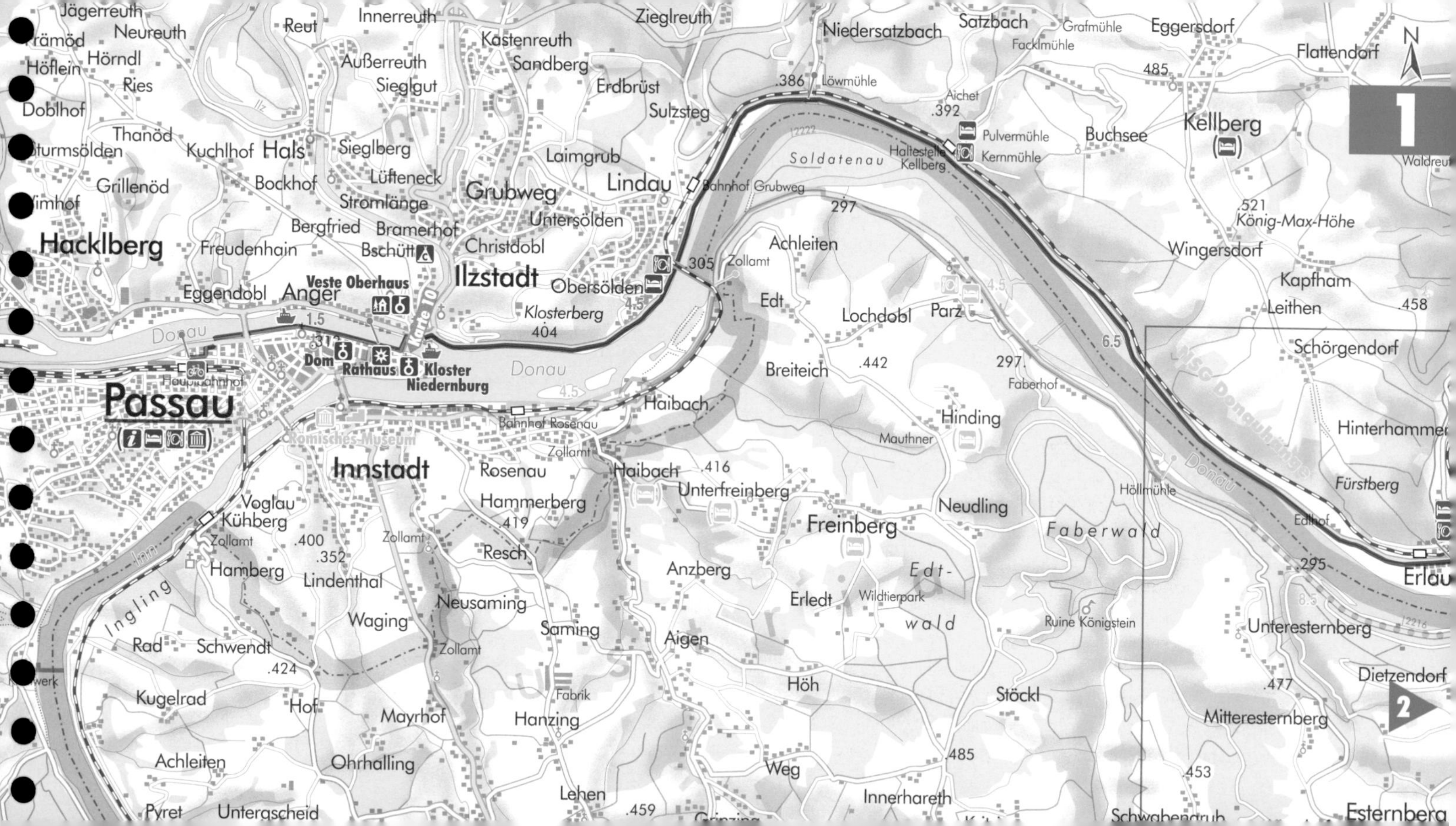

Passau
Hacklberg
Ilzstadt
Innstadt
Grubweg
Hals
Lindau
Anger
Veste Oberhaus
Dom
Rathaus
Kloster Niedernburg
Hauptbahnhof
Donau
Inn
Bahnhof Rosenau
Bahnhof Grubweg
Haltestelle Kellberg
Kellberg
Freinberg
Haibach
Soldatenau
Achleiten
Zollamt
Erlau
Faberwald
Edt-wald
Ruine Königstein
Wildtierpark
Römisches Museum
NSG Donauhänge
1
2

10:30, 14 and 19:25, Sat also 15:30.

- **Neue Residenz**, Residenzplatz. Built in the early 18th century according to the prince-bishop's taste, on the site of the early-medieval royal court. The simple facade is an important example of Viennese early-classicism in Passau.
- **Nibelungenhalle**, Kleiner Exerzierplatz. Built in 1935, the hall is the traditional venue of "European Weeks," an annual demonstration of west-occidental culture that was started in 1952 and originally aimed at the Iron Curtain. Since the political shifts of 1989, a festival held in lower Bavaria, upper Austria, Böhmen and Passau.
- **Stadttheater (city theater)**, Innbrücke. The former prince-bishop's opera house was built in 1783 and is Bavaria's only surviving early-classical theatre.
- **Veste Oberhaus**, Georgsberg. One of the three major structures that dominate the cityscape, along with the cathedral and the pilgrimage church Mariahilf. Construction of the mighty complex began as the bishopric's defenses against a popular revolt in 1219, and continued to completion of the fortifications in the 19th century.
- **Veste Niederhaus**, over the mouth of the Ilz River. Probably built in the 14th century, at the foot of the Oberhaus. In the 17th century it served as a prison, later as a factory, today privately owned.
- **St. Severin**, near the Inn landing. The church dates back to the 5th century and contains chambers once used by St. Severin.
- **Niedernburg Monastery**, on the eastern tip of the city. Niedernburg is one of Bavaria's oldest monasteries in continuous use. Its grounds include the graves of Gisela, the beatified queen and wife to the Hungarian King Stephan.

***Passau**, the City of Three Rivers, has long been regarded as one of the most beautiful cities in Germany. The confluence of the Danube and the Inn rivers, plus the waters of the Ilz river from the north, created optimal conditions for the growth of the city. Its rich history as bishopric and one of the centers of power of Roman Catholicism gave Passau great cultural wealth. In the year 460 St. Severin established a monastery at the confluence. Three centuries later it became a bishopric. Pilgrim von Pöchlarn, Passau's first great bishop, is believed to have commissioned the Nibelungenlied. He was also a successful missionary in the Danube region, spreading Christianity as far as Hungary. Vienna's St. Stephan's Cathedral was established by clergy from Passau.*

The Passau of today still reflects the one-time importance of the bishopric, despite the fact that much of the city was destroyed in the great fire of 1662. After the fire, the Gothic ruins served as the foundation for a new Passau, which was built in the style of the Italian baroque to symbolize the city's power and influence.

Passau to Engelhartszell 26.5 km

The route along the left bank of the Danube crosses the river on the Luitpoldbrücke beneath the Veste Oberhaus (the castle on the left bank) ~ then turn right, ride through the tunnel and cross the Ilz.

Tip: To reach the Veste Oberhaus, turn left after crossing the Ilz and proceed up the river. Cross it again on the next bridge, and then turn right to climb the mountain.

To continue down the Danube, stay right on the **bicycle/pedestrian path** next to the main road towards Obernzell ~ proceed under the **railroad bridge** at Lindau, pass the Löwmühle and **Kernmühle** mills and continue towards Erlau.

Erlau

*The **Donauleiten nature preserve** stretches along the left bank of the Danube from Passau to the Austrian border at Jochenstein. Its six segments, with names like Fuchsberg, Fürstberg or Jochenstein together comprise 405 hectares. The steeply-rising slopes form the southern edge of the Bavarian Wald. Over the eons the Danube has cut a path that is up to 300 meters deep through the mountain ridge, which is called*

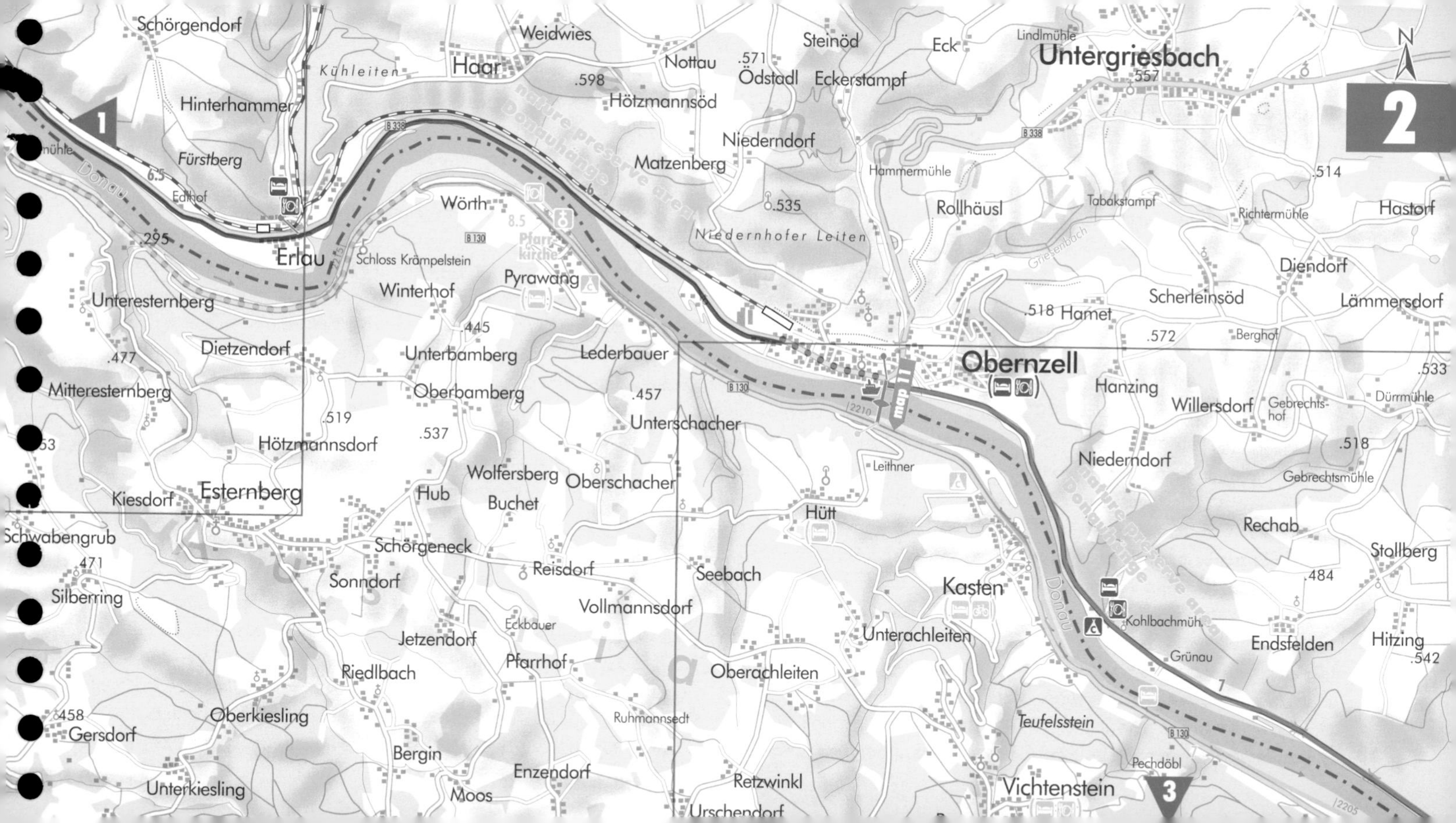

Schörgendorf
Weidwies
Haar
Kühleiten
Nottau
.571
Steinöd
Eck
Lindlmühle
Untergriesbach
.557
.598
Ödstadl
Eckerstampf
Hötzmannsöd
2
1
Hinterhammer
B 338
nature preserve area
Donauhänge
Niederndorf
Fürstberg
Matzenberg
Hammermühle
.514
Edlhof
Donau
Wörth
.535
Rollhäusl
Tabakstampf
Richtermühle
Hastorf
8.5
Pfarrkirche
B 130
Niedernhofer Leiten
.295
Erlau
Schloss Krämpelstein
Griesenbach
Diendorf
Pyrawang
Winterhof
Unteresternberg
Scherleinsöd
Lämmersdorf
.518
Hamet
.445
.572
Berghof
Dietzendorf
Unterbamberg
Lederbauer
Obernzell
.477
.533
map 11
Hanzing
Mitteresternberg
Oberbamberg
.457
Willersdorf
Gebrechtshof
Dürrmühle
2210
.519
Unterschacher
.537
.518
Hötzmannsdorf
Leithner
Niederndorf
Wolfersberg
Oberschacher
Gebrechtsmühle
Kiesdorf
Esternberg
Hub
Buchet
Hütt
Schwabengrub
Schörgeneck
Rechab
.471
Reisdorf
Stollberg
Sonndorf
Seebach
.484
Silberring
Kasten
Vollmannsdorf
Eckbauer
Kohlbachmühl
Unterachleiten
Jetzendorf
Hitzing
Endsfelden
Pfarrhof
Grünau
.542
Riedlbach
Oberachleiten
7
.458
Oberkiesling
Ruhmannsedt
Teufelsstein
Gersdorf
Bergin
Pechdöbl
Enzendorf
Retzwinkl
Unterkiesling
Moos
Vichtenstein
3
Urschendorf
2205

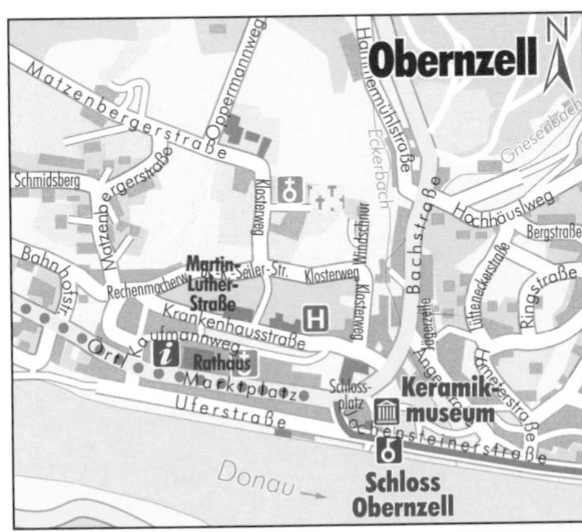

the Sauwald on the Austrian side of the river. Most of the valley's slopes are covered with mixed woods broken occasionally by stark rock outcroppings.

The strong sunshine that the south-facing slopes are exposed to has helped create an environment in which many rare, warmth-loving animals and plants thrive. The Danube's slopes, or Donauleiten, are noteworthy for the wide variety of plants from different geographical origins. For instance, many alpine and eastern-Alpine flora like cyclamen grow here, alongside broom-mugwort and knotty-grasslily from warmer, drier southern regions.

The Donauleiten's fauna are also distinguished by the presence of typical mountain dwelling animals as well as southern species. No German region has as many different reptiles: seven of the nine German species of lizards and snakes are found here, plus rare southern species like the emerald lizard and the Aesculapian viper, the largest and perhaps most beautiful snake found in Germany.

Ride through the small village of **Erlau** (across from the Krämpelstein castle), over Erlau creek and proceed close to the river onwards toward Obernzell.

Note the small church at Pyrawang across the river, where early-Gothic frescoes were uncovered in recent years.

Obernzell (D) ≈km**2210.5 L**

Postal code: 94130; Telephone area code: 08591

Tourist information, Marktpl.42, ✆ 9116119. Obernzell guided tours from May-Sept every Fri 10, 90 minutes. Meet in front of the palace.

Ferry to Kasten: 1 May-start of winter, Mon-Fri 6:15-18:15, Sat/Sun/Hol 7:30-18:15.

River cruise with the Obernzell city ship, ✆ 9116111. Departs from Wurm & Köck ship landing.

Ceramics museum, Schloss Obernzell, ✆ 1066. Open: 1 April-6 Jan, Tues-Sun 10-17. Part of the Bavarian national museums system. On display are ceramic artifacts from the early Stone Age to contemporary times, plus earthenware, stone tools, faience, porcelain and other wares. Free of charge.

Palace. Main attraction of the former second residence of the Passau bishops (16th century) is the knights room done in the style of the Passau Renaissance.

Gasthof Alte Schiffspost, Marktpl. 1. The structure was built 1805-1810 and is noteworthy for interesting putto-reliefs that show happy scenes of wine-making and sampling, reminders of Obernzell's past as a wine-making town.

Parish church, Marktplatz. Rococo church.

Public outdoor pool at the edge of town

Radsport (bicycles) Müller, Marktplatz, ✆ 2890

For many years the town was called Hafnerzell, for the many "Hafner" (potters) who worked here. This heritage is preserved in the ceramics museum in the palace.

Turn towards the river at the **palace** ~ pass the ferry and down a quiet road that runs along the Danube ~ after 3 kilometers an inn and a campground share the narrow strip between the river and the road.

Burg ***Vichtenstein*** *can be seen on the other side of the river. This mighty castle, which dates back to the 12th century, stands in front of the 895-*

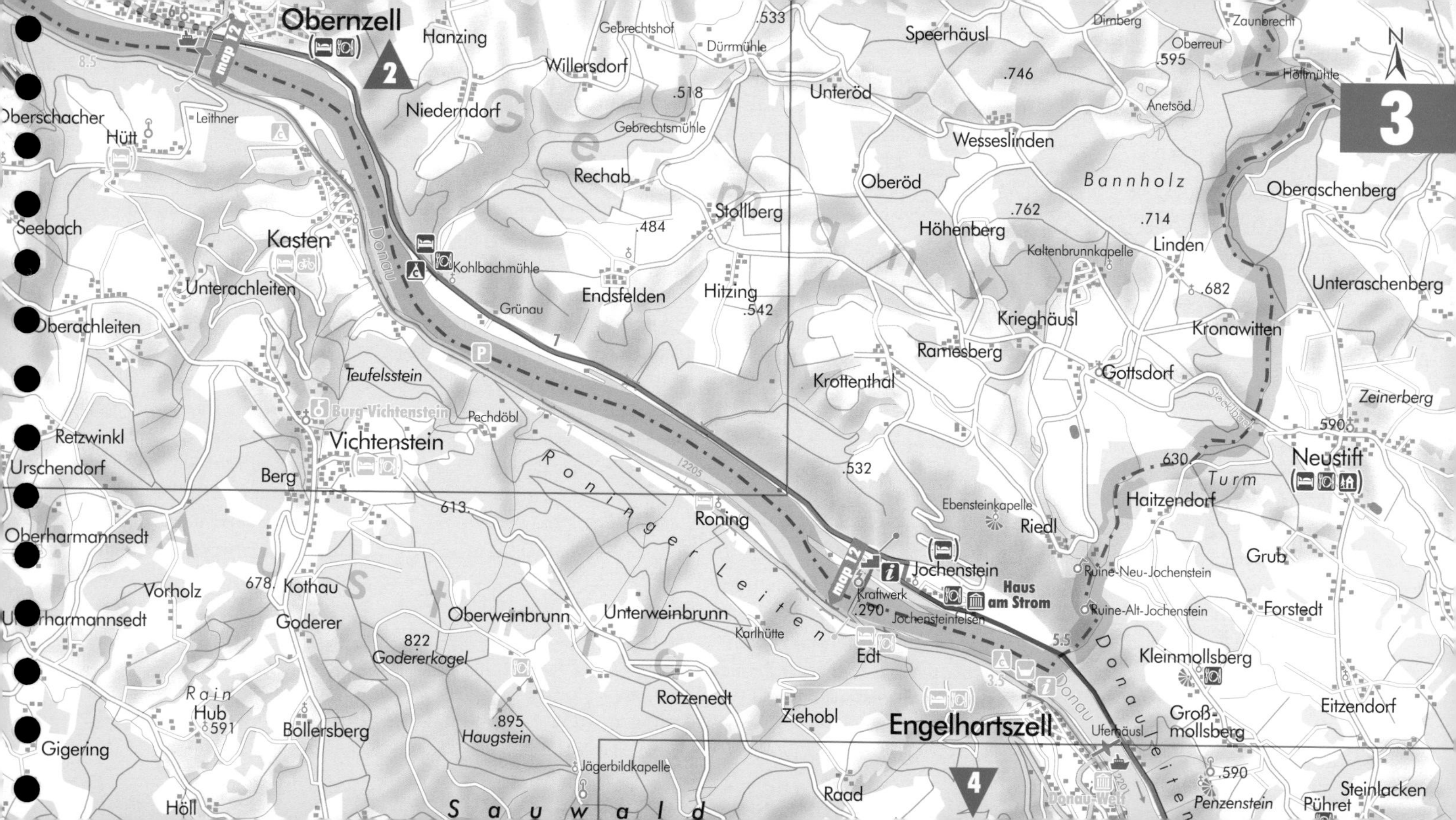

Obernzell
map 12
2
Hanzing
Willersdorf
Gebrechtshof
Dürrmühle
.533
Niederndorf
.518
Gebrechtsmühle
Oberschacher
Leithner
Hütt
Rechab
Seebach
Kasten
Donau
Kohlbachmühle
.484
Stollberg
Unterachleiten
Endsfelden
Hitzing
.542
Oberachleiten
Grünau
Teufelsstein
Burg Vichtenstein
Pechdöbl
Retzwinkl
Vichtenstein
Urschendorf
Berg
Roninger Leiten
613.
Roning
Oberharmannsedt
Vorholz
678.
Kothau
Goderer
Oberweinbrunn
Unterweinbrunn
822
Godererkogel
Karlhütte
Rain
Hub
591
Bollersberg
.895
Haugstein
Rotzenedt
Ziehobl
Gigering
Jägerbildkapelle
Höll
Sauwald
Raad
4
Speerhäusl
Dirnberg
Zaunbrecht
Oberreut
.595
Höllmühle
3
.746
Unteröd
Anetsöd
Wesseslinden
Oberöd
Bannholz
Oberaschenberg
.762
Höhenberg
.714
Linden
Kaltenbrunnkapelle
.682
Unteraschenberg
Krieghäusl
Kronawitten
Ramesberg
Krottenthal
Gottsdorf
Zeinerberg
Stockbach
590.
.532
630.
Neustift
Turm
Haitzendorf
Ebensteinkapelle
Riedl
Grub
Jochenstein
Ruine-Neu-Jochenstein
Kraftwerk
Haus am Strom
.290
Jochensteinfelsen
Ruine-Alt-Jochenstein
Forstedt
5.5
Edt
3.5
Kleinmollsberg
Groß-mollsberg
Eitzendorf
Engelhartszell
Uferhäusl
Donauleiten
.590
Donau-Welt
Penzenstein
Steinlacken
Pühret

meter Haugstein, the tallest peak in the region.

4 kilometers further downstream is the **river barrage at Jochenstein**.

Tip: To visit the town of Engelhartszell on the southern side of the Danube, cross the river either at the Jochenstein power plant (open 6-22) or with the ferry further downstream (see page 36).

Jochenstein (D) **≈km 2203 L**

Postal code: 94107; Telephone area code: D-08591

Tourist information Untergriesbach, Marktpl. 24, ✆ 08593/1066

Jochenstein-Engelhartszell **Danube adventure trail** with artifacts from the state exhibition.

Jochenstein information center. Open: April-Oct, Mon-Sun 9-18, Nov-March, Sat/Sun/Hol 9-16. Topics: Water power and hydraulic engineering, technology for man and nature.

Kunst im Ländlichen (Art in the countryside), a collection of wood sculptures from around the world, shown near the hiking and biking parking lot, is open year-round.

Haus am Strom (house on the river), am Kraftwerk 4, ✆ 912890. Open: Mon-Sun 9-17. Topics: All aspects of water. With Isa Gate sculpture.

Further down the north bank, past the transformer station, turn right on the small **Am Jochenstein** road ~ stay close to the river bank through the village of **Jochenstein** and then down the path paved with concrete slabs toward the Austrian border.

From here one can see the legendary ***Jochensteinfelsen*** *looming out of the river. It is the home of the Danube nixie Isa, one of the sisters of Loreley, the Rhine's famous nixie.*

Cross the **Dantlbach creek** to depart Germany and enter Austria ~ the tour now follows the old towpath, and is marked with signs for the "Oberösterreichischen Landesradwanderwegenetzes" (Upper Austrian State bicycle touring network) ~ in about 700 meters reach the **bicycle ferry** that transports cyclists across the river to Engelhartszell (from 9 to 19).

Tip: The Donaumarkt with the unique Trappist monastery is worth a visit.

Engelhartszell

Tip: We recommend returning to the northern side of the river to continue downstream towards Schlögen (about 15 kilometers away). The left bank route is quieter, while the right bank route follows the heavily-traveled state highway (see page 38).

Engelhartszell to Niederranna *10 km*

The quieter route on the left side of the Danube continues from the **Engelhartszell bicycle ferry**, and follows the well-built towpath once used by the horses that pulled ships upstream ~ continue downstream when the route joins a country lane just before the Ranna stream reaches the Danube ~ the valley is dominated by the **Rannariedl castle** ~ **in Niederranna** turn right after the church ~ continue straight at the next junction, or turn right to visit the ship landing and inn on the river.

Niederranna **≈km 2194.5 L**

Postal code: 4085; Telephone area code: 07285

Hofkirchen town office, ✆ 7011

Bicycle information center Kramesau, ✆ 07285/559. Open: Mid May-Oct, Mon-Sun 11-18.

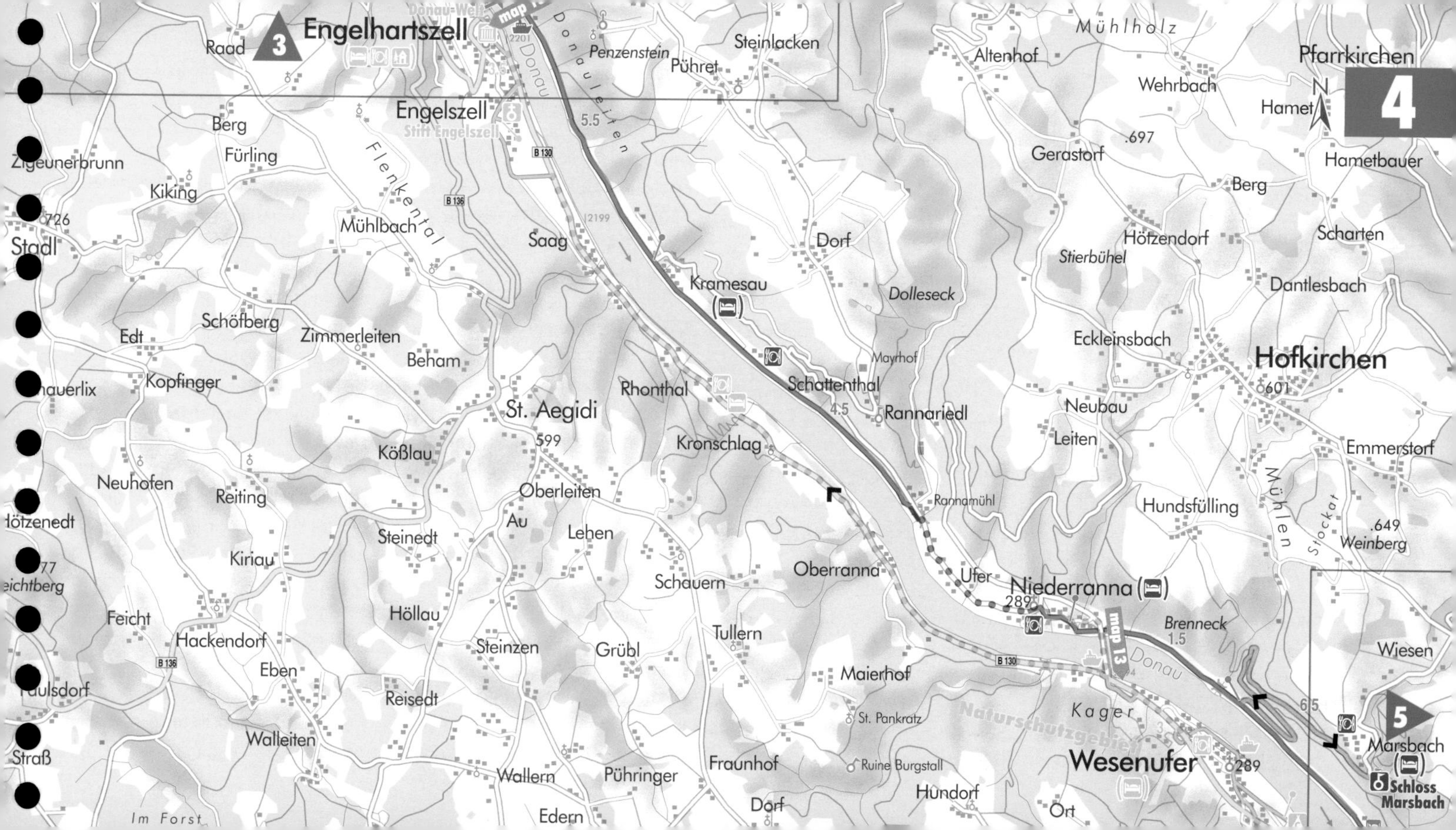

Engelhartszell
3
Engelszell
Stift Engelszell
Donau
Donauleiten
Penzenstein
Pühret
Steinlacken
Mühlholz
Altenhof
Pfarrkirchen
Wehrbach
Hamet
4
Raad
Berg
Fürling
Zigeunerbrunn
Kiking
Flenkental
Mühlbach
Stadl
Saag
Dorf
Gerastorf
Hametbauer
Berg
Hötzendorf
Scharten
Stierbühel
Kramesau
Dolleseck
Dantlesbach
Schöfberg
Edt
Zimmerleiten
Beham
Kopfinger
Rhonthal
Schattenthal
Mayrhof
Rannariedl
Eckleinsbach
Hofkirchen
Neubau
St. Aegidi
Kößlau
Kronschlag
Leiten
Emmerstorf
Neuhofen
Reiting
Oberleiten
Rannamühl
Hundsfülling
Au
Lehen
Steinedt
Kiriau
Mühlen
Stockat
Weinberg
Oberranna
Schauern
Ufer
Niederranna
Feicht
Hackendorf
Höllau
Steinzen
Grübl
Tullern
Brenneck
Wiesen
Eben
Maierhof
Donau
Reisedt
St. Pankratz
Kager
Naturschutzgebiet
5
Marsbach
Walleiten
Straß
Wallern
Pühringer
Fraunhof
Ruine Burgstall
Wesenufer
Schloss Marsbach
Hundorf
Dorf
Edern
Ort
Im Forst

Rannariedl castle. Falkenstein property until 1357/58, after which it belonged, with interruptions, to the Passau prince bishops. The residential wing with courtyard dates to the 16th century. The tall keep is medieval.

Tip: The route down the left side of the river is quieter, but the right bank features the town of Wesenufer and the nature preserve around the Klein Klößlbach stream. Take the bridge from Niederranna to visit Wesenufer. We recommend returning to the left bank to continue downstream. Alternatively, one can ride along the main road to Schlögen.

Niederranna to Obermühl 14.5 km

At the eastern edge of Niederranna the route swings to the right and passes under the Danube bridge ~ the route follows a narrow road along the river bank ~ after 6 kilometers along the Danube you reach Au/Schlögen ~ the route leads directly to the famous Schlögen bend, where the river makes a sharp turn and for several hundred meters flows back towards its source. The town of **Schlögen** and its large hotel are visible across the river on the right bank.

Tip: The next 700 meters offer three ferries with which cyclists can cross the river. The first is the Schlögen bicycle ferry (open: April, 10-17; May-Sept, 9-19; Oct, 10-17). Two other ferries depart from the town of Au a few hundred meters further downstream: The bicycle ferry "Zur Fährfrau" (open: April, 7:30-19; May-Sept, 7-20; Oct 7:30-19:30) and the "Santa Maria" (open: May-second weekend in Oct, Mon-Sun 9-18). The "Santa Maria" departs Au and travels 5 kilometers down the Danube's S-curve to dock on the left bank at Grafenau and at Inzell on the right bank. The Danube bicycle route continues downstream from those towns on both sides of the Danube.

Obermühl ≈km 2178 L

Postal code: 4131; Telephone area code: 07286

Tourism association Obermühl-Kirchberg, Gasthof Aumüller, ✆ 07286/7216

Ferry: March, April, Oct, Nov 7:30-17, May-Sept 7:30-18, June, July, Aug 7:30-19.

Grain silo, on the eastern edge of the town, was built with a conspicuous 16-meters high roof in the year 1618, and served as a customs post. The silo was almost lost when the power generating plant was constructed. Now the roof of this important economic asset from the Renaissance has been lovingly restored.

Obermühl to Aschach 19.5 km

In Obermühl ride past the historic grain silo and the ferry ~ proceed 7 kilometers to the next settlement, the **inn in the Exlau** ~ continue along a narrow paved ribbon of road through the Danube's curves at Hinteraigen ~ ride under the bridge just before the Große Mühl joins the Danube.Cross the stream.

Untermühl ≈km 2168 L

Ferry: May-Aug, 9-19, Sept, 9-18.

Partenstein castle, near where the Gumpenbach joins the Danube. Built originally as a fortification to Passau, the earliest recorded mention of Partenstein dates back to 1262. Today it holds an exhibition on local history and culture.

Follow the path on the north bank uphill and past the steep slopes down to the Danube ~ continue downstream along the towpath ~ pass a small harbor before reaching the **Aschach power station**. The dam is not open to the public.

Tip: After the bridge at the intersection with the large farm, you have the option of crossing to the southern bank. The option is described on page 44.

Aschach to Ottensheim 18 km

Proceed downstream on the left bank and take the first possible right

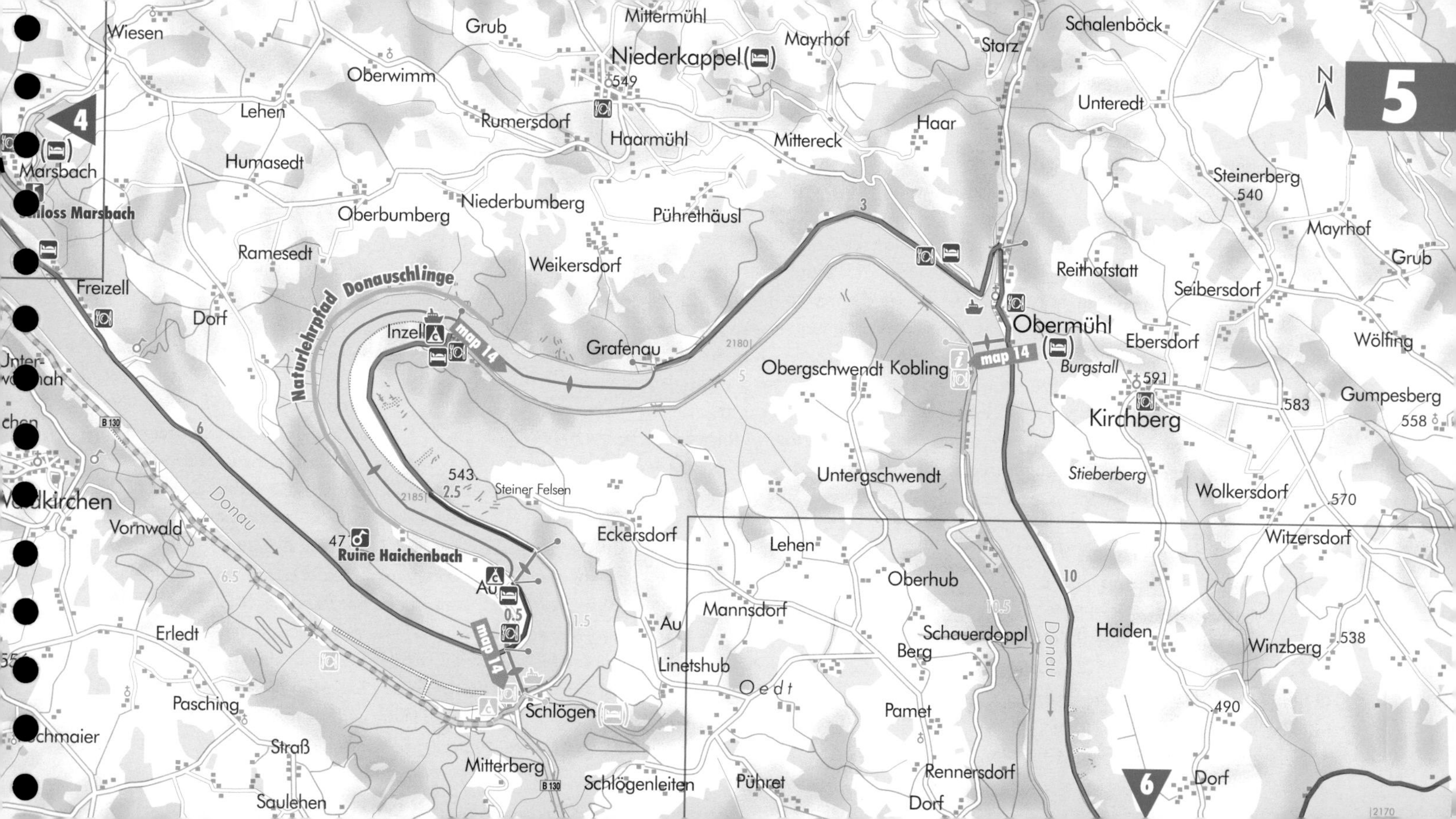

5
4
6
Niederkappel
Obermühl
Kirchberg
Schlögen
Marsbach
Schloss Marsbach
Naturlehrpfad Donauschlinge
Ruine Haichenbach
Steiner Felsen
Donau
map 14
Wiesen
Grub
Mittermühl
Mayrhof
Starz
Schalenböck
Oberwimm
Lehen
Rumersdorf
Haarmühl
Mittereck
Haar
Unteredt
Humasedt
Oberbumberg
Niederbumberg
Pührethäusl
Steinerberg
Ramesedt
Weikersdorf
Reithofstatt
Seibersdorf
Freizell
Dorf
Inzell
Grafenau
Ebersdorf
Wölfing
Obergschwendt
Kobling
Burgstall
Gumpesberg
Untergschwendt
Stieberberg
Wolkersdorf
Vornwald
Eckersdorf
Witzersdorf
Oberhub
Au
Mannsdorf
Schauerdoppl
Berg
Haiden
Winzberg
Erledt
Linetshub
Oedt
Pasching
Pamet
Straß
Mitterberg
Schlögenleiten
Pühret
Rennersdorf
Saulehen
B 130

turn ~ then turn left at the junction with the farm on the corner ~ proceed about 300 meters towards **Unterlandshaag** and follow the signs for the Danube bicycle route ~ the quiet country lane makes numerous sharp turns as it passes fields, orchards and old farmsteads ~ in Feldkirchen turn right at the first larger intersection and return to the Danube.

Feldkirchen an der Donau L

Postal code: 4101; Telephone area code: 07233

Tourism assocation, Hauptstr. 1 ✆ 7190

Parish church. The Gothic church was built in 1510.

Kneipp cures are available in the modernized Bad Mühllacken spa.

Feldkirchen recreation eldorado ("Freizeiteldorado"). Open: May-Oct. An extensive recreation facility with water skiing, camping, golf, restaurant, winery, and a hiking circuit, ✆ 6727.

Model railroad, Goldwörth (5 km south-east). Austria's largest model railroad (in 1:8 scale).

Pesenbachtal nature preserve

Tip: A detour to the Walding zoological garden is a short ride from Feldkirchen. The route to Walding is shown on the map in orange.

The **main route** down the left bank leads from **Feldkirchen** back down to the Danube ~ at the edge of town turn toward **Weidet** ~ where the route makes a sharp turn to the right ~ 300 meters further turn left at the small **wooden chapel** ~ pass a narrow woods and drainage ditch ~ and return to the towpath on the embankment ~ the route follows this straight, well-paved path as far as Ottensheim 12 kilometers downstream.

Tip: After about 1.5 kilometers you reach the Feldkirchen lakes which have, among other attractions, a water-ski towing facility in case you wish to try a different form of mobility. The lake can be reached by a narrow path that leads down from the embankment and to a narrow bridge across the ditch.

The route along the embankment is straight and impossible to lose. The power station at Ottensheim increasingly dominates the riverscape.

Tip: If you are looking for a place to take a pause, consider the second turn-off to Goldwörth, about 3 kilometers past the Feldkirchen swimming lakes. A packed-gravel path leads across two canals and then left to the village where residents used to pan for gold.

Gold and pearls from the Danube

The search for gold and pearls in the Danube may have been relatively small industries compared to main activities like fishing, shipping and energy production, but they made interesting contributions to the river's cultural history. The "pearl-fishers" especially favored the Danube's small tributaries from north. The best pearl-creeks are streams with relatively low levels of lime. The clear-as-water to reddish-green pearls grow in the approximately 10 cm long river mussel (Margaritana margaritifera) when the mussel starts depositing mother-of-pearl on a sand-corn. The process takes some 15 to 20 years, and only one in 500 to 2000 mussels produce a single pearl.

The Passau diocese organized the systematic harvest of pearls in the region, and for many years "Passau pearls" enjoyed great popularity. The pearls were treasured not just in the immediate region – the Linz bishop's miter is decorated with river pearls from the Danube.

Gold generated a similarly small but steady source of wealth. Despite the apparent futility of the activity, there is evidence of a number of gold prospectors, even from relatively recent times. In 1733, for instance, 93.3 grams of panned gold from Linz

6
5
7
Lehen
Oberhub
Mannsdorf
509
Schauerdoppl
Haiden
Winzberg
.538
.515
Partenstein
Untermühl
290
Plöcking
Ritzersdorf
.490
Falkenberg
430
Neuhaus
Schloss Neuhaus
Grub
.483
Berg
Oedt
Pamet
.499
Point
map 15
Kaiser
Pühret
Rennersdorf
Dorf
Kolleck
Dorf
.527
2170
St. Martin
Kalkenbach
Hinterhölzl
Brandtner
.531
Kolbing
Gemersdorf
Donau
Exlau
525
.480
516
Gschwendt
Donauleiten
.447
Haibach
Hinteraigen
Paching
Moos
10
10.5
Pichl
Grub
.398
Bach
Sieberstal
Komas
563
Wiesing
.509
5.5
Donau
6.5
Oberhart
.462
Guggenberger
Würting
Zagl
Mußbach
Götzling
Hinterberg
Holzer
Loidbold
B 130
Dunzing
473
Hundsdorf
Reith
Schönleiten
Ortner
.443
Zöhrerleiten
.320
Wiespointner
Stockinger
Lacken
Kraftwerk Aschach
.567
Aschach
Senghubl
Henzing
538
Ruine Stauf
Gfehret
Hart
Sommerberg

Ottensheim

was sold at the Vienna Mint, and at Mauthausen prospectors, mostly gypsies, produced a small but steady supply of gold. Place names like Goldwörth, which has a history dating back to the 11th century, testify to the long history of gold mining and panning along the Danube.

The methods used by prospectors were relatively simple. River gravel was sifted through a wooden grating. The gravel stayed in the grating, sand was washed away, while traces of gold and other minerals were caught in a woolen cloth. Then a magnet was used to extract iron ore, and the remaining gold traces were thickened with mercury. The resulting mass was put in a leather pouch through which the mercury was filtered. At the end of this arduous process a tiny amount of gold remained in the pouch. Using these methods, a successful prospector produced about one hazelnut-sized lump of gold per year. It is estimated that the total amount of gold extracted from the Danube amounts to about 20 kilograms. This small amount sufficed, however, to strike ducats in Bavaria between 1756 and 1830, and to gold-plate the communion chalices at the Kosterneuburg and Göttweig abbeys.

Continue along the embankment about 3 kilometers to a landing for motorboats just before the **Ottensheim power station** ~ then follow the path that veers off at a right angle towards Ottensheim.

Tip: Proceed straight to cross the dam and reach the right bank of the Danube near Wilhering (see page 46). If the time is past 8 p.m., you must use the speaker-phone to ask the attendant to open the gate to the dam.

The north bank route follows a long curve to the right around an arm of the Danube. A rowing club has marked out lanes in this body of water. ~ The bicycle route makes a kink into the flood-plain woods, crosses a creek and returns to the shoreline.

The trail turns inland when it reaches the small river Rodl ~ and then bends right before crossing the Rodl on a small bridge.

Tip: To reach the Rodlhof campground, proceed straight and follow the path along the Rodl.

Before the edge of Ottensheim the bicycle path turns right and returns to the Danube.

The promenade leads around the remarkable palace which stands on a slight rise above surrounding houses. At the center of the town is the landing at which an especially environmentally-friendly ferry docks. The "Rollfähre" hangs on a steel cable stretched across the Danube, and traverses the river by using its current to push the ferry from one bank to the other. The Danube's high-water marks over recent decades are recorded on the wall of a nearby house. The last disastrous flooding in this region occurred in 1954. The town's central market is also noteworthy.

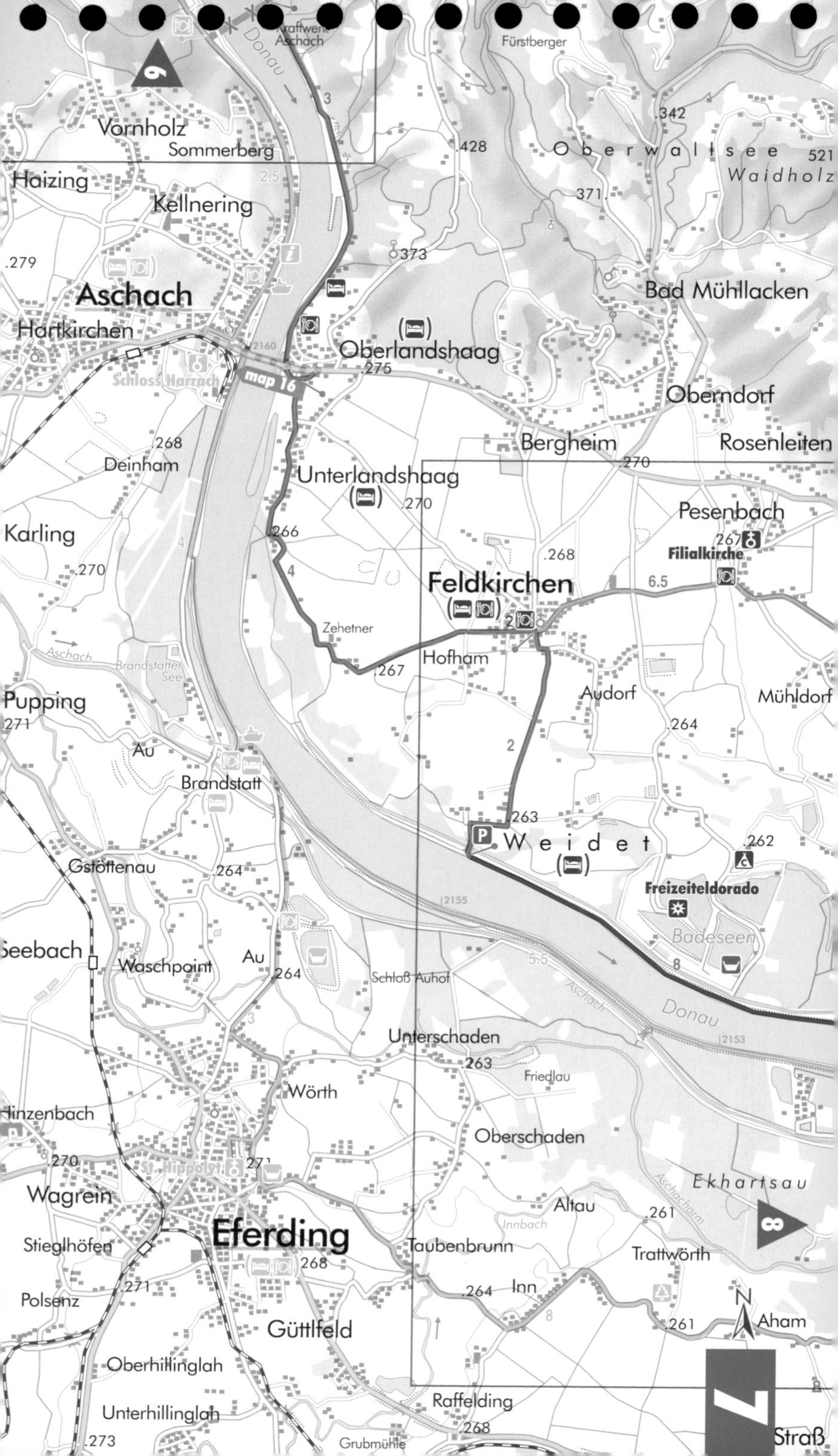

6
Kraftwerk Aschach
Donau
Fürstberger
Vornholz
Sommerberg
.428
Oberwallsee
.342
521
Waidholz
Haizing
Kellnering
.371
.279
.373
Aschach
Bad Mühllacken
Hartkirchen
.2160
Oberlandshaag
.275
map 16
Schloss Harrach
Oberndorf
.268
Deinham
Bergheim
Rosenleiten
.270
Unterlandshaag
.270
Pesenbach
Karling
.266
.268
.267
Filialkirche
.270
Feldkirchen
6.5
4
Zehetner
2
Aschach
Brandstätter See
Hofham
.267
Pupping
271
Audorf
Mühldorf
.264
Au
Brandstatt
2
.263
Weidet
.262
Freizeiteldorado
Gstöttenau
.264
2155
Badeseen
Seebach
Waschpoint
Au
.264
Schloß Auhof
5.5
Aschach
8
Donau
2153
Unterschaden
.263
Friedlau
Wörth
Hinzenbach
Oberschaden
.270
St. Hippolyt
.271
Ekhartsau
Wagrein
Altau
.261
Aschacharm
Innbach
8
Eferding
Taubenbrunn
Trattwörth
Stieglhöfen
.268
.271
.264
Inn
Polsenz
.261
N
Aham
Güttlfeld
Oberhillinglah
7
Unterhillinglah
Raffelding
.273
.268
Grubmühle
Straß

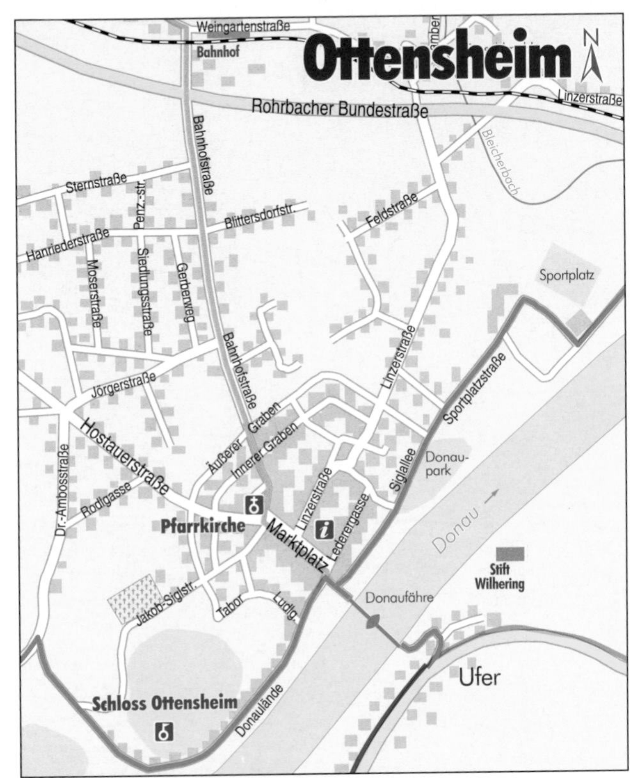

Ottensheim ≈km 2144 L

Postal code: 4100; Telephone area code: 07234

Tourist information, Donauländе 4, ✆ 83622

Ottensheim-Wilhering ferry: Mon-Sun 6:30-19:30, last departure for Wilhering 19:15, last departure to Ottensheim 19:20. First departure Son/Hol 8:00.

Ottensheim Castle. The keep and the north and east wings are all that remain of the medieval fortress that originally served as a Babenberger frontier outpost. Closed to the public.

Historic market. Despite repeated market fires, a number of interesting houses have survived, including the "Kindlhaus" which plays a key role in one of the legends about the foundation of Ottensheim.

Parish church, Marktplatz. Built 1450-1520. The Nepomuk Chapel was added in the late 19th century. The oldest part of the church is the crypt with bones recovered from the old cemetery, and the mummified remains of a noblewoman.

Ottensheim to Linz 9.5 km

The **main bicycle route** downstream from Ottensheim follows the **left bank**. There is no bicycle trail on the south (or right) bank.

Tip: The Cistercian abbey complex with its main church in Wilhering on the southern side of the Danube are well worth the detour across the river. Cyclists who are comfortable sharing the road with automobiles may then consider proceeding to Linz on the road that follows the right bank of the

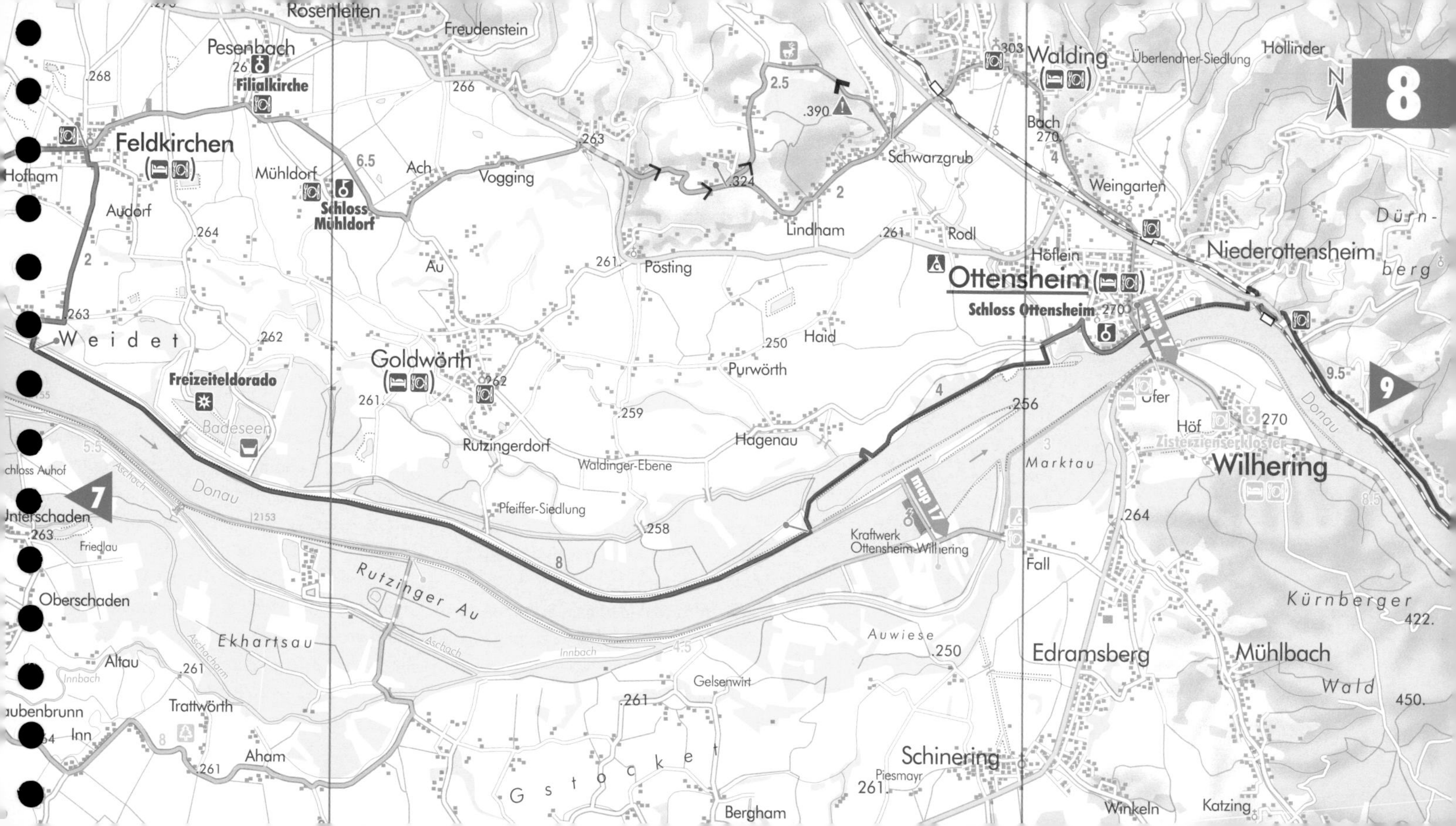
8
9
7
Rosenleiten
Freudenstein
Pesenbach
Filialkirche
Feldkirchen
Hofham
Audorf
Mühldorf
Schloss Mühldorf
Ach
Vogging
Au
Pösting
Lindham
Rodl
Schwarzgrub
Walding
Überlendner-Siedlung
Hollinder
Bach
Weingarten
Höflein
Niederottensheim
Dürnberg
Ottensheim
Schloss Ottensheim
Weidet
Freizeiteldorado
Badeseen
Goldwörth
Haid
Purwörth
Rutzingerdorf
Waldinger-Ebene
Hagenau
Pfeiffer-Siedlung
Ufer
Höf
Zisterzienserkloster
Wilhering
Marktau
Kraftwerk Ottensheim-Wilhering
Fall
Schloss Auhof
Unterschaden
Friedlau
Oberschaden
Donau
Aschach
Rutzinger Au
Ekhartsau
Innbach
Altau
Trattwörth
Inn
Aham
Gelsenwirt
Auwiese
Edramsberg
Mühlbach
Kürnberger Wald
Schinering
Piesmayr
Gstocket
Bergham
Winkeln
Katzing
map 17

Danube. The bicycle trail on the north bank is not particularly scenic.

Depart from the ferry station in **Ottensheim** (on the north bank) and follow the hiking/biking path along the river ~ behind the sports complex the path turns away from the river and goes over a narrow wooden bridge ~ then pass underneath the road and cross an unguarded railroad crossing ~ and follow the green signs to Linz ~ the cycle route dips underneath the main road again just before it enters a tunnel.

Tip: The chestnut-shaded terrace in front of the Dürnberg Gasthaus offers a lovely final view upstream towards Ottensheim and the Danube river valley.

Tip: While the stretch from Dürnberg to Linz is perfectly safe, it closely follows a heavily-traveled main road and is not scenic. If you wish to skip this section, it is possible to board a train in Dürnberg for the short trip to Linz.

Go left after the railroad station ~ pass underneath the road a third time ~ and continue along the cycle path that runs parallel with the main road ~ and reach the edge of **Puchenau** in about 4 kilometers.

Puchenau ≈km 2139 L

Stay to the left of the street as you pass two larger intersections ~ as the route enters Linz the bicycle trail goes underneath the road and down to the riverfront ~ there are two inviting-looking outdoor cafés on the river just before the Nibelungenbrücke ~ the **Danube bike trail** proceeds straight along the river.

To visit Linz, turn away from the river before the bridge and ride up around the new **city hall** to the bridge, which has bicycle lanes in both directions ~ continue straight off the bridge to reach the **Hauptplatz** (main square) with the column of the Holy Trinity. The Hauptplatz leads in to the Landstraße, which goes directly to the main train station. The mountain train up to the Pöstlingberg departs from the Mühlkreisbahnhof in the northern part of the city.

Linz see page 46

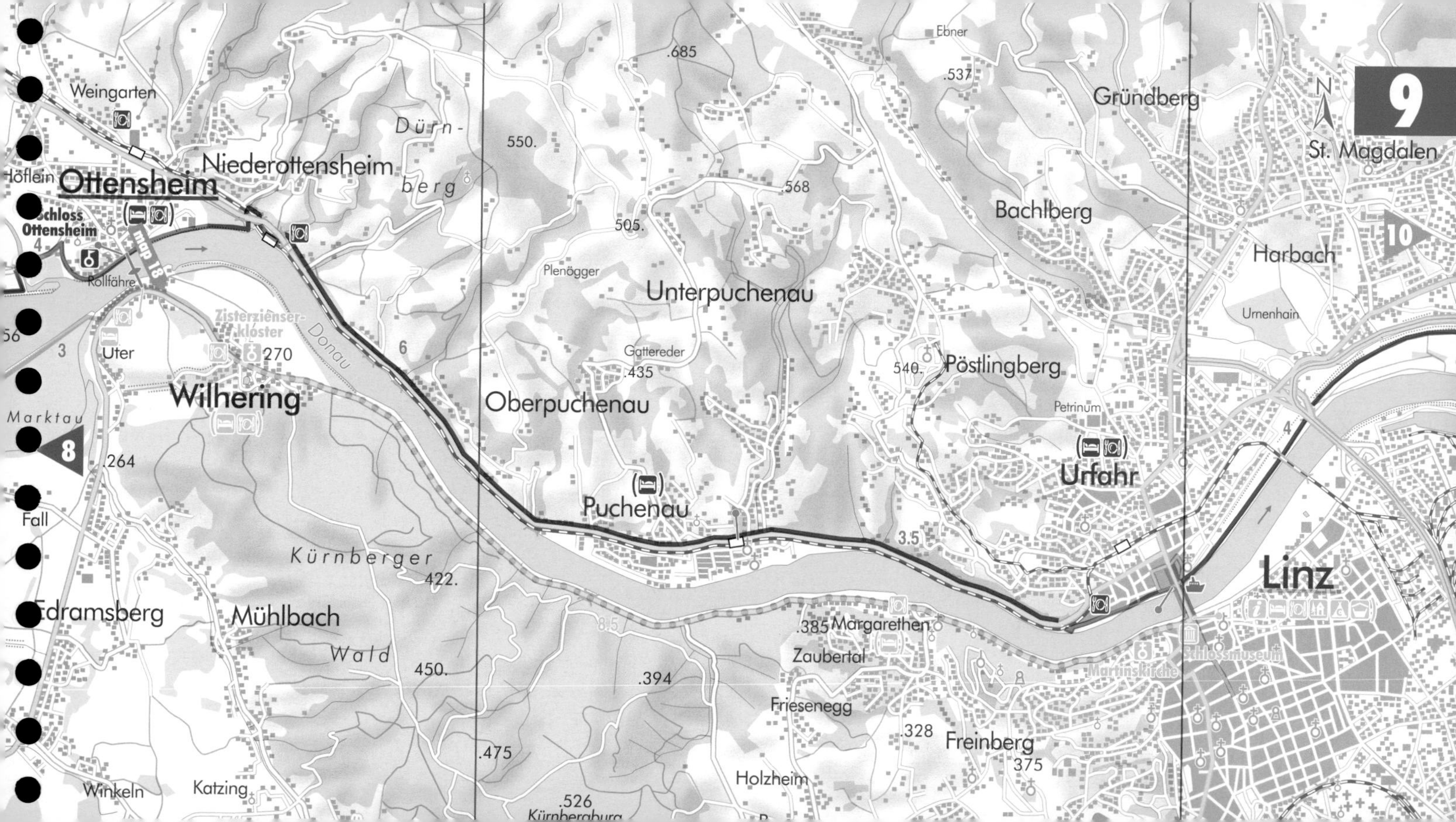

9
10
8
map 18
Weingarten
Höflein
Ottensheim
Niederottensheim
Schloss Ottensheim
Rollfähre
Dürnberg
Uter
Zisterzienser-kloster
270
Donau
Wilhering
Marktau
.264
Fall
Edramsberg
Mühlbach
Kürnberger
Wald
422.
450.
.475
Winkeln
Katzing
.526
550.
.685
505.
.568
Plenögger
Unterpuchenau
Gattereder
.435
Oberpuchenau
Puchenau
.394
Holzheim
Ebner
.537
Gründberg
Bachlberg
540.
Pöstlingberg
Petrinum
Urfahr
3.5
8.5
6
.385
Margarethen
Zaubertal
Friesenegg
.328
Freinberg
375
St. Magdalen
Harbach
Urnenhain
Linz
Schlossmuseum
Martinskirche

Passau to Linz along the right bank 98 km

The bicycle route along the right, or southern, bank of the Danube begins in Passau, the city at the confluence of the rivers Inn, Danube and Ilz. After a short distance the route enters Austria and skirts the edge of the Sauwald, through Engelhartszell to Schlögen, where the river winds through an extreme S-curve, the Schlögener Schlinge (loop). At Aschach the Danube then enters the fertile Eferdinger Basin, where it passes through vegetable gardens and imposing old farms. This stage of the Danube cycle tour ends in Linz.

Good bicycle trails are available only for parts of the route along the right bank. Several sections, especially between Engelhartszell and Schlögen, and the final kilometers into Linz, share the heavily-traveled main road with motorized traffic. There are frequent opportunities to cross the river to the quieter left bank route. This stage is completely flat, with no hills worthy of mention.

10
Passau
Hacklberg
Ilzstadt
Innstadt
Grubweg
Lindau
Hals
Anger
Dom
Rathaus
Kloster Niedernburg
Römisches Museum
Veste Oberhaus
Hauptbahnhof
Bahnhof Rosenau
Bahnhof Grubweg
Haltestelle Kellberg
Donau
Inn
Ilz
Soldatenau
Kellberg
Freinberg
Haibach
Achleiten
Edt
Lochdobl
Parz
Breiteich
Hinding
Neudling
Faberhof
Höllmühle
Erlau
Edlhof
Unteresternberg
Mitteresternberg
Dietzendorf
Esternberg
Faberwald
Edt-wald
Wildtierpark
Ruine Königstein
Nature preserve area Donauhänge
Fürstberg
Hinterhammer
Schörgendorf
Leithen
Kapfham
Wingersdorf
König-Max-Höhe
Buchsee
Pulvermühle
Kernmühle
Löwmühle
Aichet
Satzbach
Grafmühle
Facklmühle
Eggersdorf
Flattendorf
Niedersatzbach
Zieglreuth
Innerreuth
Reut
Kastenreuth
Sandberg
Erdbrüst
Sulzsteg
Außerreuth
Sieglgut
Sieglberg
Lüfteneck
Stromlänge
Laimgrub
Untersölden
Obersölden
Christdobl
Klosterberg
Bramerhof
Bschütt
Bergfried
Bockhof
Kuchlhof
Freudenhain
Eggendobl
Jägerreuth
Neureuth
Prämöd
Hörndl
Höflein
Ries
Doblhof
Thanöd
Sturmsölden
Grillenöd
Wimhof
Zollamt
Rosenau
Hammerberg
Resch
Unterfreinberg
Anzberg
Erledt
Aigen
Höh
Stöckl
Mauthner
Voglau
Kühberg
Hamberg
Lindenthal
Neusaming
Saming
Waging
Ingling
Rad
Schwendt
Kugelrad
Hof
Mayrhof
Fabrik
Hanzing
Achleiten
Ohrhalling
Lehen
Weg
Innerhareth
Schwabengrub
Pyret
Untergscheid
Grinzing
Kritzing
Waldreut
.386
.392
485
.521
.458
.305
297
4.5
6.5
297.
.442
1.5
404
.416
.419
.400
.352
.424
295
8.5
.477
.485
.453
.459
2
map I

Passau to Engelhartszell along the southern bank 26.5 km

The ride along the southern bank of the Danube first leads to Passau's second river, the Inn ⇝ take Schustergasse from the **Domplatz** in Passau's old city and ride to the left down the narrow Innbrückgasse to the Inn. Cross the river on the **Marienbrücke**.

Tip: Bicycle routes along the Inn River are described in the ***bikeline* guide books "Inn Radweg"** (parts 1 + 2). These are available in German.

From Kirchplatz on the southern side of the bridge turn left on Straße **Löwengrube**.

Tip: To reach the Roman museum turn right on Lederergasse.

From Löwengrube turn left down a widely-spaced stairs with a ramp down to the Inn ⇝ ride along the railroad tracks and a short stretch on a gravel path to reach the Rosenau train station ⇝ turn left over the tracks just before the station building and then right on Rosenauer Weg ⇝ at the end of this alley take the hiking and biking trail that passes the edge of a cluster of allotment gardens.

After the gardens the path becomes quite narrow ⇝ stay to the left of the tracks ⇝ behind an old warehouse to a sidestreet ⇝ after crossing the main road take the bicycle lane towards Achleiten ⇝ a new bicycle trail to the left of the main road begins in Achleiten ⇝ after about one kilometer the trail switches to the other side of the road and follows the edge of the forest.

After one kilometer a wide bicycle trail branches off to the right away from the road ⇝ near the Gasthaus Faberhof the route returns to the main road, which it follows as far as the former Gasthaus Höllmühle ⇝ here the bicycle trail ends and the route joins the main road for about 4 kilometers ⇝ the road follows the shoreline and leads past **Krämpelstein castle** ⇝ a new bicycle trail begins about 200 meters past the former customs station and leads through Wörth to Pyrawang ⇝ in the village the trail runs parallel to the main through street.

Tip: If you have time, take a look at the interesting church in Pyrawang.

Pyrawang ≈km 2213 R

Postal code: 4092; Telephone area code: 07714

- **Esternberg district office**, ✆ 665510
- **Parish church.** The small church contains early Gothic frescos discovered in 1982.
- **Bicycle Taxi (Radtaxi)** Johann Wallner, Esternberg, ✆ 0663/9170321. Pick-up service from Vienna or Linz, as well as other service and transport.

Take the new bicycle trail out of Pyrawang and proceed along the main road ⇝ after 3 kilometers the trail reaches the **Obernzell ferry** landing (open: 1 May-25 Sept Mon-Fri 6:15-18:15, Sat, Sun/Hol 7:30–18:15).

Tip: An interesting museum on ceramics documents Obernzell's past as a center of pottery making. The museum is on the Bavarian side of the river.

Tip: The ferry gives you the option of crossing to the northern bank of the river. See page 22 for the route description.

After the ferry landing the bicycle trail continues downstream on the left side of the road.

Tip: The campground in Kasten is equipped with bathrooms for cyclists.

The road to **Vichtenstein** branches off to the right from Kasten. It is a serpentine road that only uphill-freaks can enjoy.

The mighty castle at Vichtenstein and the 895-meter Haugstein, the tallest peak in the region, dominate the valley.

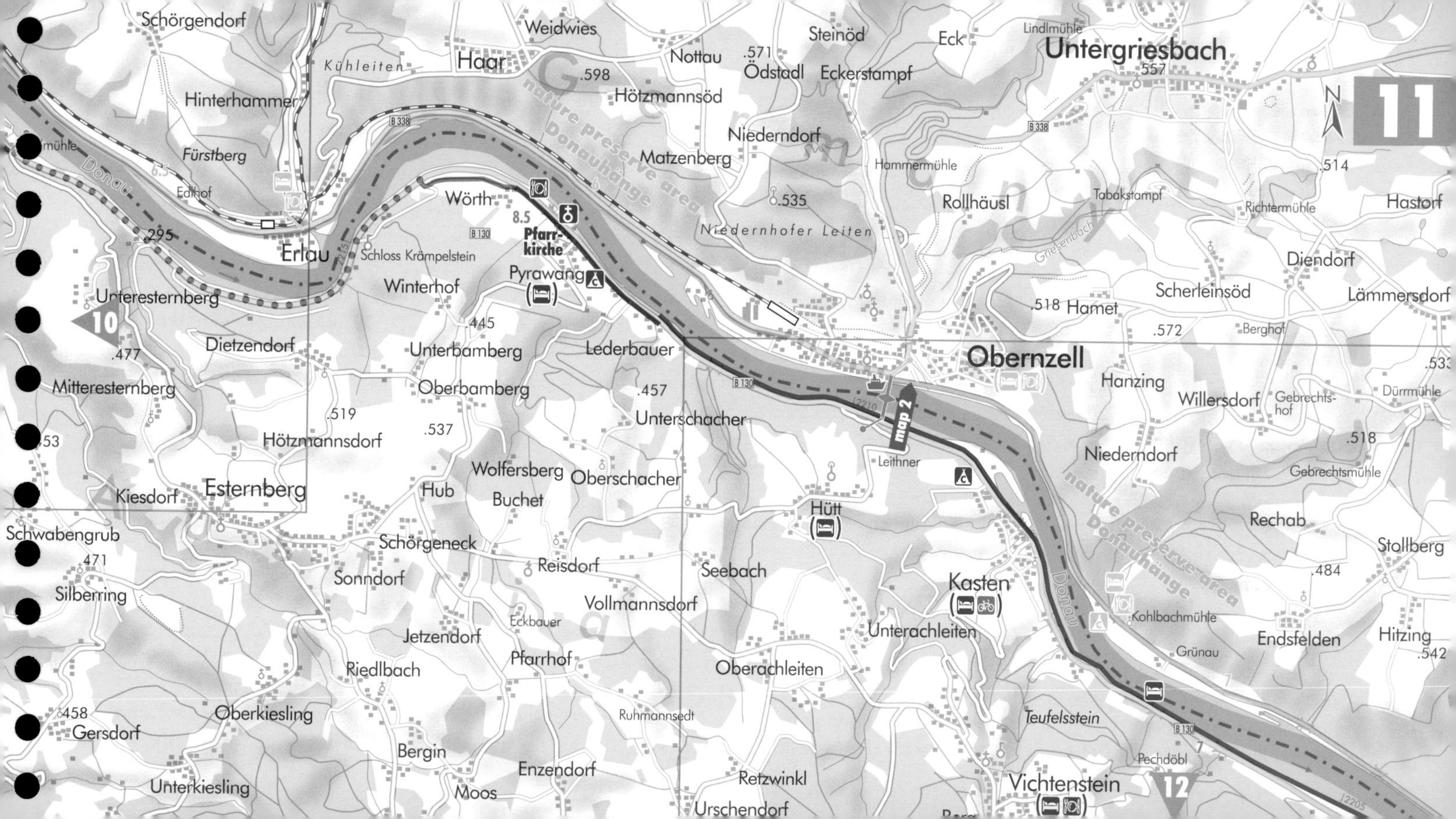
11
Schörgendorf
Weidwies
Steinöd
Eck
Lindlmühle
Untergriesbach
Kühleiten
Haar
Nottau
Ödstadl
Eckerstampf
Hinterhammer
Hötzmannsöd
Niederndorf
Matzenberg
Hammermühle
Fürstberg
Edlhof
Wörth
Rollhäusl
Tabakstampf
Richtermühle
Hastorf
Donau
nature preserve area Donauhänge
Niedernhofer Leiten
Pfarrkirche
Erlau
Schloss Krämpelstein
Pyrawang
Griesenbach
Diendorf
Winterhof
Unteresternberg
Scherleinsöd
Lämmersdorf
Hamet
Berghof
10
Dietzendorf
Unterbamberg
Lederbauer
Obernzell
Hanzing
Mitteresternberg
Oberbamberg
Willersdorf
Gebrechtshof
Dürrmühle
map 2
Unterschacher
Hötzmannsdorf
Leithner
Niederndorf
Gebrechtsmühle
Wolfersberg
Oberschacher
Esternberg
Kiesdorf
Hub
Buchet
Hütt
Rechab
Schwabengrub
Schörgeneck
Stollberg
Reisdorf
Seebach
Sonndorf
Kasten
Silberring
Vollmannsdorf
Kohlbachmühle
Eckbauer
Unterachleiten
Endsfelden
Hitzing
Jetzendorf
Grünau
Pfarrhof
Riedlbach
Oberachleiten
Oberkiesling
Ruhmannsedt
Teufelsstein
Gersdorf
Bergin
Pechdöbl
Enzendorf
Retzwinkl
Vichtenstein
12
Unterkiesling
Moos
Urschendorf
B 338
B 130
.598
.571
.557
.514
.535
.295
.518
.572
.533
.445
.477
.457
.519
.537
.518
.484
.471
.542
.458
8.5
6.5
2210
2205

Kasten ≈km **2209 R**

Postal code: 4091; Telephone area code: 07714

- **Tourism association Vichtenstein**, ✆ 80550
- **Ferry to** Obernzell: 1 May-25 Sept, Mon-Fri 6:15-18:15, Sat/Sun/Hol 7:30-18:15.
- **St. Jakob church.** Small church features reliefs dating from 1548, and was renovated in the baroque style.
- **Vichtenstein Castle**, at the foot of the Haugstein. The mighty fortifications go back to the 12th century. The main buildings in their current form were built in the 16th century. The Romanesque keep, the 2 residential towers, and the castle chapel are especially well-preserved. The castle is not open to the public.
- **Bike rental, M.-E. Pointner**, Kasten 22, ✆ 63100

The fortified castles along the Danube and in other parts of upper Austria mostly date back to the 11th to 13th centuries. They were built and occupied by the nobility as the Bavarian Ostmark, the precursor to Austria, was reestablished following the defeat of the Magyar invaders at Unstrut in 933 and on the Lechfeld near Augsburg in 955.

Proceed along the Danube to the hamlet of **Roning**.

Tip: The Jochenstein power station is just past Roning. Cyclists can cross the dam between 6 and 19 o'clock to reach the northern side of the river, where there is a long and steep stairs (see page 22).

The next landmarks are the **campground** and **outdoor pool** on the western edge of Engelhartszell. Information boards along the way describe the Roman limes in upper Austria ~ at the campground the route turns away from the river because the riverbank only has a narrow hiking path ~ cross the main road and use the cycle lane that runs to the right of the road. In Engelhartszell the route follows a service lane.

Tip: The Engelhartszell bicycle ferry landing is near the first major intersection when entering the town from the west. The ferry operates from 9-18 in the off-season, and between 8-20 in peak times. We recommend switching to the Danube's north bank at Engelhartszell because traffic is heavy on the main road on the southern bank. See page 22 for the route description.

Tip: If you wish to explore the center of Engelhartszell, turn right at the ferry and stroll through the market. Plaques on the sides of houses describe the town's history. Use the next crossing street to return to the main road.

Engelhartszell ≈km **2201 R**

Postal code: 4090; Telephone area code: 07717

- **Tourism association**, ✆ 8245 (Sparkasse)
- **Tourism office, Upper Danube Valley**, ✆ 805511
- **Ferry**: ✆ 07714/6764. Open: Daily 9-19
- **Danube passenger ship service** to Passau or Linz, ✆ 0851/929292
- **Engelhartszell Danube world (Donau-Welt)**, with eight interesting stations about the market's history.
- **Engelszell Abbey**. Established in 1293, it is the only Trappist monastery in Austria.
- **Church**. The monastery church was consecrated in 1764, and represents a highpoint in 18th century rococo stucco decoration. There are also impressive frescos in the nave.
- **Maria Himmelfahrt** parish church, town center. Nave and choir loft of the formerly Gothic market church were built between 1459-1503.
- **Imperial customs office** in a 14th century building with a mural about the history of the old mar-

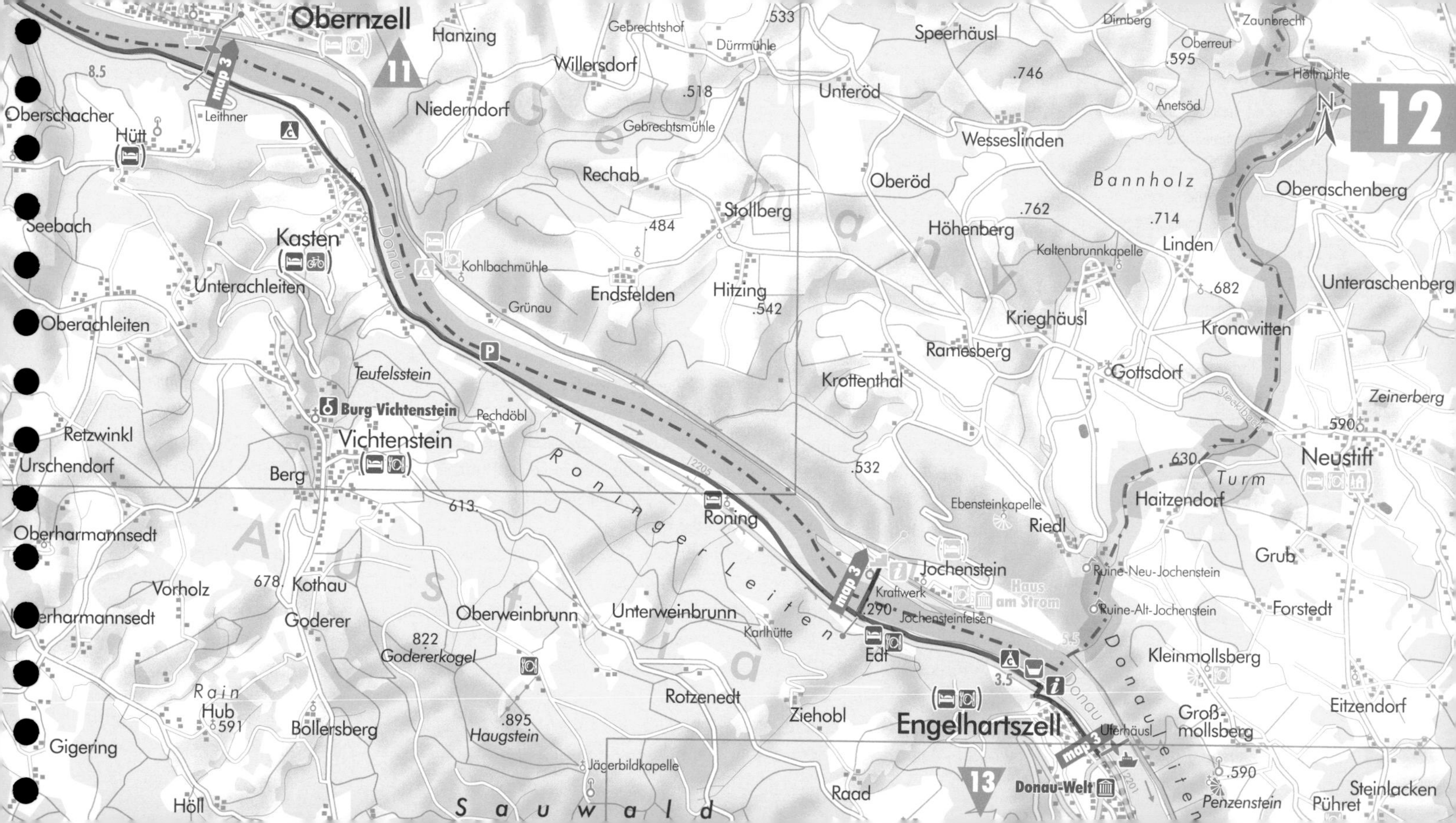

Obernzell
Hanzing
Willersdorf
Gebrechtshof
Dürrmühle
Speerhäusl
Dirnberg
Zaunbrecht
Oberreut
Höllmühle
12
11
Niederndorf
Unteröd
Wesseslinden
Anetsöd
Oberschacher
Hütt
Leithner
map 3
Gebrechtsmühle
Rechab
Oberöd
Bannholz
Oberaschenberg
Seebach
Kasten
Stollberg
Höhenberg
Linden
Kaltenbrunnkapelle
Donau
Kohlbachmühle
Unterachleiten
Endsfelden
Hitzing
Grünau
Krieghäusl
Kronawitten
Unteraschenberg
Oberachleiten
Ramesberg
Teufelsstein
Krottenthal
Gottsdorf
Zeinerberg
Burg Vichtenstein
Pechdöbl
Retzwinkl
Vichtenstein
Roninger Leiten
Neustift
Urschendorf
Berg
Turm
Haitzendorf
Roning
Ebensteinkapelle
Riedl
Oberharmannsedt
Grub
Jochenstein
Ruine-Neu-Jochenstein
Vorholz
Kothau
Kraftwerk
Haus am Strom
Forstedt
Goderer
Oberweinbrunn
Unterweinbrunn
Jochensteinfelsen
Ruine-Alt-Jochenstein
Karlhütte
Edt
Kleinmollsberg
Godererkogel
Rain
Hub
Rotzenedt
Ziehobl
Engelhartszell
Groß-mollsberg
Eitzendorf
Bollersberg
Haugstein
Uferhäusl
Gigering
Jägerbildkapelle
13
Donau-Welt
Penzenstein
Steinlacken
Höll
Sauwald
Raad
Pühret
Donauleiten

ket, and high-water marks from historic floods. A special culture exhibit in the cellar.

- **Jochenstein power generating station.** Dam open for crossings: 6-22; Guided tours: ✆ 8032 (DKJ Passau). Built between 1952 and 1956, the dam made the Danube more easily navigable for 30 kilometers upstream.
- **Outdoor pool,** ✆ 0664/8708787
- **Bike rental**, Donau-Radfreunde, ✆ 8182
- **Bike rental**, Tankstelle (petrol station) Strassl, ✆ 8037

The history of the **Engelhartszell** *market, an important border and customs post since medieval times, is closely tied to the development of the* **Engelszell monastery**. *Founded as a Cistercian monastery in 1293 by the bishops of Passau, the monastery for many years served as a refuge for travelers and the summer residence of Passau's rulers. In the course of reforms instituted by Kaiser Josef II, the monastery was closed in 1786, after which its ownership changed repeatedly.*

Religious life returned to the monastery in 1925, when it was occupied by German Trappists who had been driven out of Alsace. The strict rules by which this reformist Cistercian order lives – silence, vegetarian food, early waking hours – give the monastery an aura of otherworldly asceticism. That the Trappists' are not completely alienated from life is shown by their world-famous production of liquor.

Just past the end of the town turn right to reach the Engelszell abbey ~ ride past the monastery ~ the small road leads back down to the main road ~ turn right and continue down the heavily-traveled Bundesstraße towards Wesenufer.

Wesenufer ≈km **2192 R**

Postal code: 4085; Telephone area code: 07718

- **Tourism association Waldkirchen/Wesenufer,** ✆ 72550
- **"Tal des Kleinen Klößlbaches"** (valley nature preserve). Guided tours: ✆ 805516

Continue down the main road to Schlögen.

Tip: For a quieter ride consider switching to the northern bank. See page 24 for route description.

If you stay on the right bank, continue along the **B 130** as far as the Danube's famous loops at Schlögen.

Haibach-Schlögen ≈km **2187 R**

Postal code: 4083; Telephone area code: 07279

- **Tourism association Haibach-Schlögen,** ✆ 8235.
- **Excavations of the Roman fort Joviacum.** The fort's west gate has survived, and is the only existing Roman gate along the Danube in Austria.

Schlögen

From Passau to Aschach the Danube has cut a deep and meandering course through the tough Bohemian granite. The river does not follow the geological border between the Bohemian massif and the Bavarian-Austrian foothills, but found its own course over the eons, though not exactly by choice. The Danube had cut its curving course through the soft soils of the tertiary basin, and following the rise in the land, the river dug itself a 200 meters deep valley – today the scenic narrow valley downstream from Passau. But where the river reaches Schlögen it met a granite ridge that turned its course back 180 degrees for a short distance before finding a different route towards the sea. Geologists today still speculate about how this was possible.

The inaccessibility of the wooded slopes has helped create an environment in which many species of flora and fauna can be found. The spring and fall are seasons in which the Danube valley presents itself in especially vibrant colors, giving the valley a touch of wilderness. This impression is countered by the many inviting looking meadows and inns along the riverbank, which testify to the valley's centuries-long use.

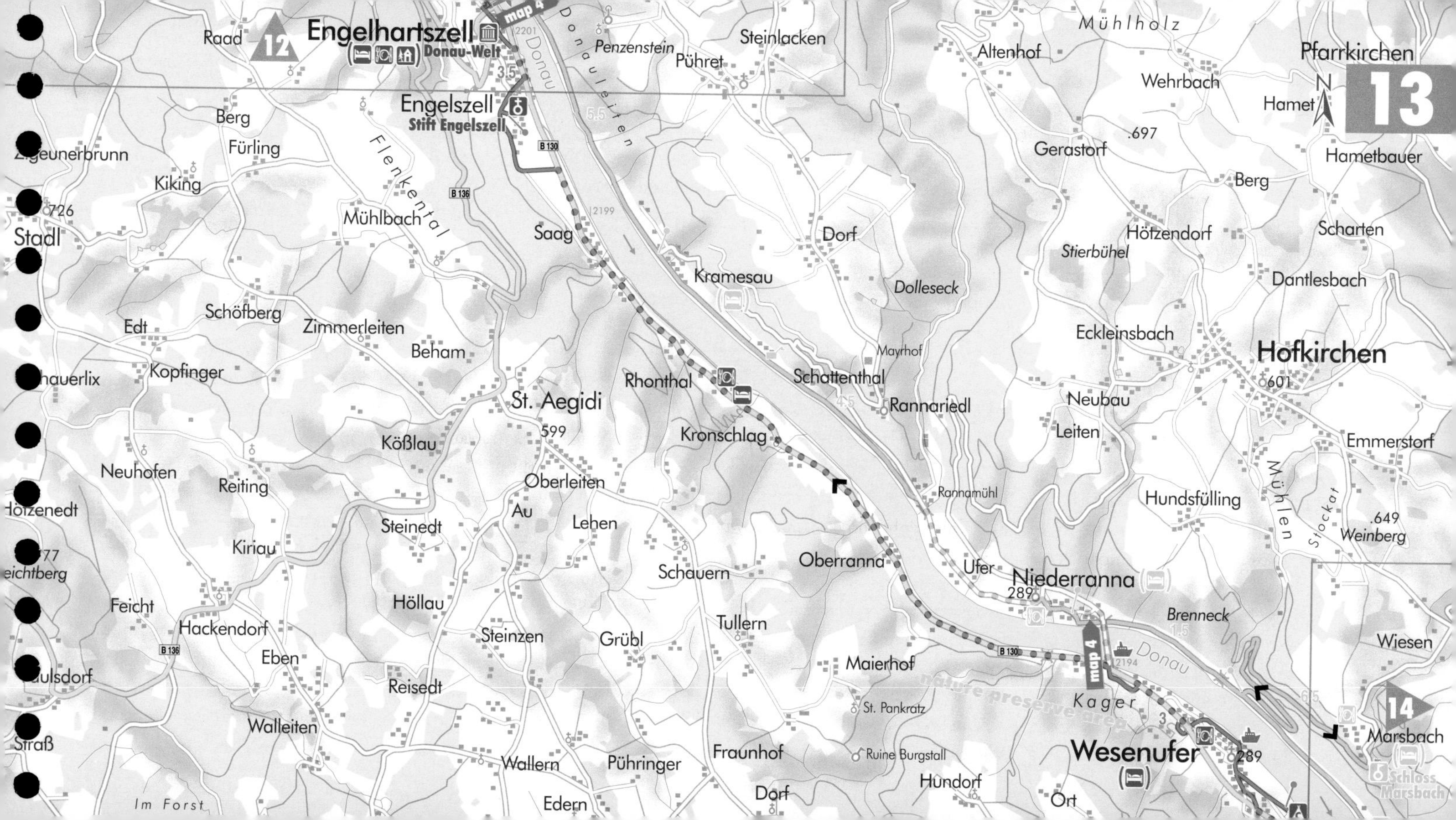

13
12
14
map 4
Engelhartszell
Donau-Welt
Engelszell
Stift Engelszell
Raad
Berg
Fürling
Zigeunerbrunn
Kiking
Stadl
726
Mühlbach
Flenkental
Saag
Donau
Donauleiten
Penzenstein
Pühret
Steinlacken
Altenhof
Mühlholz
Pfarrkirchen
Wehrbach
Hamet
Gerastorf
.697
Hametbauer
Berg
Scharten
Hötzendorf
Stierbühel
Dorf
Kramesau
Dolleseck
Dantlesbach
Eckleinsbach
Hofkirchen
601
Schöfberg
Edt
Zimmerleiten
Beham
Kopfinger
Rhonthal
Mayrhof
Schattenthal
Rannariedl
Neubau
Leiten
St. Aegidi
599
Kößlau
Kronschlag
Emmerstorf
Neuhofen
Reiting
Oberleiten
Rannamühl
Hundsfülling
Mühlen
Stockat
.649
Weinberg
Au
Lehen
Steinedt
Kiriau
Schauern
Oberranna
Ufer
Niederranna
289
Brenneck
Feicht
Hackendorf
Höllau
Steinzen
Grübl
Tullern
Maierhof
Wiesen
Eben
Reisedt
St. Pankratz
Kager
nature preserve area
Marsbach
Walleiten
Wallern
Pühringer
Fraunhof
Ruine Burgstall
Wesenufer
289
Schloss Marsbach
Straß
Im Forst
Edern
Dorf
Hundorf
Ort
B 130
B 136
2199
2201
2194
3.5
5.5
4.5
1.5
6.5
3

Between Schlögen and Grafenau the **Danube bicycle route** is present only on the right bank ~ a quiet idyllic road leads along the river through the river's bends ~ the **Haichenbach ruin** with its tower accents the verdant landscape ~ after 3.5 kilometers the route reaches the village of **Inzell**.

Inzell ≈km **2183 R**

Postal code: 4083; Telephone area code: 07279

Tourism association Haibach, ✆ 8235 and bicycle station, Gasthof Steindl ✆ 8328 and Gasthof Reisinger ✆ 8581

St. Nikolaus church. The renovated small church was reputedly established by a count after his rescue from the river here in the year 1155.

In the village the route returns to the river ~ where the bicycle trail resumes ~ after the next bend in the river the town of **Obermühl** comes into sight on the northern side of the Danube.

The distinctive grain silo from the Renaissance can be recognized by its tall hat-shaped roof. The structure has only barely survived the river's rise following construction of the dam downstream.

Kobling **R**

Postal code: 4083; Telephone area code: 07279

Tourism association Haibach-Schlögen, ✆ 8235 and Bicycle station Kobling ✆ 8624

Ferry to Obermühl. Open: April, Oct, 8-17, May, Sept, 8-18, June-Aug, 8-19.

Tip: In Kobling you can switch to the left bank of the river. See description on page 24.

Kobling to Aschach *18.5 km*

The Sauwald bicycle route branches off from the Danube bicycle route in **Kobling**, just past the tourist information office ~ stay left through a young woods to return to the Danube riverbank ~ and proceed down the comfortably-paved towpath to the Danube's next sharp bend near **Hinteraigen** ~ about 10 kilometers from Kobling the route reaches the next ferry.

*Above **Untermühl**, on the northern bank, stands the remarkable tower that belongs to **Neuhaus castle**. It is one of the largest castles in the upper Austrian Danube valley, and includes handsome Renaissance structures that are occupied to this day.*

At the **Gasthaus Kaiserhof**, which includes a large campground, there are several benches with fine views across the Danube ~ the landing place for the ***ferry to Untermühl*** is nearby (Open: May-June, 9-19; July-Aug, 9-20; Sept, 9-20).

Leave the Kaiserhof on the narrow street that serves residents along the river ~ when the Aschach dam comes in sight stay right at the fork in the path ~ at the **Aschach power station** there is a board posted with information about local accommodations. The dam is closed to the public and cannot be used to cross the river ~ a short distance further the route reaches Aschach.

The many well-groomed houses along the Danube recall the market's tradition as a center of shipping and shipbuilding.

Aschach ≈km **2160 R**

Postal code: 4082; Telephone area code: 07273

Tourism association, ✆ 635512 or 7000

Bicycle information, near the power station, ✆ 7000. Open: May-Oct, Mon-Sun 13-19.

Historic town center. Most of the old houses with their charming courtyards and arbors are built in the Gothic or Renaissance styles. Many of the facades bear stucco work from the 18th and 19th centuries.

Harrach castle, southern end of the market. The complex dates to 1606, to mark the marriage of

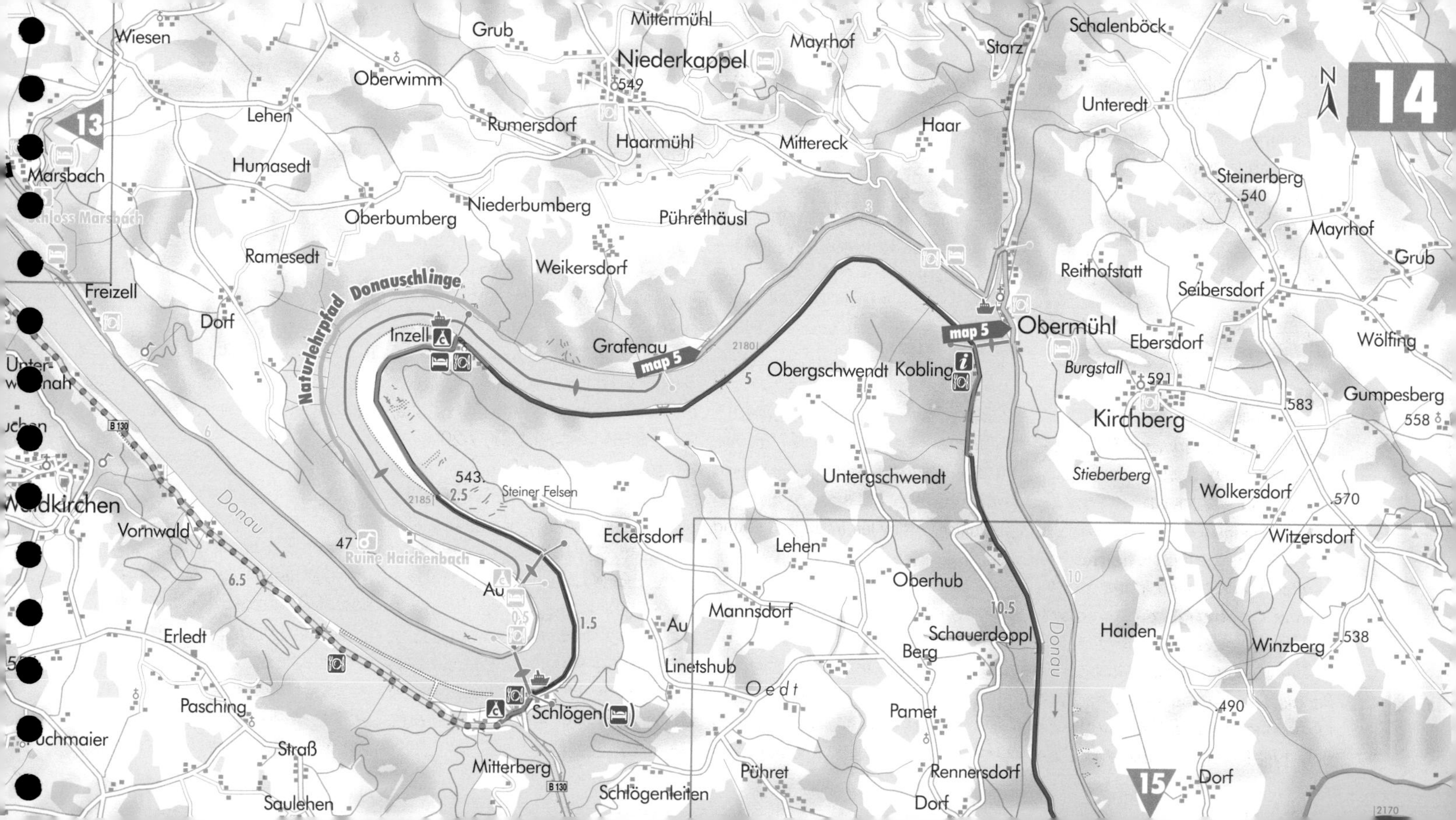
14
13
15
N
Wiesen
Grub
Mittermühl
Mayrhof
Starz
Schalenböck
Niederkappel
549
Oberwimm
Lehen
Rumersdorf
Haarmühl
Mittereck
Haar
Unteredt
Marsbach
Humasedt
Schloss Marsbach
Oberbumberg
Niederbumberg
Pührethäusl
Steinerberg
540
Mayrhof
Ramesedt
Weikersdorf
Reithofstatt
Grub
Seibersdorf
Freizell
Naturlehrpfad Donauschlinge
Dorf
Inzell
Grafenau
map 5
Obergschwendt
Kobling
Obermühl
Ebersdorf
Wölfing
Burgstall
591
Kirchberg
583
Gumpesberg
558
B 130
543
Steiner Felsen
2.5
2185
2180
5
3
6
Untergschwendt
Stieberberg
Wolkersdorf
570
Waldkirchen
Donau
Vornwald
47
Ruine Haichenbach
Eckersdorf
Lehen
Witzersdorf
6.5
Au
0.5
1.5
Oberhub
10
10.5
Mannsdorf
Au
Erledt
Schauerdoppl
Haiden
Winzberg
538
Berg
Linetshub
Oedt
Pasching
Schlögen
Pamet
490
Straß
Mitterberg
B 130
Pühret
Rennersdorf
Dorf
Schlögenleiten
Saulehen
Dorf
2170

Bicycle ferry at Schlögen

Karl von Jörger. It is one of the most significant secular Renaissance structures in upper Austria. A major reconstruction was carried out in 1709 under the architect Lukas von Hildebrandt.

Parish church. The Gothic structure was built in 1490, and was expanded in the 19th century according to plans drafted by Clemens Holzmeister. The altar includes the highly prized "Cross of the Danube," which washed ashore in Aschach in 1693.

Traun ship and park. The old river barge was built by 3 old shippers according to original plans for the 1994 state exhibition in Engelhartszell.

Hartkirchen parish church, (1.5 km west). Local records establish that the church existed as early as 898, making it the oldest church in the region. Around 1750 it was redecorated in the baroque style and furnished with imposing frescos, late-baroque illusionary paintings and rich decorations.

Faustschlössl, Landshaag, left bank. According to legend, Dr. Faust passed the castle as he traveled down the Danube to give Kaiser Friedrich III lessons in alchemy. Today is houses a hotel.

The old customs station at **Aschach** *was drawn into the great peasants' revolt of 1626, when rebels captured and plundered the city repeatedly. Shipping and ship building dominated the local economy until the early 20th century. Today Aschach is home to a handful of what may be the last living "Schopper," the name given to the craftsmen who build the 20-meter, up to 15-ton flat-bottomed barges that once plied the Danube.*

Tip: In Aschach it is possible to take the bridge across the Danube to the left bank (see page 24). The route down the right bank continues along a riverside path. A pleasant alternative is a detour through the vegetable gardens around Eferding. The next opportunities to cross the river come at the Ottensheim power station and the ferry from Wilhering.

To reach the left bank turn right just before the Danube bridge in Aschach ~ after 400 meters turn onto the bridge's ramp.

On the right bank, return to the hiking/biking trail that follows the shoreline and proceed under the bridge.

Aschach to Wilhering/Ottensheim on the right bank — 17 km

From the Danube bridge in Aschach the route runs directly next to the river ~ after 3 kilometers near Brandstatt swing to the right and across a minor tributary followed by a boat landing and then return to the Danube.

Brandstatt

Tip: A few hundred meters downstream from Brandstatt an alternative route branches off from the Danube route and leads to the town of Eferding. This route is partially posted with signs and passes through pleasant farmland before returning to the Danube 5.5 kilometers further downstream. Most of the excursion follows quiet country lanes. The route is colored orange in the maps.

From Brandstatt continue along the riverbank as far as the power station at **Ottensheim-Wilhering**.

Tip: Bicyclists can use the dam to cross the river. After 20:00 one must use the speakerphone to ask the attendant to open the gate. The next opportunity to cross the north bank

15
14
16
Lehen
Oberhub
Mannsdorf
509
Schauerdoppl
Berg
Oedt
Pamet
Pühret
Rennersdorf
Dorf
Kolleck
Gomersdorf
525
.447
Moos
Donauleiten
Haibach
Pichl
Grub
.398
Komas
Bach
Sieberstal
563
Wiesing
Hundsdorf
Dunzing
Hinterberg
B 130
Zöhrerleiten
.320
Aschach
.567
Henzing
Witzersdorf
Haiden
.499
Dorf
.527
Donau
Exlau
10
10.5
.515
.538 Winzberg
Partenstein
290
Untermühl
Point
map 6
.430
Neuhaus
Schloss Neuhaus
Kaiser
2170
Brandtner
Gschwendt
516
.480
Hinteraigen
Paching
.509
Mußbach
Würting
473
Stockinger
Wiespointner
Gfehret
Zagl
Holzer
Reith
Lacken
Senghubl
Plöcking
Ritzersdorf
Falkenberg
.490
Grub
.483
St. Martin
Kalkenbach
Hinterhölzl
531
Kolbing
Oberhart
.462
Guggenberger
5.5
Donau
6.5
Schönleiten
Loidhold
Ortner
.443
Kraftwerk Aschach

is the ferry in Wilhering (see page 28).

On the southern bank the bicycle route turns onto a road that leads directly away from the station gate ~ after the bridge over the Innbach take the sharp left turn before the campground ~ follow the Innbach back to the Danube and continue along the river.

Turn left immediately after the Mühlbach ~ and take the hiking/biking trail to the **ferry** to Ottensheim ~ the town of **Wilhering** with its noteworthy **Cistercian monastery** is about one kilometer away and can be reached with the bicycle trail that runs next to the main road.

Wilhering ≈km **2142 R**

Postal code: 4073; Telephone area code: 07226

Town office, Linzer Str. 14, ✆ 2255

Monastery building. Originally founded around 1200, the first major expansion of the monastery followed in the middle of the 17th century.

Abbey church Maria Himmelfahrt. Construction of the church in 1733-51 resulted in one of the most outstanding rococo church buildings in Austria. It is especially noted for the interior, an artwork of rococo decoration.

Abbey garden. Modeled on an English garden and laid out in 1833. It includes a yew believed to be 800 years old, and a large orangery in classicist Biedermeier design.

Fish study trail, on the shore trail between the power station and town. 84 signs describe native fish species and habitat (including extinct animals).

Tip: The right bank route follows the scenic but busy main road downriver from Wilhering to Linz. Cyclists who prefer to ride on designated bicycle trails should take the ferry to Ottensheim and the left bank route (see page 28).

The Danube river road to Linz and the Nibelungen bridge.

Tip: The bridge delivers you right to the middle of the city.

Linz ≈km **2135 R**

Postal code: 4020; Telephone area code: 070

Tourist information, Hauptpl. 1, ✆ 70701777

Donauschifffahrt Wurm + Köck, Untere Donaulände 1, ✆ 783607. Mid-April to Oct daily passenger ship service to Passau, Bicycles free.

Landes Galerie (Francisco Carolinum), Museumstr. 14, ✆ 774482. Open: Tues-Fri 9-18, Sat/Sun/Hol 10-17. State gallery with modern and contemporary art, exhibitions.

Ars Electronica Center, Hauptstr. 2, ✆ 72720. Open: Wed-Sun 10-18. Museum of the future, exhibits on technologies and ideas for the 21st century.

Palace museum, Tummelpl. 10, ✆ 774419. Open: Tues-Fri 9-18, Sat/Sun/Hol 10-17. Art and artifacts collections from the early middle-ages to art nouveau , plus weapons, musical instruments, furniture, crafts and folklore exhibits. No charge for families every first Sunday of the month.

City museum Linz-Nordico, Bethlehemstr. 7, ✆ 70701912. Open: Mon-Fri 9-18, Sat/Sun/Hol 14-17. Large special exhibits. Visit Tourist Information for current events.

Lentos Kunstmuseum (art museum) Linz, Ernst-Koref-Promenade 1, ✆ 7070-3600. Opened May 18, 2003. Open: Mon, Wed-Sun 10-18, Thur 10-22. An architectural jewel directly on the banks of the Danube, built to house the collections of the Linz Neue Galerie. The museum's appearance is dominated by a glass facade that is lit up at dark to make the building a visual landmark even at night.

Stifterhaus, Adalbert-Stifter-Pl. 1, ✆ 7720-1295. Open: Tues-Sun 10-15. The home of Adalbert Stifter, the author of "Nachsommer" and "Witiko," for 20 before his death in 1868. Today a museum on Stifter and upper Austrian literature.

Linz Palace, Tummelpl. 10. The former Babenberg border fortress against Bavaria underwent major reconstruction around 1600 by Rudolf II. The first Austrian Reichstag (parliament) met here. Especially noteworthy – the banquet hall and the reconstructed Weinberger palace pharmacy from 1700.

Martins church, Römerstraße. Regarded as the oldest surviving church built in the original Austrian form (known since 799). The foundations of a Carolingian king's residence were discovered above a Roman foundation.

Brucknerhaus, Untere Donaulände 7, ✆ 76120. Modern concert and congress hall, venue of the

16
15
17
map 7
Donau
Aschach
Vornholz
Sommerberg
Haizing
Kellnering
Hartkirchen
Schloss Harrach
Deinham
Karling
Pupping
Au
Brandstatt
Brandstätter See
Gstöttenau
Waschpoint
Hinzenbach
St. Hippolyt
Wagrein
Eferding
Stieglhöfen
Polsenz
Güttlfeld
Oberhillinglah
Unterhillinglah
Grubmühle
Raffelding
Fürstberger
Oberwallsee
Waidholz
Bad Mühllacken
Oberlandshaag
Oberndorf
Bergheim
Rosenleiten
Unterlandshaag
Pesenbach
Filialkirche
Feldkirchen
Zehetner
Hofham
Audorf
Mühldorf
Weidet
Freizeiteldorado
Badeseen
Schloß Auhof
Unterschaden
Friedlau
Wörth
Oberschaden
Ekhartsau
Aschacharm
Altau
Innbach
Taubenbrunn
Trattwörth
Inn
Aham
Straß

Linz Anton Bruckner Festival. Internationally renowned for its superior acoustics.

Neuer Dom, Baumbachstr. The largest Austrian church since the baroque, built 1862 to 1924 with capacity for 20,000 worshippers. Noteworthy are the painted windows with illustrations from the history of Linz.

Minorites church, Klosterstraße. Charming rococo church built in the 18th century next to the Minorite monastery (founded in 1236).

Linz parish church, Pfarrplatz. Originally a Roman basilica. The 1648 baroque new building includes a wall-mounted gravestone for the heart and entrails of Kaiser Friedrich III.

Pilgrimage church Pöstlingberg. The origin of the pilgrimage was the miraculous healing of Count Gundomer von Starhemberg. The easily-recognized church, a Linz landmark, was built 1738-47.

Landhaus, Promenade. The 16th century Renaissance Upper Austrian government offices had several interesting sights, including the courtyard with the so-called Fountain of Planets.

Column of the Holy Trinity, Hauptplatz. The 20-meter baroque column was built in 1700 in thanks for the city's survival in the face of war, plague and fire.

Mozarthaus, Altstadt 17. Wolfgang Amadeus Mozart lived in this 16th century Renaissance building as the guest of Grafen von Thun. He composed the "Linz Symphony" here.

Grottenbahn am Pöstlingberg. Open: 1 March-31 May and 1 Sept-2 Nov, daily 10-17; June-Aug 10-18; Advent Sundays 10-17. A fairy-tale world for children and adults, with stories of dwarfs, giants and enchanted princesses.

Botanic Garten, Rosegger Str. 20, ✆ 70701880. Open: Mon-Sun. Notable complex covering 4.25 hectares with more than 10,000 varieties, plus cactus collection, rosarium, alpinum and tropical house.

Pöstlingbergbahn, base station in Urfahr part of Linz. In operation since 1898, the mountain train climbs 255 meters to the pilgrimage church and a favorite Linz vantage point.

Sport Home Service, Lornstorferpl. 8, ✆ 0664/4316969. Open: Mon-Sun 10-20

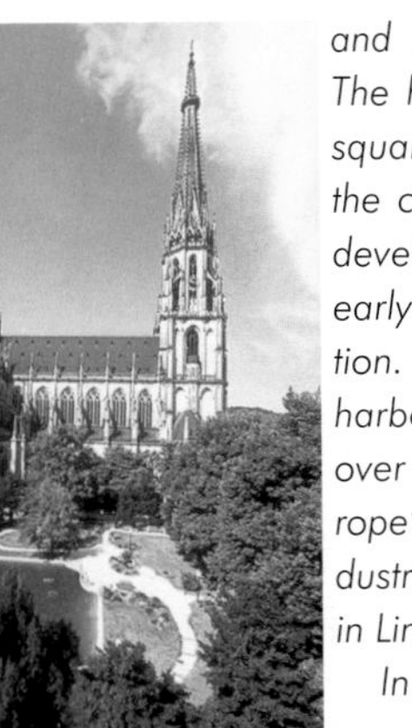

Centuries ago, when salt and iron ore were Europe's important commodities, a large market was built at the site of the Roman settlement of Lentia. Kaiser Maximilian's "Brückenbrief" in 1497 launched the developments that made Linz and its annual fair known across Europe in the 16th and 17th centuries. The huge medieval square influenced the city's economic development until early industrialization. Today the city harbor has taken over this role. Europe's first large industrial factory was in Linz.

In more recent years the city has been gaining an international reputation as a city of culture that combines the qualities of an important industry and trade city with a lively and attractive contemporary arts scene. One example is the Ars Electronica, which since 1979 has been giving renowned artists the opportunity of giving form to the newest technological advances.

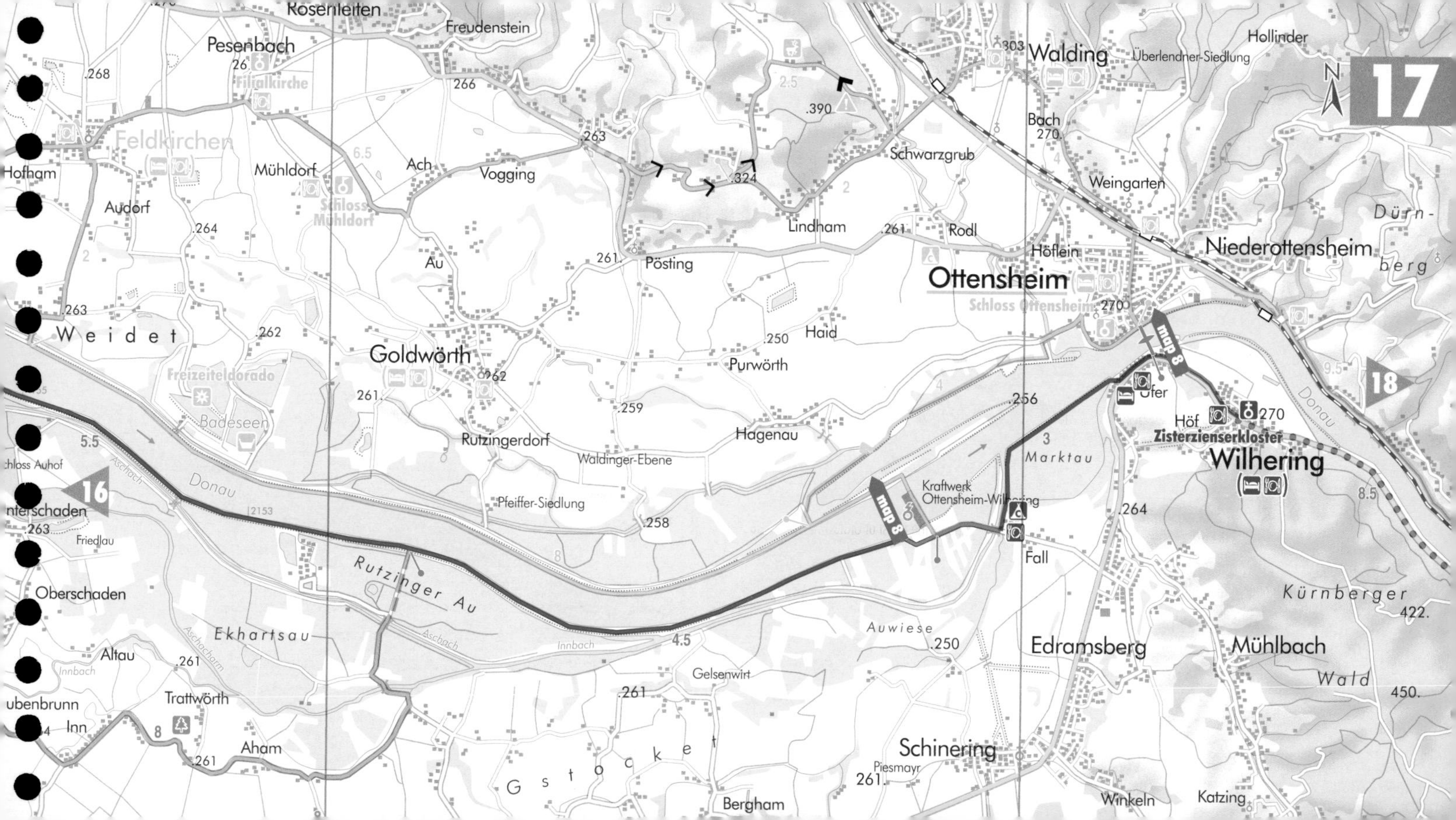

17
18
16
map 8
map 8
Rosenleiten
Freudenstein
Pesenbach
Filialkirche
Feldkirchen
Hofham
Audorf
Mühldorf
Schloss Mühldorf
Ach
Vogging
Au
Pösting
Lindham
Schwarzgrub
Walding
Überlendner-Siedlung
Hollinder
Bach
Weingarten
Rodl
Höflein
Niederottensheim
Dürnberg
Ottensheim
Schloss Ottensheim
Haid
Purwörth
Weidet
Goldwörth
Freizeiteldorado
Badeseen
Rutzingerdorf
Waldinger-Ebene
Hagenau
Pfeiffer-Siedlung
Kraftwerk Ottensheim-Wilhering
Marktau
Ufer
Höf
Zisterzienserkloster
Wilhering
Donau
Schloss Auhof
Unterschaden
Friedlau
Oberschaden
Rutzinger Au
Ekhartsau
Aschach
Aschacharm
Innbach
Altau
Trattwörth
Inn
Aham
Gstocket
Gelsenwirt
Auwiese
Edramsberg
Mühlbach
Kürnberger Wald
Fall
Schinering
Piesmayr
Bergham
Winkeln
Katzing

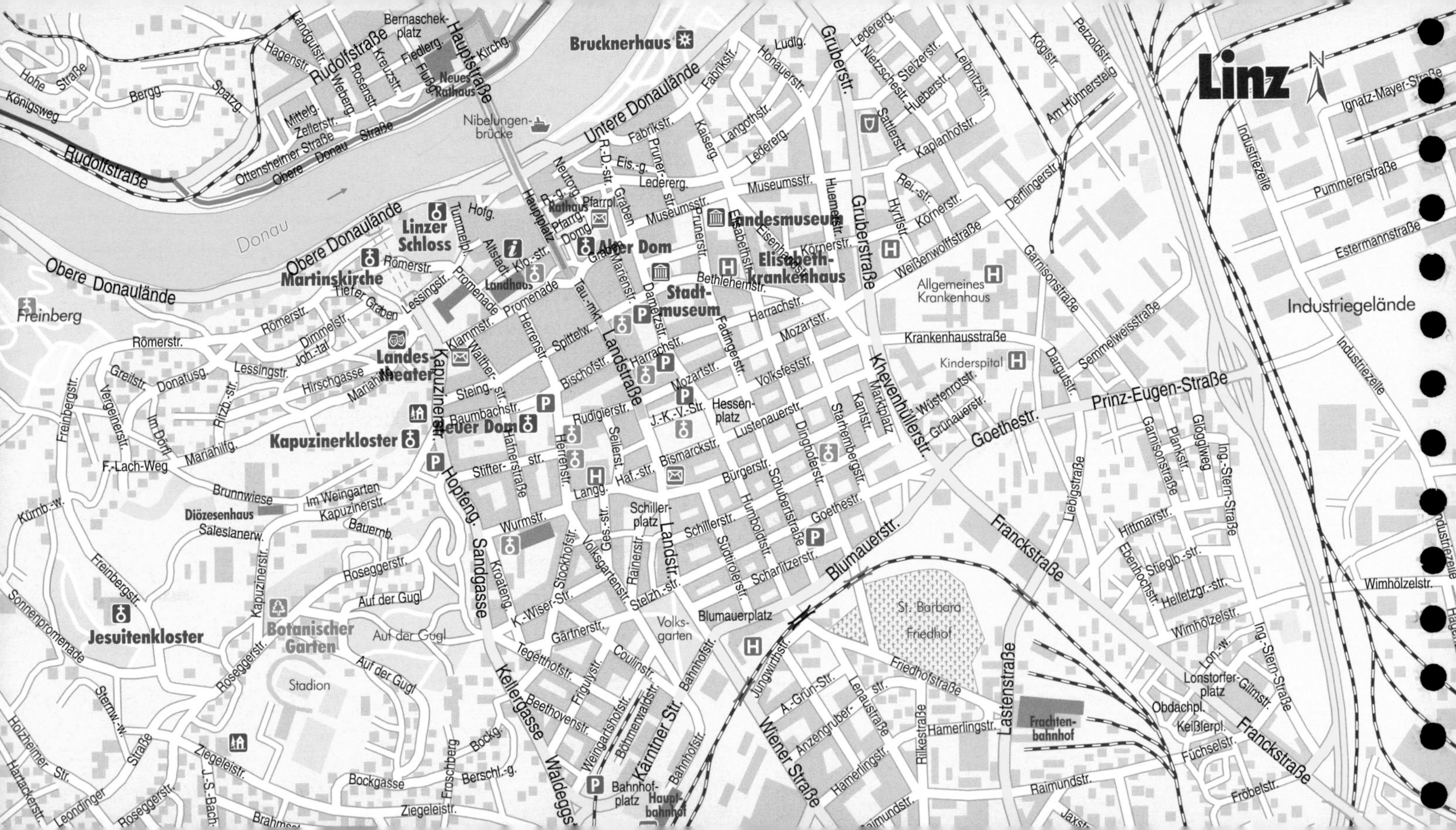
Linz
Brucknerhaus
Donau
Neues Rathaus
Nibelungenbrücke
Linzer Schloss
Martinskirche
Landhaus
Alter Dom
Landesmuseum
Elisabethkrankenhaus
Stadtmuseum
Landestheater
Neuer Dom
Kapuzinerkloster
Diözesenhaus
Botanischer Garten
Stadion
Jesuitenkloster
Freinberg
Allgemeines Krankenhaus
Kinderspital
Industriegelände
St. Barbara Friedhof
Volksgarten
Frachtenbahnhof
Hauptbahnhof
Hauptstraße
Rudolfstraße
Obere Donaulände
Untere Donaulände
Landstraße
Prinz-Eugen-Straße
Franckstraße
Blumauerstr.
Wiener Straße
Kärntner Str.
Khevenhüllerstr.
Gruberstraße
Goethestr.

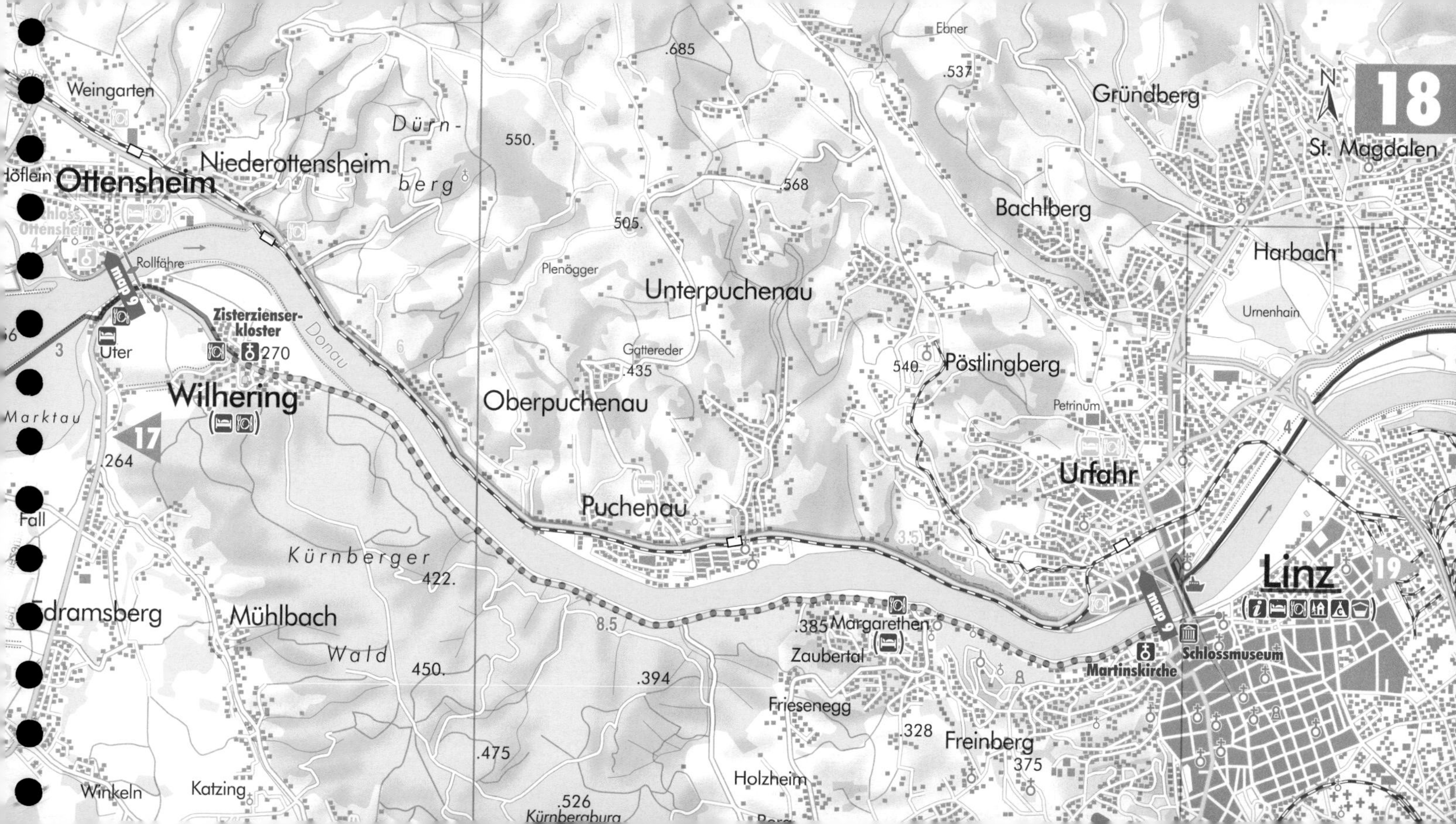
18
Weingarten
Dürn-
berg
Niederottensheim
Höflein
Ottensheim
Schloss Ottensheim
Rollfähre
map 9
Zisterzienser-
kloster
270
Uter
Donau
Wilhering
Marktau
17
.264
Fall
Edramsberg
Mühlbach
Kürnberger
Wald
422.
450.
8.5
550.
505.
Plenögger
Unterpuchenau
Gattereder
.435
Oberpuchenau
Puchenau
.685
.568
.475
.394
.526
Kürnberaburg
Holzheim
Friesenegg
.385 Margarethen
Zaubertal
.328
Freinberg
375
Ebner
.537
Gründberg
St. Magdalen
Bachlberg
Harbach
Urnenhain
540.
Pöstlingberg
Petrinum
Urfahr
3.5
Linz
19
Martinskirche
Schlossmuseum
Winkeln
Katzing

Linz to Melk along the left bank 107 km

Downstream from Linz, the Danube bicycle trail returns to the green and fertile Austrian countryside, bringing the bicycle tourist through pretty towns like Steyregg and Grein, past cultural attractions like the open-air museum in Metterkirchen, and historical sites, including the Mauthausen concentration camp, a remnant of Germany and Austria's Nazi past. The bicycle tour crosses the fascinatingly melancholy Strudengau, the much-feared narrows where the Danube churns and races, to the gentle Nibelungengau that the river passes to reach Melk.

From Linz to Abwinden the Danube bicycle route can be found only on the northern, or left, bank of the river. The route guides riders along quiet country lanes and cycle paths to Melk. The section between Grein and Persenburg is routed on public roads - traffic is somewhat heavier. The only climbs are for the excursion to Mauthausen.

Linz to Abwinden — *15.5 km*

The **Danube bicycle route** passes through the city, underneath the **Nibelungen bridge,** and down the northern bank of the river ~ as far as the steel railroad bridge, where the route leaves the shoreline and moves 100 meters "inland" before going under the bridge ~ stay right from the embankment, under the Autobahn bridge and proceed along the edge of the Pleschinger Au (flood plain).

Tip: After 2 kilometers it is possible to ride up to the crown of the embankment and down to the Pleschinger See (lake) with its beaches, campground, restaurant, nudist-area and various recreational facilities.

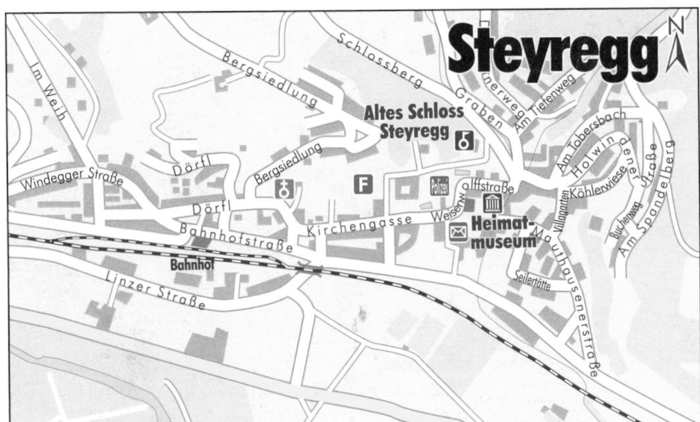

On the right bank of the river lie Linz harbor and the city's industrial zone, which includes Voest Alpine Stahl steelworks and the Chemie-Linz AG chemicals plant. Since 1991 Linz has had the lowest air pollution values of all Austrian provincial capitals – the result of extensive investments that have also helped create numerous jobs.

The bicycle route passes between these sharply contrasting landscape features toward the town of Steyregg and another railroad bridge – about one kilometer past the railroad bridge there is a mostly-paved 1.5 kilometer excursion route into the likeable town of Steyregg and its imposing old castle.

Steyregg L

Postal code: 4221; Telephone area code: 0732

Municipal office, Weißenwolffstr. 3, ✆ 640155 or 640082

Small museum in the city tower, with artifacts from Steyregg's stone age settlement.

St. Stephan church, Kirchengasse. This 14th century church includes early frescos that were rediscovered in 1951.

Old castle, Schlossberg. Castle from the second half of the 12th century, includes extraordinary frescos in the castle's chapel (14th century).

Pulgarn abbey, 2 km east of the Danube cycle route. Established in 1303 as a hospital for the sick and needy. Today part of the St. Florian canonical abbey. The one-time chapel space includes impressive frescos from the time of the abbey's founding. The late-Gothic abbey church (1512) is distinguished by its excellent acoustics and interior spaces.

Proceed along the former towpath past the Steyregg-Rosenau marina towards the Abwinden-Asten power generating station.

Across the river, the confluence of the ***Traun****, an important tributary of the Danube, can be seen. The flat Machland plateau opens up to the east, interrupted only by the lonely 400-meter high Luftenberg.*

Steyregg – city tower

⚠ 2 kilometers after Steyregg the bicycle route makes a dangerous and hard-to-see right turn around a marina.

Tip: A gravel path branches off the main route exactly on this curve. It leads to the Ringelau lakes 1.5 kilometers away.

20
19
21
map 30
Steyregg
Götzelsdorf
Lehen
Pürach
Knierübl
Denneberg
Pulgarn
Gröbetsweg
Knollmühle
Kloster Pulgarn
Kutzenbergsiedlung
Altau
Kruckenberg
Hannerlhaufen
Luftenberg
St. Georgen
Ringelau
Staizing
Meierhof
Kirchberg
Hintberg
Frankenberg
Luftenberg
Resch
Bahnhof St. Georgen
Steining
Abwinden
Gusen
Langenstein
Donau
Neuau
Traun
Weikerlsee
Angererhaufen
Raigerhaufen
Förgenhaufen
Haltestelle Ebelsberg
Klettfischer
Ufer
Donaukraftwerk-Abwinden-Asten
Posch
Ausee
Hochhauser
Adamshaufen
Schlossau
Ebelsberg
Schiltenberg
Pichling
Lang Au
Pichlinger See
Bahnhof Asten-St. Florian
Raffelstetten
Enghagen
B3
B1
A1

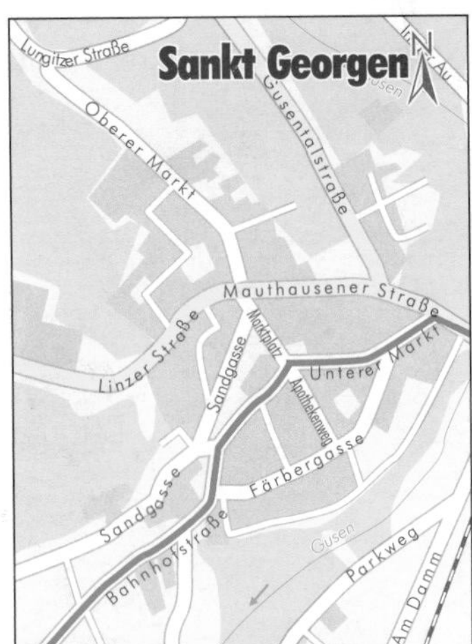

Proceed along the well-built embankment trail.

Tip: Just upstream from the Abwinden-Asten generating station the Danube bicycle route offers several options. The left bank route branches off from the Danube towards Mauthausen on the northern side of the river. The Mauthausen concentration camp memorial site is a short distance off the northern cycle route. The right bank route is also an attractive option, with an excursion route to the monastery at St. Florian and an alternative route to Enns. One can also select quiet country lanes to ride directly to the historic city of Enns or to the ferry to Mauthausen. The various routes converge again either at the Mauthausen bicycle ferry or at the Danube bridge downstream from Enns/Mauthausen.

Please go to the next section, page 74, Map 31 for a description of the routes on the southern bank.

Abwinden to Mauthausen 9 km

The **left bank route** branches away from the river before it reaches the **Abwinden-Asten power station** ~ proceed across an arm of the Danube and under the main road ~ and turn right towards Abwinden.

Abwinden

The town has numerous comfortable inns and inviting restaurants ~ continue straight on the main road past the train station at **St. Georgen a. d. Gusen**.

Mauthausen

Tip: The train station has interesting rail connections for excursions into the charming Mühlviertel region north of the Danube.

Go under the railroad and follow the road towards St. Georgen.

St. Georgen a. d. Gusen L

Postal code: 4222; Telephone area code: 07237

Town office, ✆ 22550

Turn right across the small river Gusen and cross the tracks next to the train station ~ and follow this street out of St. Georgen towards Langenstein.

*Tourists with an interest in archaeology might take note of the 12-meter hillock about one kilometer south of Gusen. This "**Berglitzl**" is a memorial to the region's prehistoric settlers – a granite formation that was able to defy the river's wearing powers and protect a camp used by hunters at the end of the last Ice Age (about 12,000 BC). It is the oldest proven human settlement in upper Austria.*

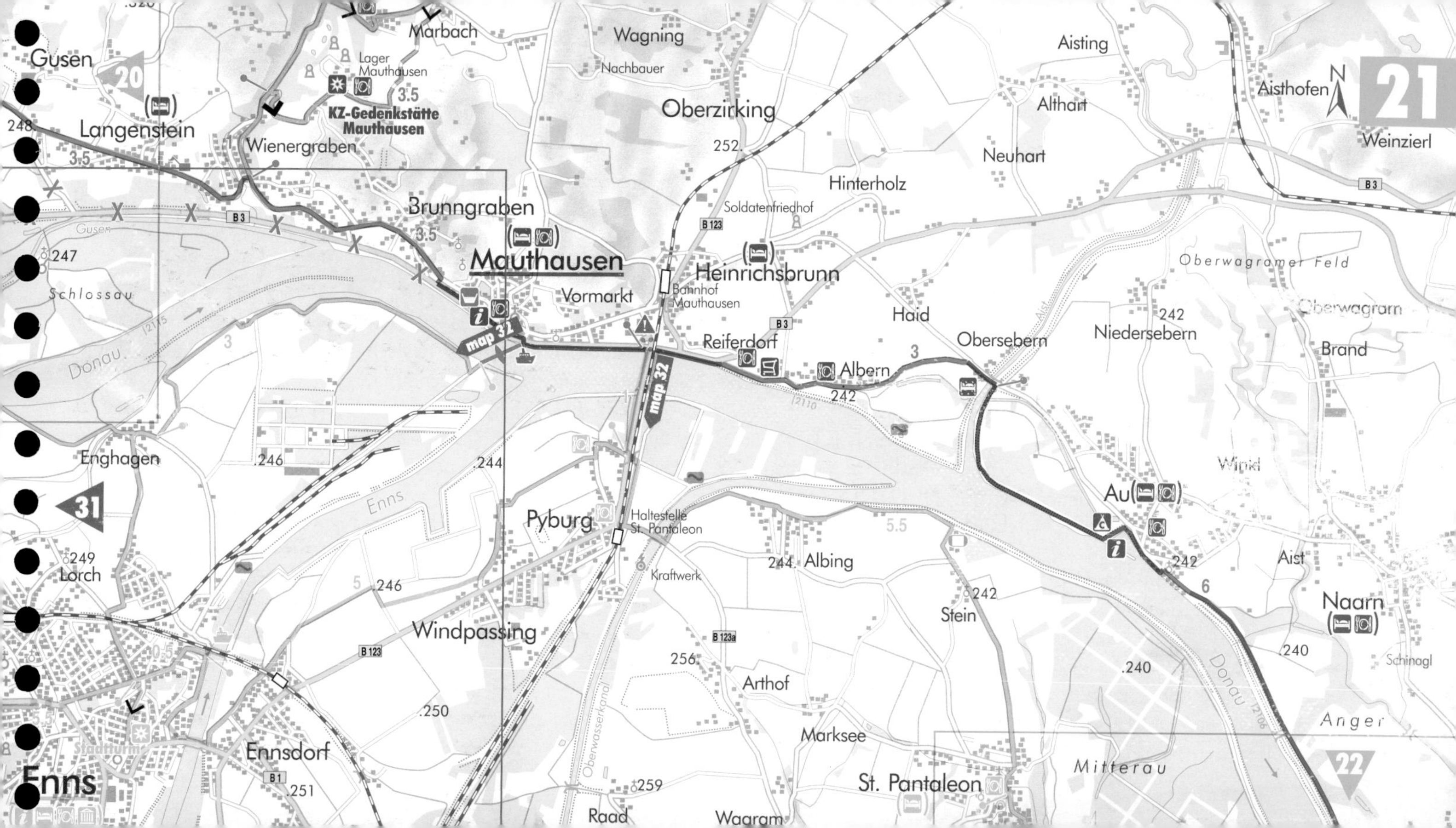

21
20
31
22
Gusen
Langenstein
Marbach
Lager Mauthausen
KZ-Gedenkstätte Mauthausen
Wienergraben
Brunngraben
Mauthausen
Vormarkt
map 32
Wagning
Nachbauer
Oberzirking
Soldatenfriedhof
Heinrichsbrunn
Bahnhof Mauthausen
Reiferdorf
Albern
Haid
Hinterholz
Neuhart
Aisting
Althart
Aisthofen
Weinzierl
Obersebern
Niedersebern
Oberwagramer Feld
Oberwagram
Brand
Au
Aist
Naarn
Schinogl
Anger
Mitterau
Donau
Enns
Aist
Schlossau
Enghagen
Lorch
Pyburg
Haltestelle St. Pantaleon
Kraftwerk
Albing
Stein
Windpassing
Arthof
Marksee
St. Pantaleon
Ennsdorf
Enns
Stadtturm
Raad
Waaram
Oberwasserkanal
B 3
B 123
B 123a
B 1

Langenstein

Postal code: 4222; Telephone area code: 07237

Town office, ✆ 2370

Ride straight through the next town, **Langenstein** ⁓ after a long gradual curve across the Rieder creek before it joins the Danube.

Tip: Turn left just after the creek if you wish to visit the concentration camp memorial at Mauthausen.

The main route continues to the right.

Mauthausen memorial 5.5 km

Almost one kilometer up the valley of the Rieder creek (Wienergraben).

Tip: There are two routes to the former concentration camp. The first is shorter and follows a "Road of Memories" that winds to the right. After a 14-percent incline and one kilometer one reaches the site.

The second route is less strenuous but somewhat longer. It follows the Rieder past two quarries in which concentration camp inmates once worked.

A short distance further near the inn turn right on **Marbachstraße** ⁓ and go uphill through two switchbacks ⁓ to the newly-renovated **Marbach palace**.

At the palace turn right on Kardenweg, which initially has a poor surface but is paved a short distance later ⁓ past several farms and into a distinctive right curve behind which the former camp can be seen. Open: 8-18, admission to 17:00.

The quiet and tidy landscape of the Mühlviertel section of the Danube river valley belies the horrors that occurred here during the Nazi dictatorship. Uncounted victims were "shot while escaping," plunged from the granite quarries' cliffs or died in the gas chambers and crematoriums in Mauthausen, Gusen and Melk. It is estimated that between 1938 and 1945 about 123,000 people were murdered at the ***Mauthausen concentration camp****.*

Tip: If your bicycle is equipped with good brakes front and rear, take the short steep route to return to the valley floor and the main Danube bike route.

Marina in Au a. d. Donau

The route reaches the town of Mauthausen a short distance after the detour to the memorial site ⁓ after passing the playing fields turn right on **J. Czerwenka Straße** toward the ferry ⁓ turn left before the main road and take the cycle trail directly into the quaint old town's center.

Mauthausen ≈km **2112 L**

Postal code: 4310; Telephone area code: 07238

Tourism association, Heindlkai, ✆ 2243

Bicycle information office, Heindlkai, ✆ 3860

Mauthausen Danube bicycle ferry, ✆ 0664/

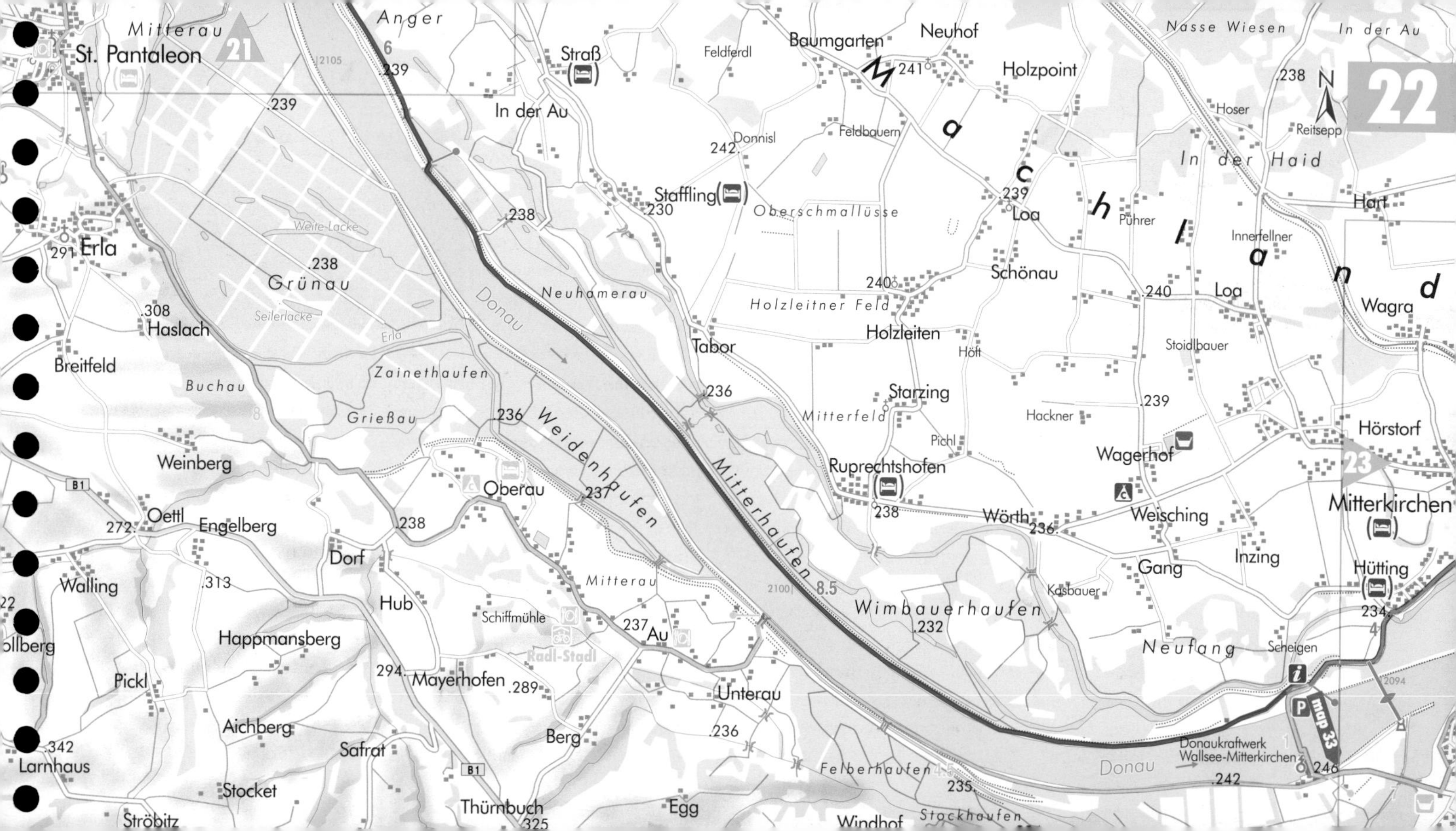

22
21
23
St. Pantaleon
Mitterau
Anger
Straß
In der Au
Baumgarten
Neuhof
Holzpoint
Feldferdl
Nasse Wiesen
In der Au
Hoser
Reitsepp
Machland
Donnisl
Feldbauern
In der Haid
Staffling
Oberschmallüsse
Loa
Pührer
Hart
Innerfellner
Erla
Weite Lacke
Grünau
Seilerlacke
Schönau
Loa
Wagra
Haslach
Neuhamerau
Holzleitner Feld
Donau
Breitfeld
Tabor
Holzleiten
Höft
Stoidlbauer
Zainethaufen
Buchau
Starzing
Grießau
Mitterfeld
Hackner
Hörstorf
Weidenhaufen
Mitterhaufen
Pichl
Weinberg
Wagerhof
Ruprechtshofen
Oberau
Mitterkirchen
Oettl
Engelberg
Wörth
Weisching
Dorf
Inzing
Gang
Hütting
Walling
Mitterau
Kasbauer
Hub
Wimbauerhaufen
Schiffmühle
Au
Radl-Stadl
Happmansberg
Neufang
Scheigen
Pickl
Mayerhofen
Unterau
Aichberg
Berg
Safrat
Larnhaus
Felberhaufen
Donau
Donaukraftwerk Wallsee-Mitterkirchen
map 33
Stocket
Thürnbuch
Egg
Windhof
Stockhaufen
Ströbitz
B1

2797272. Open: May, June, Aug 9-19; July, 9-20; Sept, 9-18. On weekends the Enns city landing in the Enns harbor is also open.

- **Mauthausen concentration camp memorial,** 4 kilometers north-west. Open: April-Sept, 8-18 (admission to 17:00), Feb, March, Oct-Dec, 8-16 (admission to 15:00).
- **St. Nikolaus church.** The late-Gothic church features a handsome altar painting by Martin Johann Schmidt "the Kremser," painted 1796-97.
- **Karner.** Traces of figurative and ornamental wall paintings from the late 13th century can be seen in the circular Romanesque structure.
- **Town center.** Especially noteworthy are the stately houses along the Danube, with their playful facades, most of which are done in 17th century baroque style.

The earliest known historic mention of the **Mauthausen** *market dates to the year 1208. Local legend has it that Frederick Barbarossa wrecked the town after townspeople demanded a toll when he and his army of crusaders passed through Mauthausen. Not all travelers contested the toll as vigorously, a fact shown by the late Gothic church and other splendid structures that were financed by income from tolls.*

Mauthausen to Mitterkirchen 20.5 km

The riverfront bicycle path heads east out of **Mauthausen**.

Tip: Danube bicycle tourists face a decision at the bridge between Heinrichsbrunn and Pyburg. The northern route passes underneath the bridge and continues through the Au (flood plain) and along the river's embankment to the power station at Wallsee-Mitterkirchen. Note the times that the dam is open for crossing the river: Mon-Sun 6–9, 11–14, 16–21.

As an alternative, tourists can cross the bridge and join the southern route, which offers a pleasant ride on quiet country lanes from village to village. The southern route at this point enters the province of Lower Austria (Niederösterreich) for the first time (see page 79).

The left bank route continues along the river after the bridge ~ after 500 meters the route turns away from the embankment and onto Dorfstraße through the village of Albern.

Open-air prehistory museum, Mitterkirchen

Albern

After the hamlet turn right on a right-of-way street ~ cross the Aist river on a bicycle bridge and then turn right towards Grein ~ ride along the top of the embankment to where the Aist joins the Danube and continue downstream ~ one kilometer later the route winds around a widening of the river near Au ~ there is an information board near the campground ~ stay right at the main road and follow the towpath.

Au a. d. Donau / Naarn ≈km 2107 L

Postal code: 4331; Telephone area code: 07262

- **Naarn local office,** Pergerstr. 2, ✆ 58255
- **River study path,** halfway between Au and Naarn. A hiking path posted with information about the plants and animals found in the river plain.

At the end of the village continue on the path along the embankment ~ after 1.5 kilometers cross a flood-protection canal and return to the embankment ~ and proceed 8 kilometers to the **Wallsee-Mitterkirchen** power station where there is a bicycle-tourist rest area with information boards and water.

Tip: The dam across the river can be used to cross to the southern route

23
Hart
Hofstetten
Freilicht-museum
Lehen
Wagra
Labing
Mitterkirchen
Kaindlau
Hütting
Mettensdorf
Pitzing
Froschau
Haselbauer
Saxendorf
Hofkirchen
Eizendorf
Rosenhaufen
Hollerau
Wetzelsdorf
Patzenhof
Windhirn
Knappetsberg
Dornach
Winklinger-Haufen
Hackfeld
Schwaighofer
Mitterhaufen
Weidenhaufen
Häundlhaufen
Hochau
Donau
Winkling
Brandhof
Fuchshof
Bockreut
Ardagger Markt
Grenerhaufen
Bach
Au
Kirchfeld
Ufer
Mühlhaufen
Wallsee
Hagenau
Hundertleiten
Unterau
Roßwiese
Sindelburg
Sommerau
Empfing
Leitzing
Hummelberg
Moos
Doppstein
Hinterholz
Stephanshart
Pfaffenberg
Aigen
Groppenberg
Zehenthof
Hofing
Hörzenleiten
Schneckenreit
Salvetär
Hebmannsberg
Geisthof
Kälbersberg
Weg
Igelschwang
Schweinberg
Dorf
Zeitlbach
Ardagger Stiftskirche

(see page 82). The next opportunity to cross the river is at Grein.

Mitterkirchen to Grein on the northern bank 16 km

The **left bank Danube bicycle route** passes through the flat Machland ~ turn left on Werksstraße ~ across a bridge over an old arm of the river and through the village of **Hütting** ~ the lightly-traveled road leads to Mitterkirchen, signs indicate where the main route branches off to the right before it reaches the busy road ~ if you miss the turn-off, stay to the right towards Mettensdorf and rejoin the route after the Naarn bridge.

Mitterkirchen in the Machland L

Postal code: 4343; Telephone area code: 07269

- **Town office**, No. 50, ✆ 82550
- **Bicycle information**, near the power station, ✆ 30373. Open: May to mid-Oct, Mon-Sun 11-19.
- **Open-air prehistory museum**, Lehen (2 km from Mitterkirchen), ✆ 6611. Open: Mid-April to Oct, Mon-Sun 9-17. The remains of a large barrows field from the Hallstatt period (around 700 BC) were discovered here in 1980. Excavations lasted 10 years, and exposed sensational discoveries that drew international attention to the site. Today a reconstructed Celtic village provides insights into the lifestyle of the Danube's ancient residents.
- **Parish church.** From 1482 with Gothic arches and modern stations of the cross by Th. Pühringer.
- **Swimming lake near Hörstorf**, about 1.5 km from the Danube bicycle route, is the main beach in the Donauland-Strudengau region.

The official Danube bicycle route makes a small detour and crosses the Naarn, one of the main rivers of the Mühlviertel, south of the road ~ turn left on the other side and then turn right on the country lane out of town.

Tip: About one kilometer later the main route turns to the right towards Mettensdorf. One can also turn left to visit the open-air prehistory museum in Lehen. From Lehen one can return to the main route, or continue on the somewhat more strenuous alternative route through the town of Klam and on to Grein. This excursion has several climbs, and is shown on the map in orange.

Wallsee-Mitterkirchen power station

The **main route** stays in the flat Gefilden and leads to **Mettensdorf** ~ after 1.5 kilometers turn left at the crossing street and after crossing a minor stream continue to the right.

Mettensdorf L

A narrow road leads out of the village ~ turn right after the farms of **Pitzing** on the intersecting street at the edge of **Eizendorf**.

Eizendorf

Turn right to leave the street and head for the Danube ~ 500 meters further cross a branch of the Naarn and go left around the **swimming lake** ~ this stretch of the route is lined with signs bearing information about the Strudengau region ~ turn left when you reach the Danube ~ the Au and Machland end at **Dornach**, where the Danube enters the picturesque Strudengau.

Dornach

The route crosses a bridge at the **Dornach Station**.

Tip: The village and a small bathing pond are straight ahead.

The main route turns right onto the towpath just before the rail line ~ and closely follows the tracks past

24
Grein
Greinburg
Standreith
Hehenberg
Föhren-
wald
Thanhof
Gauninger
Holz-
Gauning
Linden
Klam
Burg Clam
Purghofer
Lettental
Unterhörnbach
Oberhörnbach
Haushofer
Gstettenbauer
Teichhäuseln
Mühlberger
Ponegger
Pötzlehner
Mayerhofer
Kolbing
Amesbach
Siebermühle
Ruine Außenstein
Schneckenreitstal
Schneckenreitsberg
Burgstall
Achatzberg
Letten
Schacherbauer
Herdmann
Wiesen
Bahnhof
Grein-Bad Kreuzen
Ufer
Gobelwarte
Plank
Gipfelstein
Kühberger
Kren
Nomberger
Baumgartner
Lärchbaumer
Oberbergen
Stadler
Oberberger
Fischecker
Deiming
Steindl
Obergassolding
Hintermühle
Saxen
Kirchbichl
Au
Mitterholz
Bruderau
Untergassolding
Stiftskirche
Baumgartenberg
Winkelgraben
Hofkirchen
Gschwendt
Zehethofer
Windhörr
Tiefenbach
map 35
Froschau
Haselbauer
Saxendorf
Patzenhof
Windhirn
Mayerhofer
Wetzelsdorf
Knappetsberg
Lärchbauer
Innerzaun
Freilicht-
museum
Mettensdorf
Eizendorf
Pitzing
Dornach
Donau
Rosenhaufen
Hollerau
Winklinger-
Haufen
Felleismühle
Hackfeld
Schwaighofer
Mitterhaufen
Weidenhaufen
Hochau
Winkling
Zehent
Oberh
23
25
B3
B119

Dornach ~ the trail makes a hook to the right and crosses a narrow bridge ~ the valley here becomes narrower quickly and the trail nears the narrows that river navigators so fear ~ the Danube bridge upstream from **Grein** is 4.5 kilometers further.

Tip: Grein is a pretty town worth visiting, but the route further down the left bank shares the pavement with busy roads and bicycle lanes are scarce. Consider using the bridge before Grein and continuing the Danube bicycle tour on the right bank route as far as Ybbs. That route is described beginning page 86.

Follow the riverside bicycle trail in to Grein ~ ride around the small harbor ~ pass the campground and turn right on the main road ~ turn left after 300 meters to reach the town square.

Grein a.d. Donau ≈km **2079 L**

Postal code: 4360; Telephone area code: 07268

Tourism association, ✆ 7055

Oberösterreichisches Schifffahrtsmuseum (ship museum), Greinburg, ✆ 7007. Open: June-Sept, Tues-Sun 10-18; May, Oct, Tues-Sun 10-12 and 13-17. Describes the history of shipping on the Danube, Traun, Salzach and Inn rivers, with many detailed and accurate models of most types of ships as well as shipping-related river facilities and machines.

Greinburg castle, ✆ 7007. Open: May-Oct, by appointment. Today's enclosed castle was completed in the early 17th century. The courtyard is especially attractive, and several decorated rooms and the chapel with its marble alter from 1625 are also noteworthy. The "Sala terrena" or stone theatre can be seen on guided tours.

Old Rathaus. Unchanged since its construction in 1563 by the Italian architect M. Canaval. The adjacent grain silo was transformed into the famous Bürgertheater in 1791.

Old city theater, ✆ 7055. Tours: April-Oct, Mon-Sun at 9, 11, 13:30 and 16. Built in 1791, this rococo structure is the oldest original bourgeois theater in the country.

St. Ägidius city church. A late-Gothic, heavily-rebuilt church with a baroque altar that includes a painting by Bartolomeo Altomonte (1749).

Town center. Most of the houses in the center of town date to the 16th and 17th centuries, though many have baroque facades. The town's bourgeois flair is especially evident in the 19th century inns and taverns.

Stillensteinklamm, Gießenbach, 2 km east. The 200 meters deep Bachtal with its impressive stone formations.

Grein – old city theater

The small medieval city's location at the entrance to the perilous Struden made it the base for river pilots and a popular place to transfer freight. As a result, Grein prospered. In 1790 the town built a small theatre adjacent to the Rathaus. It could seat 160 people, with individually locked folding seats in the first rows reserved for the town's most important citizens. There was, however, also a viewing slit through which inmates in the local jail could see performances. It is the oldest theatre in Austria to survive in its original form.

Grein to Persenbeug on the north bank 20 km

The bicycle route on the north bank of the Danube follows the busy Bundesstraße. Some parts of the stretch have a bicycle lane. The route is not marked with signs, but is virtually impossible to lose.

25
Grein
Greinburg
St. Nikola
Struden
Burg Werfenstein
Wörth
Hößgang
Sarmingstein
Schlosskogel
Predigtstuhl
Gloxwald
Schwarze Wand
Strudengau
Donau
Wiesen
Dachberg
Peham
Rühring
Elserkogel
Sand
Nöchling
Hochhart
Lehmgrub
Nabegg
Oberschlag
Wolfödhöhe
Gipfelstein
Brandstetterkogelhütte
Schlagberg
Schlaghof
Niederhard
Faschingleiten
Bahnhof-Grein-Bad Kreuzen
Ufer
Gobelwarte
Plank
Baumgartner
Lärchbaumer
Oberbergen
Stadler
map 36
Tiefenbach
Schweighof
Großberg
Kegler
Hinterleiten
Riegel
Spitzhof
Hirschenau
Haltestelle-Hirschenau-Nöchling
Meierhof
Sooshof
Zierhof
Burgruine
Lindmühl
Freyenstein
Koxödt
Schauberg
Au
Bernhard
Weg
Schaltberg
Zehethofer
Windhirn
Mayerhofer
Innerzaun
Fellner
Berg
Neustadtl
Steinödt
Oberhofstad
Burgkogel
Kremslehen
Geißstein
Dörfl
Willersbach
Gschirnbauer
Berghof
Reith
Winthan
Luegerkapelle
Oberholz
Winklinger Haufen
Felleismühle
Winkling
Zehent
Tanninger
24
26
Mühlberger
Ponegger
Pötzlehner
Mayerhofer
Ramersböck
Hofstätter
Reitbauer
Burgner
Eichberg
Bahnhof-St. Nikola-Struden
Bauerngruber
Kienberg
Bichl
B 119
B 3

Tip: After 2.5 kilometers, near an old railroad viaduct, a smaller road branches off to the nearby Stillensteinklamm, where the waters of the Gießenbach shoot through the rocky narrow gorge.

Proceed down the B 3 towards **Burg Werfenstein**, which once protected the toll at the narrowest part of the Strudengau ⇝ pass through the village of Struden and arrive in St. Nikola.

St. Nikola **≈km2075 L**

Postal code: 4381; Telephone area code: 07268

Town office, ✆ 8155

Schiffer church. Originally a Romanesque church, which then went through Gothic and baroque (17th century) renovations. The 4 Gothic reliefs of the side altar (c. 1500) on the left are especially noteworthy.

Burg Werfenstein, Struden. Werfenstein is an example of the castles and towers that were built in the narrowest parts of the river and had the capacity to block the river to traffic. Earliest recorded mention of the castle dates to 1242.

Ride through St. Nikola and continue down the **B 3** ⇝ 3 kilometers past **Sarmingstein**, across from the **Hirschenau station,** turn right onto the quieter towpath ⇝ at the parking lot 3 kilometers later the route returns to the **B 3**.

Tip: The parking lot is at the end of the beautiful Ysper valley, and entrance to the wild and romantic Waldviertel. The region's excellent bicycle touring opportunities are described in the **Waldviertel bike atlas from** *bikeline* (available in German).

Cross the Ysper and after one kilometer turn left away from the road ⇝ cross the tracks and go slightly uphill into **Weins** ⇝ at the end of the village the route returns to the main road and proceeds to the **Ybbs-Persenbeug power station**.

Tip: The power station dam can be crossed to reach the southern side of the river. Description starts on page 88.

Coming from the northern end of the Ybbs-Persenbeug station, go left around the castle and then go right off the Bundesstraße ⇝ the route through Persenbeug's narrow streets follows the Schlossstraße and the Hauptstraße.

Persenbeug **≈km 2059.5 L**

Postal code: 3680; Telephone area code: 07412

Town office, Rathauspl. 1, ✆ 52206

Castle. The complex on the steep rock outcropping attained its current form after reconstruction by Eusebius v. Hoyos 1617-21. Owned by the Habsburgs since 1800.

St. Florian and St. Maximilian parish church. The massive late-Gothic structure (c. 1500) contains a choir room and a high altar of multicolored marble.

Town center. Among the numerous original Biedermeier houses – the Kleine and Große Schiffsmeisterhaus (small and large shipmasters' houses).

Market linden, Rathauspl. The huge linden tree next to the Floriani chapel is said to have been planted in 1300.

Schloss Persenbeug

*Under the shipmaster Matthias Feldmüller (1801-50), **Persenbeug** was the most important shipbuilding town on the lower Danube. The town's "schopper" built about 20 ships a year. At the time the Danube carried about 850 ships and 25 rafts from Feldmüller downstream each*

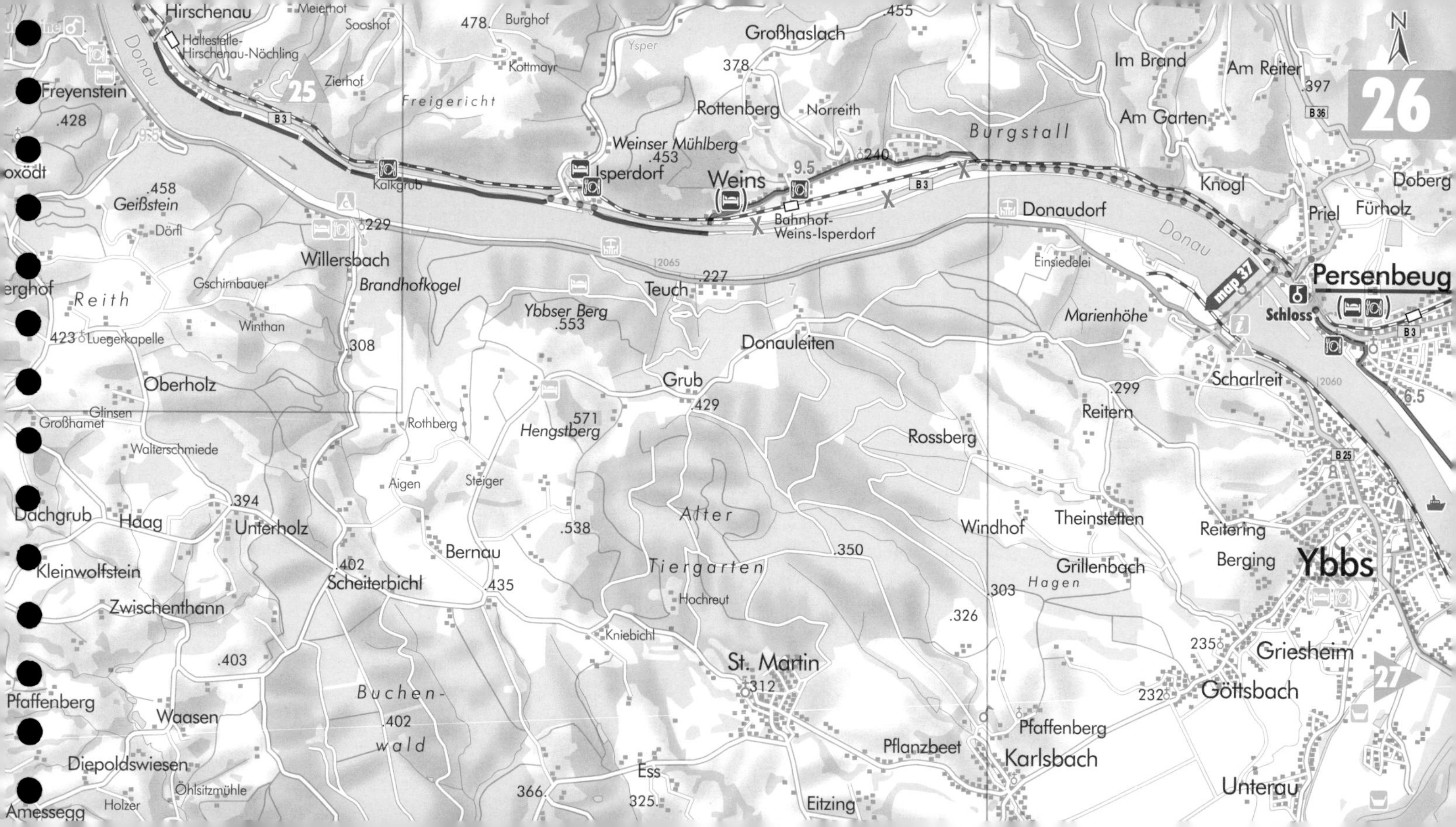

26
25
27
map 37
Donau
Hirschenau
Haltestelle-Hirschenau-Nöchling
Meierhof
Sooshof
Burghof
Kottmayr
Zierhof
Freigericht
Großhaslach
Ysper
Rottenberg
Norreith
Weinser Mühlberg
Isperdorf
Weins
Kalkgrub
Bahnhof-Weins-Isperdorf
Burgstall
Im Brand
Am Reiter
Am Garten
Knogl
Doberg
Priel
Fürholz
Donaudorf
Einsiedelei
Persenbeug
Schloss
Marienhöhe
Scharlreit
Freyenstein
Geißstein
Dörfl
Willersbach
Brandhofkogel
Gschirnbauer
Reith
Winthan
Luegerkapelle
Oberholz
Glinsen
Großhamet
Walterschmiede
Teuch
Ybbser Berg
Donauleiten
Grub
Rothberg
Hengstberg
Aigen
Steiger
Rossberg
Reitern
Alter
Tiergarten
Hochreut
Windhof
Theinstetten
Reitering
Berging
Ybbs
Grillenbach
Hagen
Dachgrub
Haag
Unterholz
Bernau
Kleinwolfstein
Scheiterbichl
Zwischenthann
Kniebichl
St. Martin
Griesheim
Göttsbach
Pfaffenberg
Buchen-wald
Waasen
Pflanzbeet
Karlsbach
Diepoldswiesen
Ess
Öhlsitzmühle
Eitzing
Unterau
Amessegg
Holzer
B 3
B 36
B 25

Ybbs-Persenbeug power station

across a flat peninsula, the Hagsdorfer Scheibe ~ take the first turn left in **Hagsdorf** and then right at the intersection with the shrine ~ follow the paved lane, which goes to the right after 1.5 kilometers ~ and then turns left at the next the cluster of houses ~ the next town

year. About 350 ships were dragged back upstream by horses using the towpath.

Persenbeug to Marbach 10.5 km

Turn right on **Rollfährestraße**, a side street at the Gasthof zum Weißen Lamm. The next goal is Melk ~ turn right again after 400 meters, into **Kinostraße** ~ and then take the trail along the shoreline out of town ~ the small city of Ybbs can be seen on the opposite bank.

The left bank route continues is Gottsdorf, with a distinctive onion-roof church steeple.

Gottsdorf

The route joins a street along the shoreline at the edge of the village ~ proceed straight along Donaustraße ~ turn right just before the fire station ~ the bicycle route then runs between the shoreline and the Bundesstraße ~ in the town of **Granz**, ride past the campground, the harbor and a sign marking the start of the **Nibelungengau** ~ in Marbach there is also a ship landing.

Marbach ≈km 2049 L

Postal code: 3671; Telephone area code: 07413

- **Tourism office**, Marbach 28, ✆ 7045
- **Former manor house.** Built in 1575, the Habsburg manor house with its two round corner towers bears the coats of arms of the families Starhemberg-Schaumburg-Löwenstein-Wertheim.

Marbach – Maria Taferl pilgrimage church

Tip: In Marbach it is possible to start an interesting excursion into the southern Waldviertel, with stops at Maria Taferl, Artstetten castle or Burg Leiben. This tour follows quiet country roads that include several daunting climbs. It is also possible to reach Maria Taferl by bicycle-taxi, which can bring bicycle and baggage straight to the place of pilgrimage. Return to the main route either through Klein-Pöchlarn or through Weitenegg, just before Melk. The excursion is shown in the maps in orange color. Tourists who are satisfied with a distant view of the pilgrimage church at Maria Taferl can continue along the shoreline trail.

Marbach to Emmersdorf 14 km

The left bank **Danube bicycle tour** stays on the towpath and passes **Krummnußbaum** and the Danube river railroad ~ ride along the embankment or go right to the towpath where the main road veers away from the river ~ information boards can be found near the campground ~ proceed 5 kilometers to the Danube bridge past Pöchlarn ~ the village of **Klein-Pöchlarn** is to the left.

Tip: Klein-Pöchlarn is another entrance to the pretty Waldviertel trail to the north. The ***bikeline*** **"Waldviertel Radatlas"** (available in German) contains detailed information about bicycle tours in this charming region north of the Danube.

Klein-Pöchlarn **≈km 2044 L**

Continue along the top of the embankment after the bridge ~ proceed 3.5 kilometers to the fork in the trail near the village of **Ebersdorf**.

Tip: Tourists who wish to visit Melk continue straight and cross the river on the Melk power station dam. After Melk, take the Danube bridge to return to the northern bank (see page 90).

To stay on the left bank, take the left fork off the embankment and ride along the main road to Weitenegg ~ this route accompanies an arm of the Danube which is clean enough for swimming ~ there is a romantic ruin in **Weitenegg,** and a fine view at the imposing **Melk abbey** across the Danube.

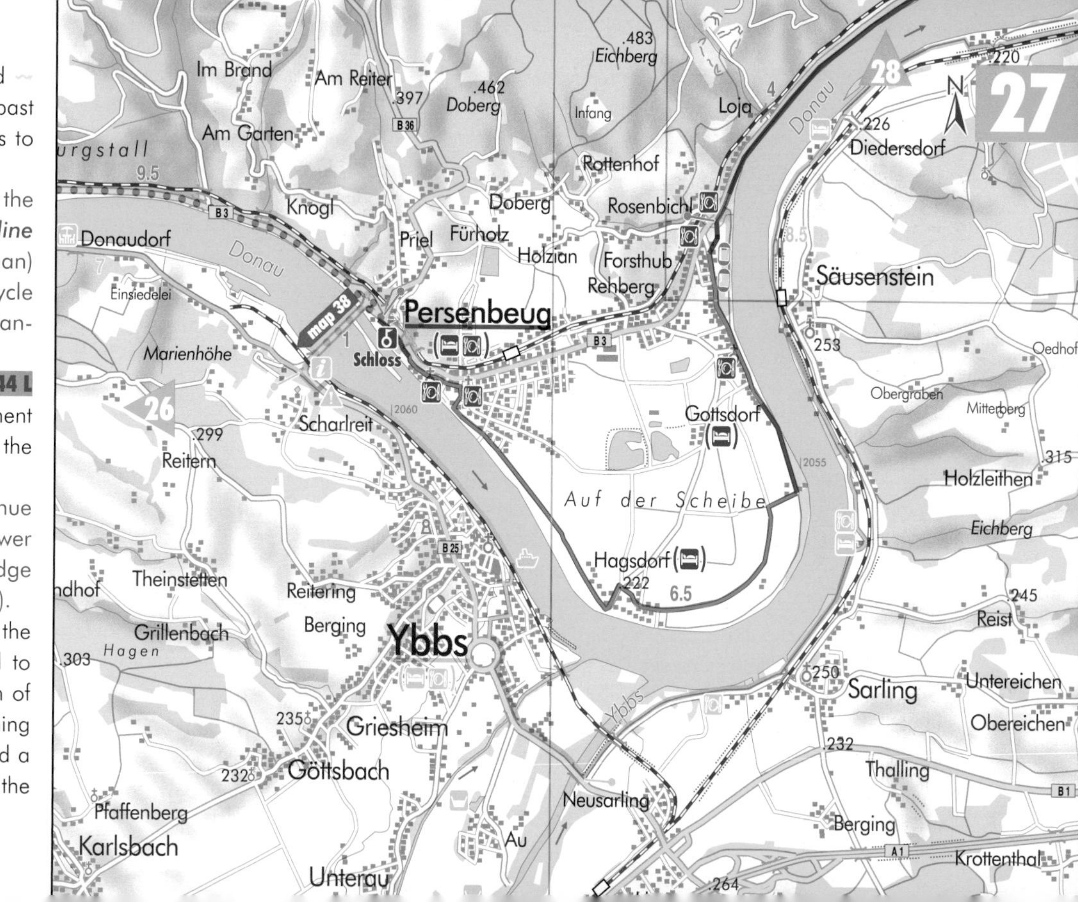

"Light house" in Luberegg

Weitenegg

Danube bicycle route signs now indicate Krems as the next most distant destination, 36 kilometers away ~ near **Luberegg castle** in the next village there are two squat old towers that once served as light and signal towers for rafts and barges on the Danube ~ continue on down the Danube to Emmersdorf, where the bicycle trail connects with the main through road.

Emmersdorf ≈km 2035 L

Postal code: 3644; Telephone area code: 02752

Town office, ✆ 71469

Luberegg palace museum, Hain, ✆ 71755. Open: April-Oct, Mon-Sun 9-17:30. Permanent exhibition on "Kaiser Franz and his times – from the French revolution to the Congress of Vienna."

Luberegg palace, Hain. Built in 1780, the small palace was Kaiser Franz I's favorite residence. The late-baroque decoration on the outside is supplemented by the early classicist linen wall-papering inside. Recently renovated, open to the public since 1991.

Chapel of St. Maria Magdalena, Hauptplatz. A picturesque stairs lead to the late-Gothic chapel (after 1516) with its arches and stone gallery.

Town center. The enchanting, stretched-out main square is surrounded by distinctive houses characteristic of the 16th to early 19th centuries.

Tip: The left bank route downstream from **Emmersdorf**, through the Wachau, is regarded as the main route, passing through a series of the region's prettiest and best known villages and towns. The right bank route follows public roads as it winds through small winemaking villages.

The bridge offers another opportunity to visit the **abbey at Melk** (see page 90).

After crossing the bridge to the right bank, either take the steps down to the riverfront road, or continue straight to the intersection and turn right ~ immediately turn right again and follow the busy road to the riverfront road, where you can turn left to visit the center of **Melk** or turn right to continue downstream on the southern bank.

To reach the abbey, proceed straight on the side street, turn left on **Johann-Steinböck-Straße** and then right on **Wiener Straße** to reach the abbey ~ the river road, called **Wachauer Straße** here, leads to Melk left, or right to the next downstream town, Schönbühel.

Melk see page 90

28
Artstetten
Eichberg
Trennegg
Ferdinand-Museum
Hasling
Hausäcker
Obersteinbach
Pargatstetten
Grubholz
.554
.372
Reitern
.639
Im Aschern
Hilmanger
Obererla
Unterthalheim
Ziegelstadl
Erlanghofholz
Langäcker
Unterbierbaum
Reuter Feld
6.5
.324
4
Wolfseck
Kundles
Angerwiese
Wimm
.514
Hirschensprung
Untererla
Maria Taferl
Oberthalheim
Schlossäcker
Heideck
Grub
Im Graben
Rindfleischberg
.388
Tonberg
29
4.5
Kogel
Wallfahrtskirche
2
Klosterberg
.355
Grammern
Toberl
Zinn
Auratsberg
Hinterbrühl
Saulackenberg
.361
Rotenberg
Klein-Pöchlarn
Krummnußbaum
-an der Donauuferbahn
Steinwand
3.5
Friesenegg
Mühlberg
.509
Marbach
4.5
B3
map 39
Kracking
Autenberg
.366
Bauernfeld
Granz
5.5
Wört
Am Rechen
Oskar-Kokoschka-Geburtshaus
Wallenbach
Krummnußbaum
Annastift
.220
.219
Pöchlarn
Kirchbühel
Donau
Loja
.226
Diedersdorf
Neuda
Brunn
.213
Ornding
Kellerhäuser
Hinterleiten
Grießgrub
8.5
.309
27
Neustift
Golling
Neupöchlarn
.219
Steinwand
B1
A1
Säusenstein
Hühnerberg

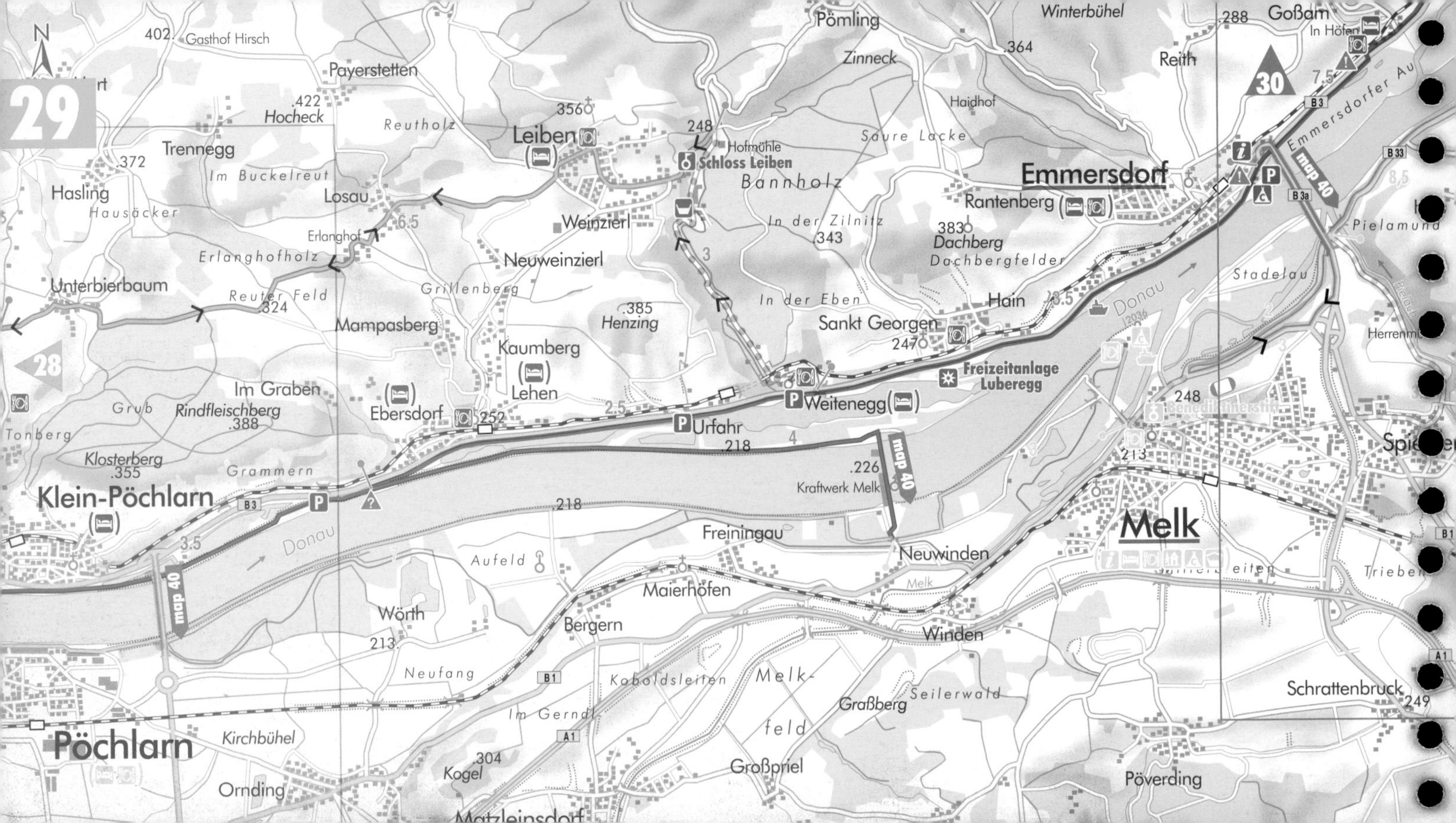

29
30
28
Gasthof Hirsch
Payerstetten
Hocheck
Reutholz
Leiben
Trennegg
Im Buckelreut
Hasling
Hausäcker
Losau
Erlanghof
Erlanghofholz
Unterbierbaum
Reuter Feld
Mampasberg
Im Graben
Grub
Rindfleischberg
Tonberg
Klosterberg
Grammern
Klein-Pöchlarn
Donau
Wörth
Neufang
Pöchlarn
Kirchbühel
Kogel
Ornding
Im Gerndl
Koboldsleiten
Melk-feld
Großpriel
Graßberg
Seilerwald
Winden
Bergern
Maierhöfen
Aufeld
Freiningau
Neuwinden
Kraftwerk Melk
map 40
Urfahr
Weitenegg
Ebersdorf
Lehen
Kaumberg
Grillenberg
Henzing
Neuweinzierl
Weinzierl
Hofmühle
Schloss Leiben
Bannholz
In der Zilnitz
In der Eben
Sankt Georgen
Freizeitanlage Luberegg
Hain
Dachberg
Dachbergfelder
Rantenberg
Emmersdorf
Emmersdorfer Au
Saure Lacke
Haidhof
Zinneck
Pömling
Winterbühel
Goßam
In Höfen
Reith
Pielamund
Stadelau
Herrenmb
Melk
Spie
Trieben
Schrattenbruck
Pöverding
Matzleinsdorf
B3
B1
A1
B33
B3a

Linz to Melk along the right bank 107 km

The Danube bicycle route on the southern side of the river leaves the capital of Upper Austria, Linz, and proceeds into the fertile Machland. Especially noteworthy here are the St. Florian monastery and, of course, Enns – Austria's oldest city. The route then passes through the enchanting "most" region with its distinctive farms. The Danube becomes narrower and faster before reaching Grein and then rushes through the thrilling Strudengau. The crowning conclusion to this stage is the town of Melk and its world-famous Benedictine abbey.

Between Linz and Abwinden there is no Danube bicycle route on the right, or southern, bank. In Abwinden you can cross to the right bank and proceed along quiet country lanes, farming roads and bicycle trails. This stage has no serious climbs and no stretches along busy roads.

St. Florian abbey

Tip: There is no bicycle route along the southern bank between Linz and Abwinden. Turn to page 53 and map 19 for descriptions of the northern route between Linz and Abwinden.

Abwinden to Enns on the southern bank — 8 km

On the right bank continue south on the wide asphalt road ~ turn right on the narrow path 1.5 kilometers from the river. Signs indicate the cycle path to Enns.

Tip: You can continue straight ahead and follow the green signs to St. Florian.

Excursion to St. Florian

This outing leads to the magnificent baroque abbey St. Florian as well as an excellent open-air farm museum.

A wide asphalt road leads south from the power station at Abwinden-Asten and past the turn-off to Enns ~ about one kilometer later turn left across the railroad ~ and turn left after 500 meters onto the bicycle trail along the Ipfbach (creek), which leads to the center of Asten.

Asten

Cross the B 1 on the pedestrian stripes at the church and continue straight on **Ipfbachstraße** ~ past a number of old farms and then left across the bridge ~ turn right ~ and cross the main road and proceed to the left ~ this road leads into St. Florian, past the market square and take the first right to the monastery.

St. Florian — R

Postal code: 4490; Telephone area code: 07224

Tourism association, Marktpl. 3, ✆ 5690

Historic fire house, Stiftstr. 2, ✆ 4219. Open: May-Oct, Tues-Sun 9-12 and 14-16. The museum presents the development of fire-fighting technologies as well as the social organization of fire departments.

Schloss Hohenbrunn hunting museum, 2 km southwest, ✆ 8933. Open: April-Oct, Tues-Sun 10-12 and 13-17. The art of hunting, and especially hunting traditions of Upper Austria, are presented in this baroque palace from 1722-32.

Monastery art collection and Anton Bruckner memorial chamber, St. Florian monastery, ✆ 8902. Guided tours: Mon-Sun at 10, 11, 14, 15 and 16; groups also by appointment. In addition to the so-called Kaiser chambers, which are still furnished as in the 18th century, exhibits include furnishings that belonged to the composer Bruckner, and works by numerous well-known artists.

Augustine canonical abbey, ✆ 8902. Guided tours: April-Oct, for groups of 10 and more Mon-Sun at 10, 11, 14, 15 and 16 and by appointment. The monastery existed as early as Carolingian times, and was transferred to the canons in 1071. The great courtyard, part of new buildings constructed in the 17th and 18th centuries, are among the most beautiful south-German baroque creations (Carlone and Prandtauer). Especially noteworthy: the Sebastian Altar by A. Altdorfer, 1518.

Maria Himmelfahrt abbey basilica. The baroque church's consummately festive decoration is considered C.A. Carlone's masterpiece. The Bruckner organ built by Franz Xaver Krismann 1770-74 is among the most famous organs of its time.

Bruckner organ performances Sun-Fri 14:30.

Museum train, ✆ 4333-11. Operation: May-Sept, Sun/Hol. Former electric train between St. Florian and Linz (1913-1973) can be rented for any occasion.

Altes Schloss
Steyregg
Götzelsdorf
Lehen
Pürach
Knierübl
Denneberg
30
Pulgarn
Kloster Pulgarn
Gröbetsweg
Knollmühle
Kutzenbergsiedlung
Kruckenberg
Altau
Neuau
Donau
Hannerlhaufen
Luftenberg
St. Georgen
Ringelau
Staizing
Meierhof
Traun
Weikerlsee
Luftenberg
400
Hintberg
Resch
Kirchberg
Frankenberg
Bahnhof St. Georgen
Steining
Angererhaufen
Abwinden
Fall
Gusen
Raigerhaufen
map 20
Langenstein
Haltestelle Ebelsberg
Förgenhaufen
Klettfischer
Ufer
Ausee
Donaukraftwerk-Abwinden-Asten
Posch
Hochhauser
Adamshaufen
Schlossau
Ebelsberg
Schiltenberg
Pichling
Lang Au
Pichlinger See
Bahnhof Asten-St. Florian
Raffelstetten
Donau
Enghagen

In the middle-ages the abbey emerged as the spiritual and economic center of the region. Its schools for writing and painting were famous throughout Europe, and monastery organist Anton Bruckner (1845-55) brought even greater fame to St. Florian.

From the monastery hill take the next crossing street to return to the main street ~ turn left and ride out of town by the route you entered ~ turn right on the street to Samesleiten, cross the narrow-gauge tracks of the **museum train** and proceed to the open air museum.

Samesleiten R

🏛 **OÖ. Sumerauerhof open air museum**, Samesleiten, ✆ 8031. Open: Easter to mid-May, Oct, Sat/Sun/Hol 10-12 and 13-17. Mid-May to Sept, Tues-Sun 10-12 and 13-17. One of the largest and most beautiful of the "Vierkanthöfe" common to the region. The farm has been associated with the monastery since the early 13th century. Museum exhibits include farm furnishings from four centuries, a "Most" museum, a stable, bakery and wagons.

The country lane leads from Samesleiten past a handsome brick farm and to a right-of-way street where the route turns to the right ~ turn left at the next opportunity and proceed underneath the Autobahn ~ after 2 kilometers arrive at the edge of Enns and follow the bicycle trail that follows the main road ~ after 400 meters the cycle lane ends and the route joins the main street ~ stay left on **Stadlgasse** at the main intersection where the bicycle trail resumes.

Although the cycle route signs point to the right at the yellow cemetery wall, it is easier to proceed straight to **Mauthausener Straße** and turn right toward the **main square** with the city tower. There is a short climb. ~ At the other end of the square take **Stiegengasse** to a terrace which offers magnificent views of the Danube's flood plains and the Voralpenvorland.

If you do not take the Markt Sankt Florian excursion, the right bank main route simply follows signs for the TOP-path towards Enghagen ~ where the route splits with the left fork leading to the bicycle ferry to Mauthausen, and the right fork going to the pretty historic city of Enns.

The route to Enns proceeds over a small creek ~ at the intersection with the **large farm complex** the TOP-path to Enns branches off to the right.

Enns R

Postal code: 4470; Telephone area code: 07223

ℹ **Tourism association**, Hauptplatz 1, ✆ 82777

ℹ **Hotel Lauriacum**, ✆ 82315

⛴ **Mauthausen bicycle ferry**, ✆ 0664/2797272. Open: May-Aug, 9-19, Sept, 9-18.

🏛 **Museum Lauriacum**, Hauptpl. 19, ✆ 85362. Open: April-Oct, Tues-Sun, Nov-March, Sun/Hol 10-12 and 14-16, groups also anytime by appointment. Austria's most important museum on Roman civilization and culture. Includes unique ceiling frescos and Austria's oldest city law document. 1989 winner of the Austrian Museum Prize.

✲ **City tower,** Hauptpl. The guard and watch tower built 1565-68 is a masterpiece of Renaissance construction and a distinctive symbol of the

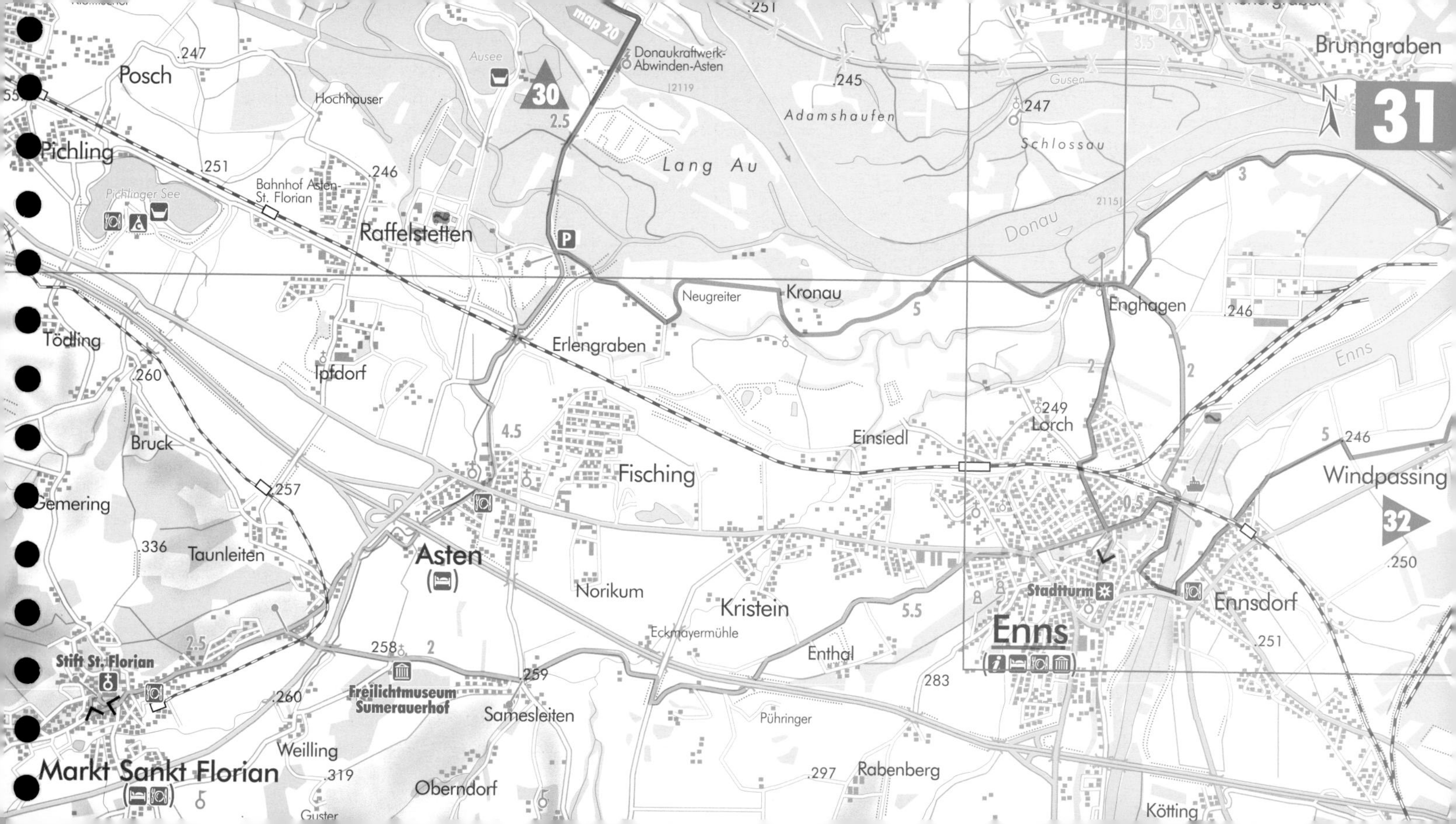

map 20
Donaukraftwerk-Abwinden-Asten
Brunngraben
Posch
.247
Ausee
30
Hochhauser
.245
Adamshaufen
Gusen
.247
Schlossau
31
Pichling
.251
Bahnhof Asten-St. Florian
.246
Lang Au
Pichlinger See
Raffelstetten
Donau
Neugreiter
Kronau
Enghagen
.246
Tödling
Erlengraben
Ipfdorf
Enns
.260
.249
Lorch
4.5
Einsiedl
Bruck
.246
Windpassing
.257
Fisching
Gemering
32
.336
Taunleiten
Asten
.250
Norikum
Kristein
Stadtturm
Ennsdorf
Eckmayermühle
5.5
Enns
Stift St. Florian
258
Enthal
.251
.259
283
Freilichtmuseum Sumerauerhof
.260
Samesleiten
Pühringer
Weilling
Markt Sankt Florian
.319
.297
Rabenberg
Oberndorf
Kötting

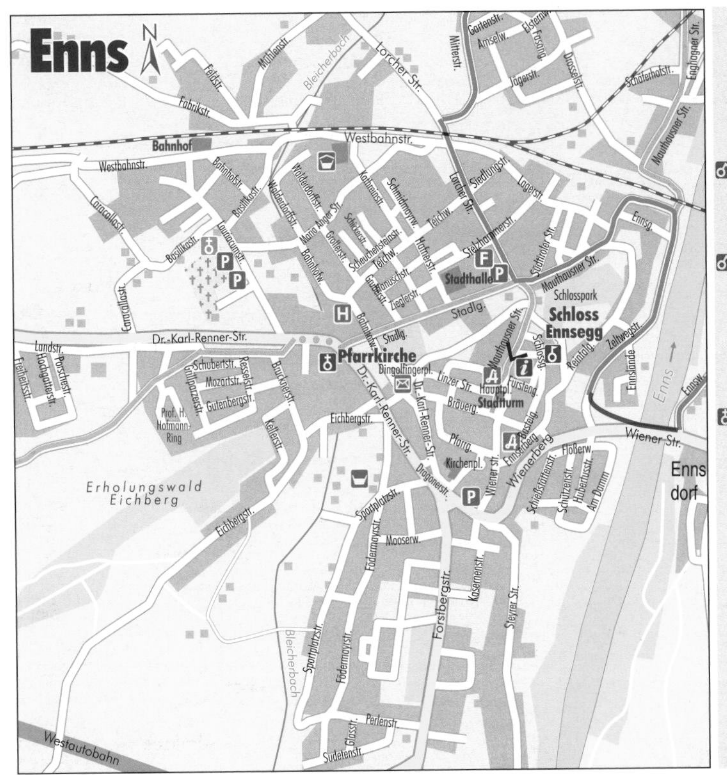

town's influence. The 56 meter tower offers outstanding views of the Alpenvorland. City tours start at the tower May-Sept, Mon-Sun 10:30 or make an appointment at the tourism association office.

Ennsegg palace, near Basteigasse in north end of town. Four-story palace with massive corner tower, built 1565.

Enns castle, Wiener Str. 9-13. Built in 1475 of three town-houses. Its Gothic elements are integrated into residential and commercial areas. The 16th century courtyard (in no. 9) is especially beautiful.

Basilica St. Laurenz-Lorch, Basilikastr., ✆ 84010 or 87412. Open: Guided tours April-Oct, Mon-Sun 16 and by appointment. No other church in Austria or Germany can boast 1,700 years of Christian continuity. The building combines Roman, early-Christian, Carolingian and medieval elements, and an accessible underground Roman city temple (c. 180 AD), plus the two largest paintings in Upper Austria – a panorama of Enns with the city's patron saints (18th century), and the Lorcher bishops.

Town square. Many well-preserved old buildings are clustered around the city tower. Most are basically Gothic structures decorated with Renaissance, baroque and rococo facades. Also noteworthy: the 16th century well that was rediscovered in 1995.

St. Marien parish church, Kirchenpl. A picturesque Gothic ensemble (most of which was built around 1270), including a main church, Wallseer chapel, cloister and Franciscan abbey.

Ennser town adventure path. An interesting trip through 2,000 years of local history – starting from a Roman encampment to the city Lauriacum to the medieval old city to today's town center. The new geology park enables visitors to explore the course of the river Enns.

Enns calls itself the oldest city in Austria, and is famous for many historic events and a wealth of important cultural edifices.

The turning point in the history of Enns was in 1212 when it earned its legal status as a city, 1,000 years after Romans established the settlement Lauriacum. During the Reforma-

tion, Enns was a bastion of Protestantism and the seat of a school for the nobility's children. The school later moved to Linz, and is regarded as the precursor to today's Linz University.

Depart Enns on **Mauthausener Straße** ~ at the intersection of Stadlgasse follow signs for the bicycle route.

Tip: If you wish to return to the north bank take the Mauthausen bicycle ferry (see page 60).

Enns to Mauthausen 5.5 km

To reach the **Enns-Mauthausen bicycle ferry** turn left on **Lorcher Straße,** cross the railroad and follow signs for Enhagen ~ turn right before the inn and after 100 meters turn left ~ the trail to the Danube runs along a shoreline woods, making one small detour around a concrete block ~ pass the arm of the Danube where fishing clubs have

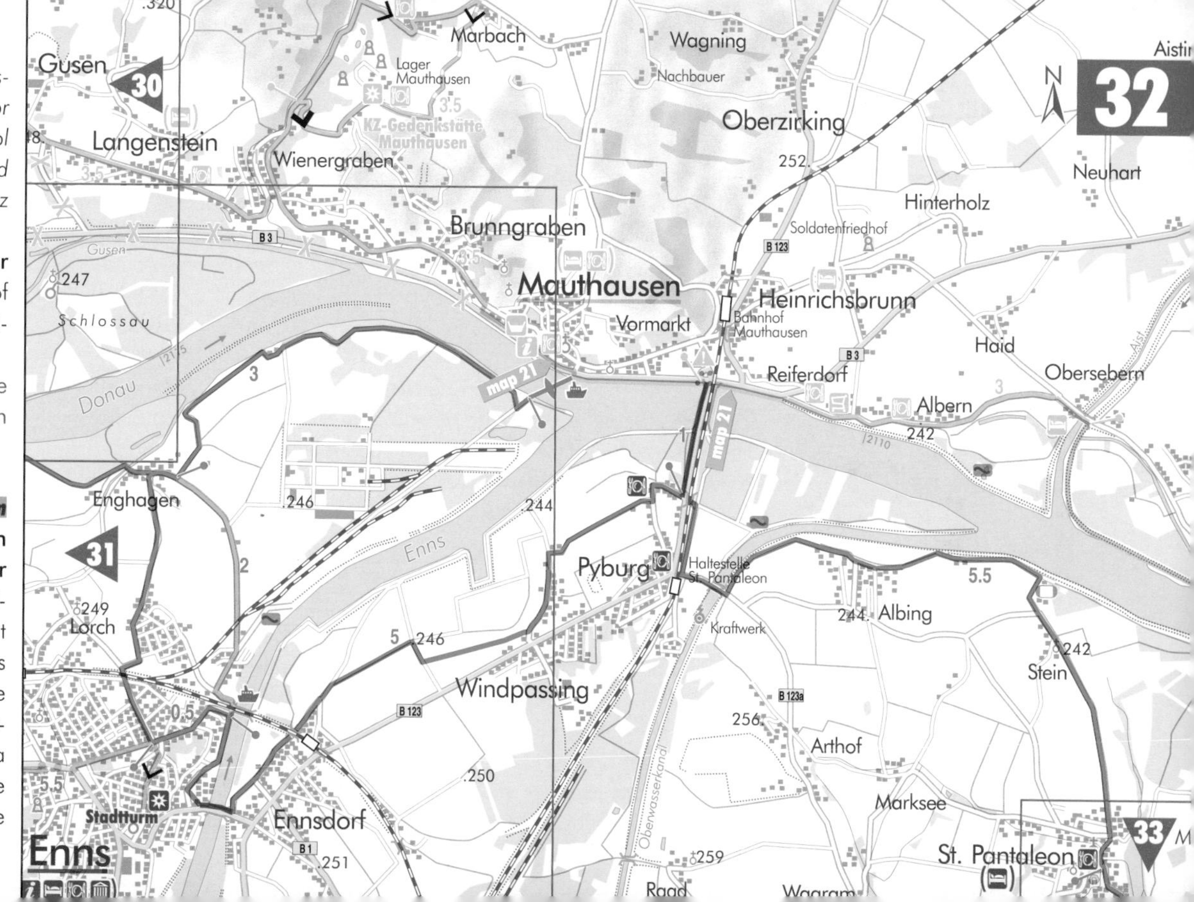

restored the natural habitat for many fish and other animals ~ pass the Tabor pond to reach the Mauthausen **bicycle ferry landing** (Open: May-Aug, 9-19; Sept, 9-18).

Enns to Wallsee along the southern bank *26 km*

To reach the Danube river bridge turn right before passing under the railroad ~ proceed to the Enns bridge and cross it on the left side ~ follow the sign "Zum Donauradweg" ("To the Danube bicycle trail") to the left ~ ride along the edge of **Ennsdorf** and under the railroad ~ turn right on the asphalt lane after the last farm ~ and turn left on the wide asphalt lane before you reach the main road ~ and again left and then right and straight into Windpassing ~ cross a recently completed railroad spur that leads to the equally new Ennsharbor ~ in **Windpassing** turn left on Dorfstraße before the large white farm ~ the street makes a kink to the right at the end of the village and continues 750 meters to a crossing street in **Pyburg**.

Pyburg

Turn left and then follow the street towards the right to another street that leads to the Danube river bridge.

Tip: If you wish to return to the northern bank, follow the narrow hiking/biking path to the left. When you reach the northern bank take the first left down to the riverside. Mauthausen is about one kilometer upstream (see page 62).

To continue down the **southern bank** from **Pyburg**, cross the road and ride under the tracks ~ immediately turn right and go along the embankment to the next underpass ~ turn left on the right-of-way road ~ and turn left after the Oberwasserkanal towards Wallsee.

The path initially follows the canal and skirts the edge of **Albing** ~ the route briefly touches the Danube where the canal meets the river, and then continues about 700 meters along the embankment.

Tip: Although the path along the river looks inviting, the following 8 kilometers are a flood-dike for irrigating the floodplain. Riding on the middle section of the dike can be very uncomfortable, even in good weather. The Danube bicycle route heads inland for a pleasant change of scenery around the edge of the flood plain.

Turn right off the dike path before the **playing fields** ~ and follow the zigzag route to the next street ~ turn left and ride through the village of **Stein** and proceed to St. Pantaleon.

St. Pantaleon

Postal code: 4303; Telephone area code: 07435

Town office, ✆ 7271

Connection to the "Mostviertelweg"

Proceed straight through St. Pantaleon and turn left at the Danube bicycle route signs at the fork near the church.

Tip: The "Moststraßentour" connects to the Danube tour in St. Pantaleon. The ***bikeline* "Mostviertel" cycling guide** (available in German) describes routes in the delightful Mostviertelregion.

Ride past the next town, **Erla**, and up the slight incline ~ cross the small bridge 2.5 kilometers after Erla ~ and proceed straight at the next intersection and follow the long gradual curve to the left ~ the route continues to the right through the farms of **Oberau** and passes an inn with a campground ~ stay to the left ~ past a row of pear trees and through the farms in Au ~ when you reach the Danube, cross the first protective dike and ride up to the bicycle path on the outer dike.

Proceed 4 kilometers along the

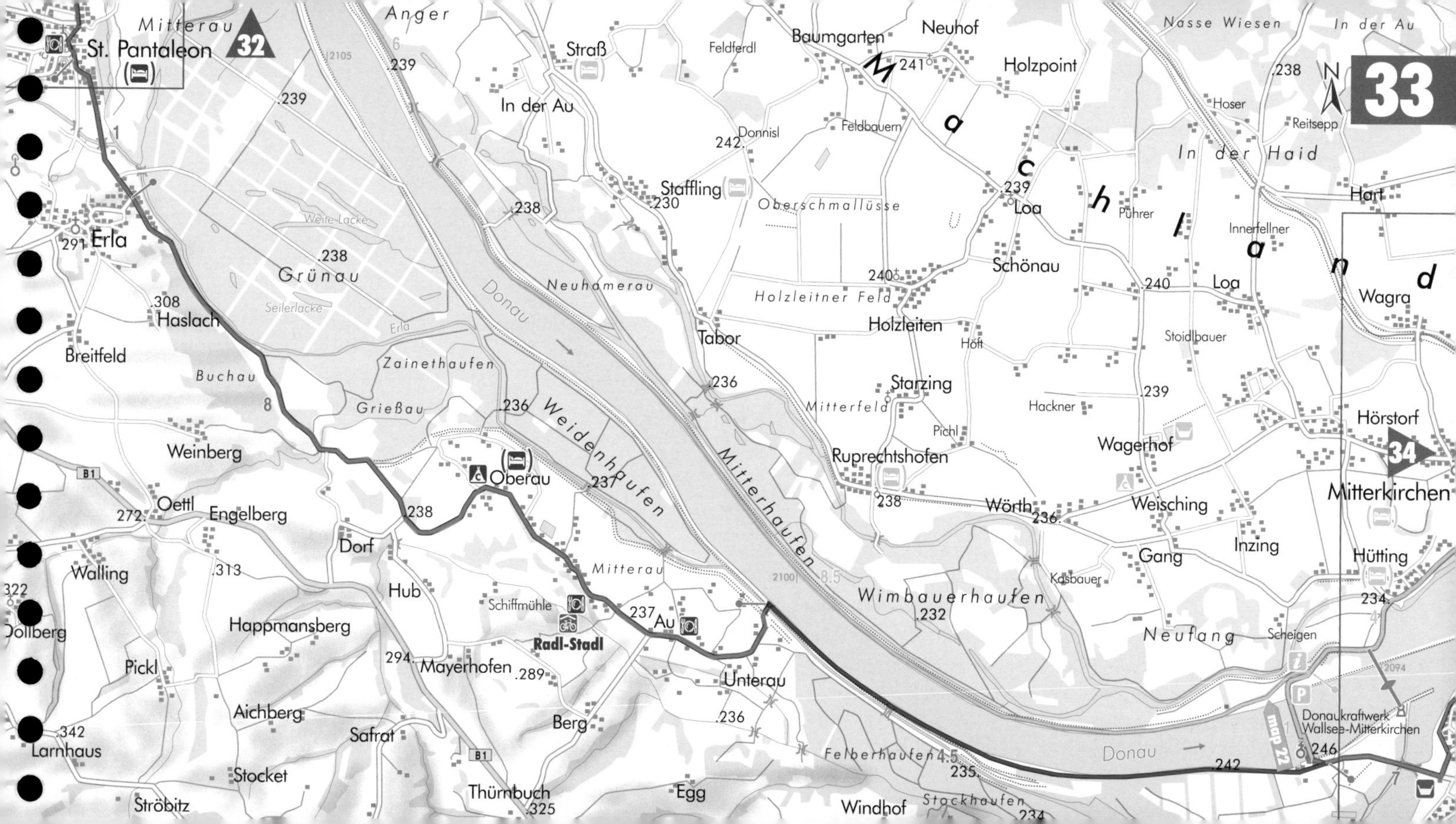
33
32
34
map 22
St. Pantaleon
Mitterau
Anger
Straß
Feldferdl
Baumgarten
Neuhof
Holzpoint
Nasse Wiesen
In der Au
Hoser
Reitsepp
In der Au
Donnisl
Feldbauern
Machland
In der Haid
Staffling
Oberschmallüsse
Loa
Pührer
Hart
Innerfellner
Erla
Weite Lacke
Grünau
Seilerlacke
Neuhamerau
Donau
Schönau
Loa
Wagra
Haslach
Breitfeld
Holzleitner Feld
Holzleiten
Tabor
Höft
Stoidlbauer
Buchau
Zainethaufen
Starzing
Grießau
Weidenhaufen
Mitterfeld
Hackner
Pichl
Hörstorf
Weinberg
Ruprechtshofen
Wagerhof
Mitterhaufen
Oberau
Wörth
Weisching
Mitterkirchen
Oettl
Engelberg
Dorf
Gang
Inzing
Hütting
Walling
Mitterau
Kasbauer
Hub
Wimbauerhaufen
Schiffmühle
Dollberg
Happmansberg
Au
Radl-Stadl
Neufang
Scheigen
Pickl
Mayerhofen
Unterau
Aichberg
Donaukraftwerk Wallsee-Mitterkirchen
Larnhaus
Safrat
Berg
Felberhaufen
Donau
Stocket
Thürnbuch
Egg
Ströbitz
Windhof
Stackhaufen
B1

Danube to the Wallsee-Mitterkirchen power station ~ continue straight as the town of **Wallsee-Mitterkirchen** and the towers of its Habsburg castle draw into sight.

Tip: The Wallsee-Mitterkirchen power station dam is open day and night, and may be used to cross the river (see page 62).

Ride along the **southern bank** towards Wallsee as far as Ardagger ~ just follow the power station service road ~ cross the old arm of the Danube ~ and ride straight toward the center before turning right ~ and curve around the castle.

Wallsee **≈km 2093 R**

Postal code: 3313; Telephone area code: 07433

- **Wallsee-Sindelburg district office**, No. 22, ✆ 2216
- **Roman museum** (Limes-Kastell-Adjuvense), ✆ 2597 or 221622. Open: 15 May-1 Oct by appointment.
- **Sindelburg parish church**, 1 km south. Built in Gothic-baroque style and includes an altar painting by "Kremser Schmidt."
- **Castle.** The castle with its 70 meter keep and a Gothic chapel was expanded between the 15th and 17th centuries. The irregular interior courtyard has a well.
- Baroque **Maria's column (**1710), a work by the Viennese sculptor Benedikt Stober.
- **Outdoor pool** (heated)

Wallsee – Maria column on Marktplatz

Wallsee to Ardagger **11.5 km**

At the right curve near the castle go straight on the street with the 30 km/h zone ~ and roll downhill to the left and then turn right on the crossing street.

Turn left on the lightly-traveled country-lane ~ in Sommerau the route crosses a drainage ditch and proceeds straight ~ at the end of the village the road makes a bend to the left ~ 2.5 kilometers pass the Gasthaus Zum Parlament, which stands on the banks of the Landgerichtsbaches (creek) ~ the bicycle route proceeds to the left.

After another 1.5 kilometers turn left towards Grein and Ardagger-Markt ~ the road curves to the right, crosses the Landgerichtsbach and continues straight towards **Ardagger-Markt** where the **Ardagger Abbey** looms handsomely on one of the many little hills over the river plain ~ cross the Ardagger-Markt bypass road before entering the town ~ turn left on the main road.

Tip: Before you enter the Danube's Strudengau, consider a short side-trip to the abbey church with its unique Margarethe windows and the Mostgallerie where local wines can be sampled.

Ardagger Markt **≈km 2084 R**

Postal code: 3321; Telephone area code: 07479

- **Town office**, Markt 58, ✆ 73120
- **Donauschifffahrt Ardagger**, yacht harbor, ✆ 64640. Open: April-Oct, Sun/Hol with river tours to the Strudengau at 14 and 16.
- **Military history museum** (Wehrmacht museum), near the yacht harbor, ✆ 7239. Open: 15 March-Oct, Mon-Sun 8:30-18. Vehicles, uniforms and weapons from 1914-1945, plus posters, flags, medals etc.
- **Farm museum**, Ardagger-Gigerreith monastery, on the B 119, ✆ 7334. Guided tours by appointment. Austria's largest folklore collection, with more than 15,000 items on handicrafts, farm living and country innovation.

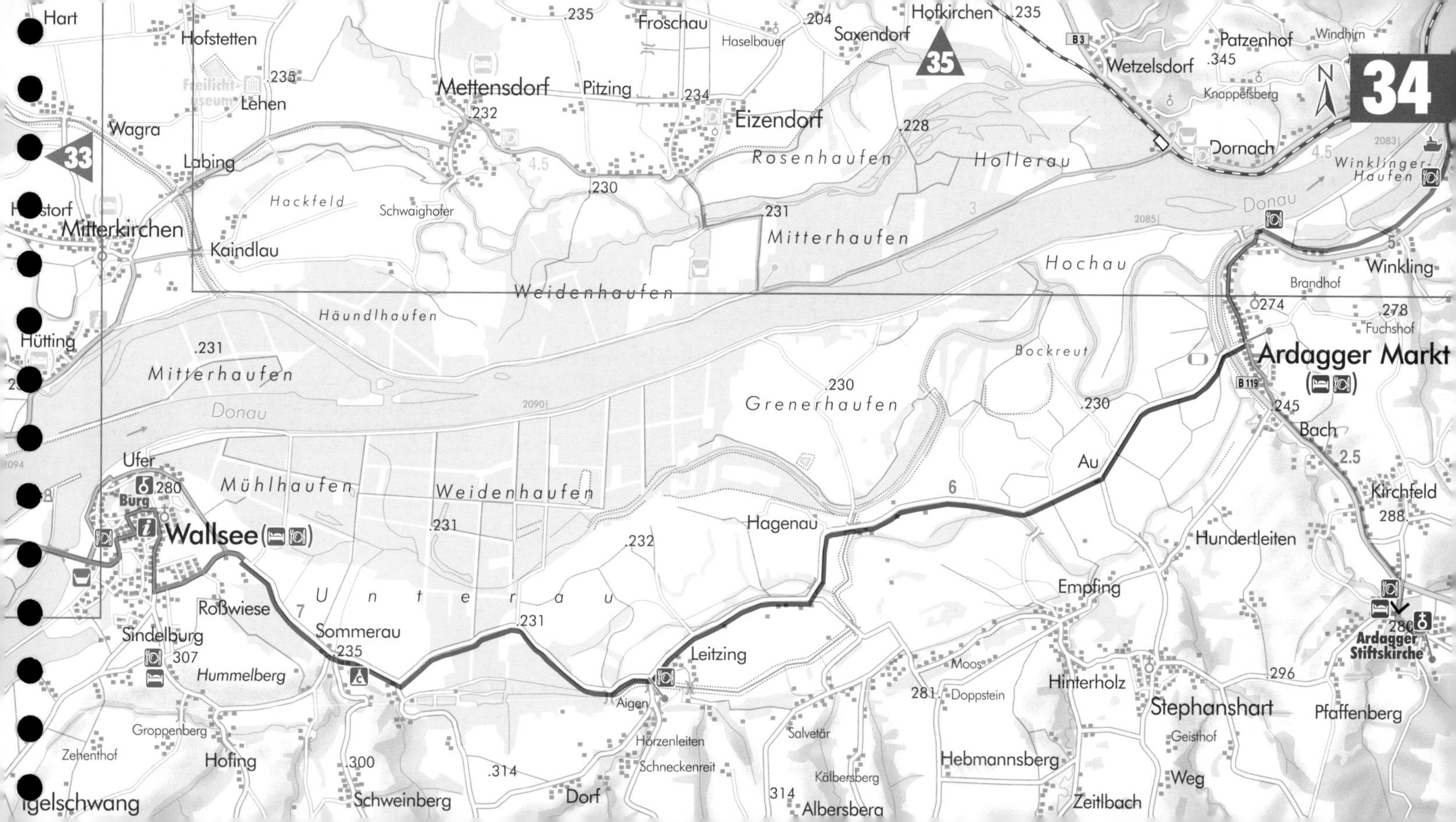
34
35
33
Hart
Hofstetten
Freilicht-museum
Lehen
Wagra
Labing
Mitterkirchen
Kaindlau
Hütting
Mettensdorf
Pitzing
Froschau
Haselbauer
Saxendorf
Hofkirchen
Eizendorf
Rosenhaufen
Hollerau
Hackfeld
Schwaighofer
Mitterhaufen
Weidenhaufen
Häundlhaufen
Donau
Wetzelsdorf
Patzenhof
Windhirn
Knappetsberg
Dornach
Winklinger-Haufen
Hochau
Winkling
Brandhof
Fuchshof
Bockreut
Ardagger Markt
Grenerhaufen
Bach
Kirchfeld
Au
Hagenau
Hundertleiten
Ufer
Burg
Wallsee
Mühlhaufen
Unterau
Roßwiese
Sommerau
Sindelburg
Hummelberg
Leitzing
Aigen
Empfing
Moos
Doppstein
Hinterholz
Stephanshart
Pfaffenberg
Ardagger Stiftskirche
Groppenberg
Zehenthof
Hofing
Igelschwang
Schweinberg
Dorf
Hörzenleiten
Schneckenreit
Salvetär
Kälbersberg
Albersberg
Hebmannsberg
Geisthof
Weg
Zeitlbach
B 3
B 119

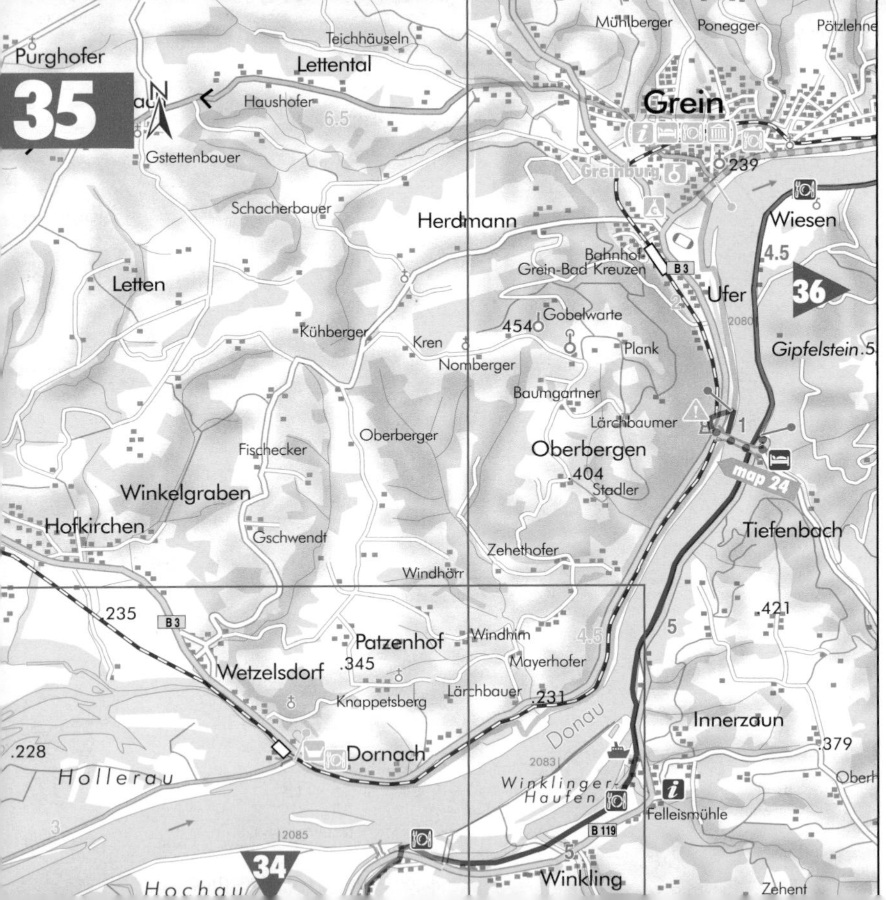

Oldtimer museum, Ardagger. Open: May - Sept, 13-18, Sun/Hol 9-18. With antique vehicles belonging to the Blindenmarkt Old-timer club.

Former abbey church. The oldest part is the Romanesque crypt from 1049. The church's main attraction is the Margarethe window from around 1240, the oldest figurative painted glass in Austria.

Mostgalerie, Stift Ardagger, ✆ 6400. Open: Easter-Oct, Mon-Sun 13-18 and by appointment. Sampling and sales of the region's best and most popular light wines (most).

On clear day one can see the Ötscher (1,893 meters) from the heigts along the Danube.

Ardagger to Grein 8 km

Take the main street out of **Ardagger Markt** towards the Danube ~ after about 500 meters cross the bypass road near the **Gasthof Raderbauer** ~ and take the service road to the right ~ go left at the fork that soon follows.

The ***Ardagger yacht harbor*** *has a snack and grill stand, a playground, an information board and a boat landing used by Danube passenger ships.*

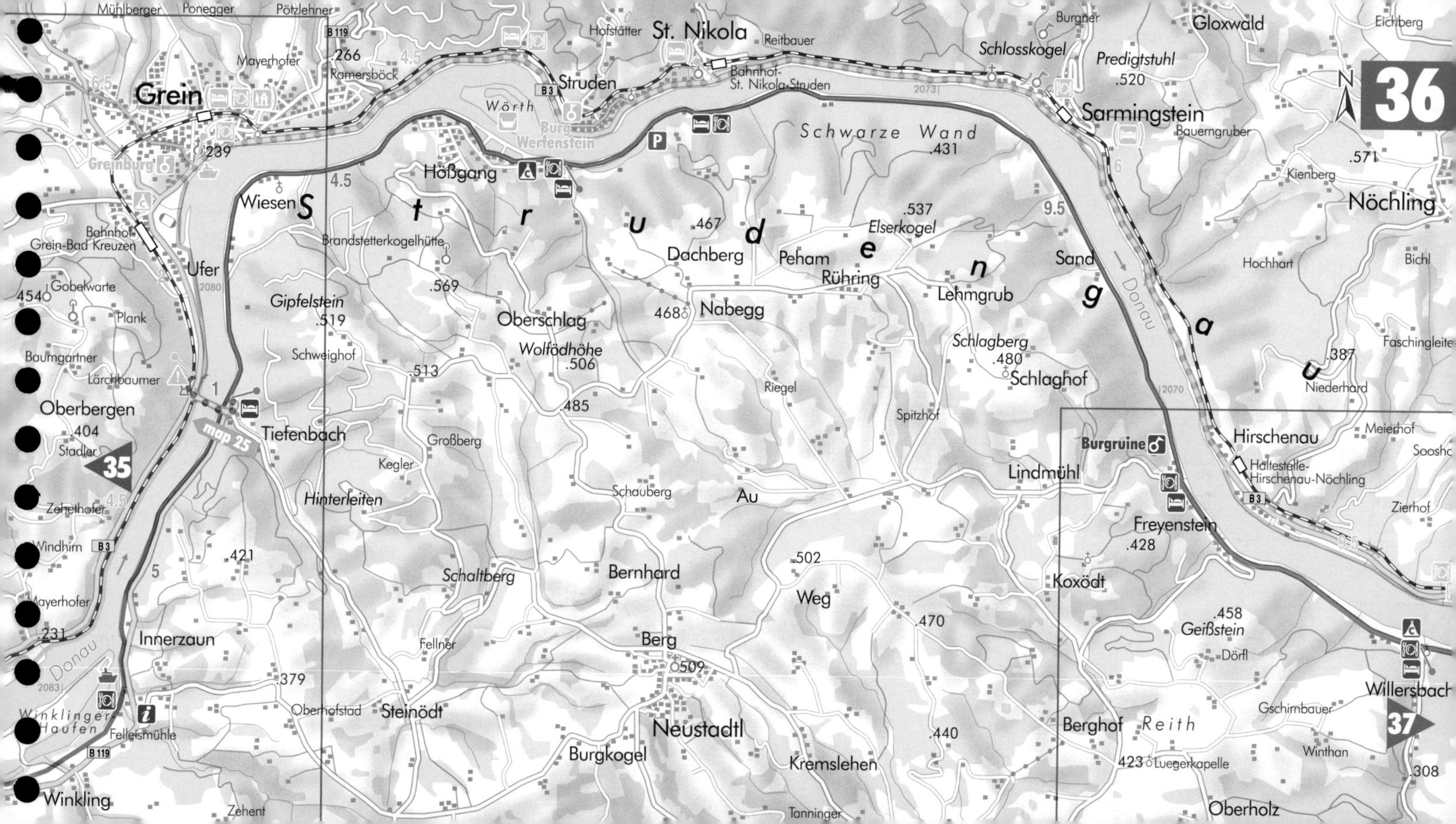

36
Grein
St. Nikola
Struden
Sarmingstein
Gloxwald
Nöchling
Strudengau
Schwarze Wand
Burg Werfenstein
Greinburg
Bahnhof-St. Nikola-Struden
Bahnhof Grein-Bad Kreuzen
Hößgang
Wiesen
Ufer
Dachberg
Peham
Rühring
Nabegg
Lehmgrub
Oberschlag
Tiefenbach
Oberbergen
Hirschenau
Haltestelle-Hirschenau-Nöchling
Burgruine
Freyenstein
Lindmühl
Koxödt
Bernhard
Weg
Berg
Neustadtl
Steinödt
Innerzaun
Winkling
Winklinger Haufen
Felleismühle
Burgkogel
Kremslehen
Berghof
Reith
Oberholz
Willersbach
Donau
map 25
35
37

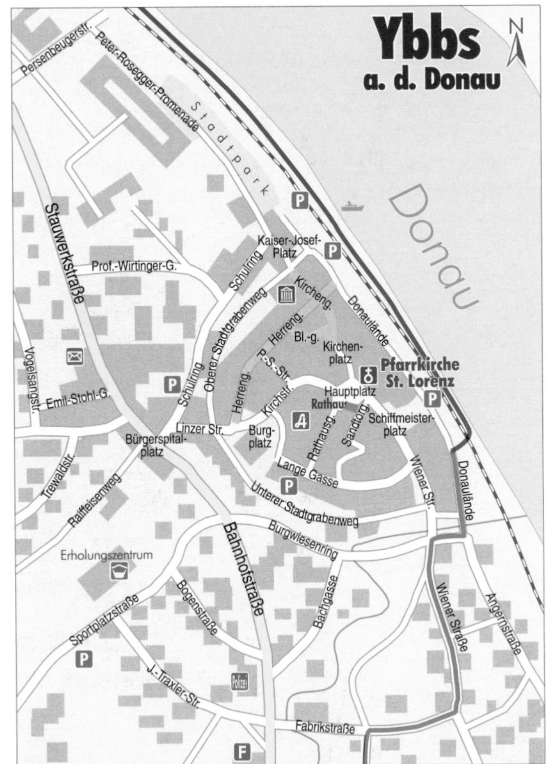

Cross a small creek and the parking lot and return to the Danube – follow the bicycle trail along the Danube and the main road until it reaches the bridge upstream from Grein.

Tip: The recommended route proceeds on a minor road down the southern bank to the town of Ybbs. Grein is an attractive town with many sights, however, and worth an excursion to the northern side of the river. Ride under the bridge and take the loop to the right to cross the river (see page 64).

Ybbs a. d. Donau

Grein to Ybbs 25 km

After the Danube bridge upstream from Grein, the southern route follows a pleasant minor road as it enters the Strudengau – the valley, and the road, become narrower downstream from the hamlet of **Wiesen**.

The route nears the dangerous narrows at Struden. The ***Hausstein rock*** *near the island of* ***Wörth*** *caused notorious eddies that made the passage especially tricky to navigate. The village of* ***Hößgang*** *is named after the canal which was excavated long ago to enable ships to bypass the river's sharp bend at Struden.*

Hößgang

The southern route veers away from the river and passes around a swimming lake – the former customs station, **Burg Werfenstein** and the towns of **Struden** and **St. Nikola** are just downstream from Hößgang.

The Danube valley becomes ever more narrow as the granite cliffs close in on the river. A floating restaurant provides an excellent platform for viewing the river while enjoying local recipes.

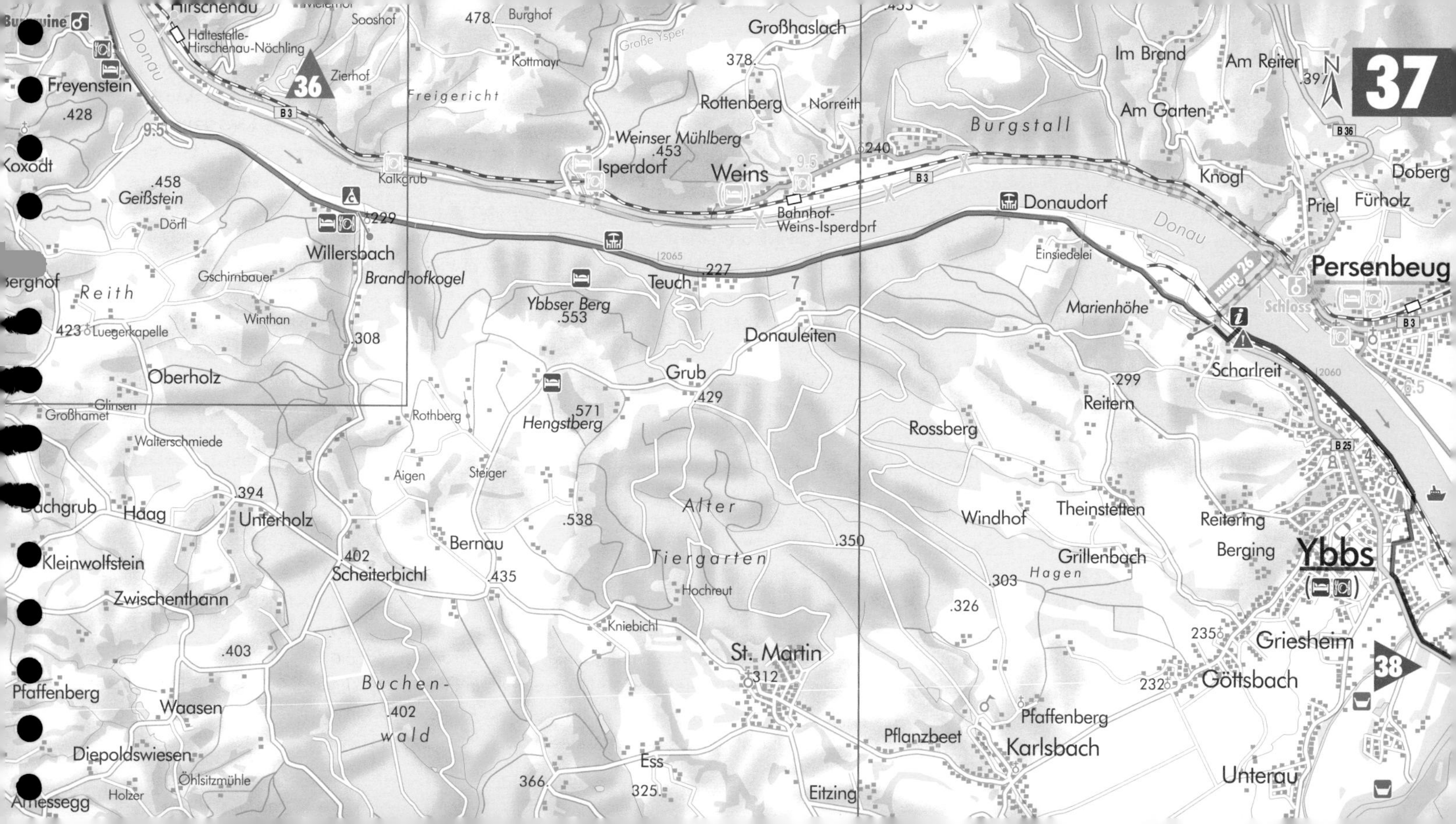

37
36
38
Donau
Persenbeug
Ybbs
Weins
Isperdorf
Donaudorf
Willersbach
Freyenstein
Großhaslach
Rottenberg
Weinser Mühlberg
Burgstall
Ybbser Berg
Donauleiten
Grub
Hengstberg
Teuch
Marienhöhe
Scharlreit
Reitern
Rossberg
Alter Tiergarten
Buchenwald
St. Martin
Karlsbach
Göttsbach
Griesheim
Unterau
Oberholz
Unterholz
Scheiterbichl
Bernau
Kleinwolfstein
Zwischenthann
Pfaffenberg
Waasen
Diepoldswiesen
Theinstetten
Windhof
Grillenbach
Reitering
Berging
Knogl
Doberg
Fürholz
Priel
Im Brand
Am Reiter
Am Garten
Bahnhof-Weins-Isperdorf
Haltestelle-Hirschenau-Nöchling
map 26

The route continues down the river to **Freyenstein**.

Freyenstein

The ruins of a castle are perched above the village on a wooded bluff over the river. It is said to be haunted by a legendary river ghost, "Prince Nöck," who comes out only by full moon and is rarely seen.

The route continues along the river to **Willersbach**, a small village with an inn and a campground ~ the river gradually becomes wider and less turbulent ~ after 7 kilometers the route reaches the bridge and **power station at Ybbs-Persenbeug** ~ there is an information board for bicycle tourists at the entrance to the bridge ⚠ Caution. Slippery surface when crossing the tracks near the information stand!

Tip: The power station road is open to traffic and may be used to cross the river. See page 66.

Ybbs to Melk — *28 km*

Stay left at the southern end of the Ybbs-Persenbeug power station ~ 50 meters after the **bicycle information board** cross the railroad tracks and ride down to the river ~ proceed 2 kilometers to the Ybbs **riverfront promenade** and turn right where the lanterns come to an end ~ pass the old city wall and turn left on **Wiener Straße** ~ before continuing the Danube tour ride to the right to take a look at the Ybbs city square and the old town.

Ybbs a. d. Donau — ≈km 2058 R

Postal code: 3370; Telephone area code: 07412

- **Tourist information**, ✆ 55233
- **St. Lorenz parish church**. Built around 1500. The pulpit, organ and the beautiful richly decorated altar date from 1730.
- **Old town.** Ybbs has been widely commended for the exemplary efforts to restore and preserve the old Renaissance houses and remaining parts of the city defenses.

Follow **Wiener Straße** out of the city ~ ride across a small stream and turn right onto the bicycle path at the next crossing street ~ when you reach the wide **Bahnhofstraße** stay left, following signs for Melk ~ cross the Ybbs river and turn left towards the Danube ~ ride down from the embankment where the Ybbs joins the Danube and continue downstream on the towpath ~ the bicycle route proceeds between the river and the railroad right-of-way to the hamlet of **Aigen** and on to Säusenstein.

Säusenstein — ≈km 2054 R

- **Theresien chapel**. The last remnants of a former Cistercian monastery (14th century), attached to a renovated baroque palace.
- **St. Donatus parish church**. The late-baroque church high above the village includes interesting wall paintings and an altar painting by Paul Troger (1746).

Continue along the riverfront to **Diedersdorf**, where the route runs closer to the railroad line ~ at the railroad underpass turn away from Dorfstraße and return to the Danube ~ the imposing **Maria Taferl pilgrimage church** can be seen beyond the Danube's opposite shore ~ at a roadside shrine in **Wallenbach**, the route turns away from the river and takes the street to the left of the railroad ~ turn left onto the towpath after passing the Krummnussbaumer harbor and proceed straight into the town.

Krummnussbaum — ≈km 2049 R

Continue down the river for 3 kilometers to where the Erlauf river joins the Danube ~ turn right and proceed to the bridge ~ cross the Erlauf and turn left to return to the Danube ~ and ride to the Danube bridge connecting Pöchlarn and Klein-Pöchlarn.

Pöchlarn — ≈km 2045 R

Postal code: 3380; Telephone area code: 02757

- **Tourism office**, ✆ 2310-11
- **Oskar Kokoschka house**, Regensburger Str. 29, ✆ 7656. Open: May-Oct, Mon-Sun 9-17. Rotating exhibits presented in the artist's birthplace.

38
Krummnußbaum
Annastift
Diedersdorf
Hinterleiten
Golling
Neustift
Säusenstein
Kirchenfeld
Sittenberg
Holzern
Oedhof
Schacherfeld
Obergraben
Mitterberg
Schacherhof
Höhlberg
Wolfring
Holzleithen
Eichberg
Ratzenberg
Maierhofen
Reist
Wolfsgrub
Sarling
Untereichen
Obereichen
Mitterndorf
Henning
Kolm
Thalling
Berging
Hohenau
Krottenthal
Unterweinzierlberg
Oberweinzierlberg
Polln
Unteregg
Neusarling
Au
Unterau
Ybbs
Griesheim
Göttsbach
Karlsbach
Pflanzbeet
Pfaffenberg
Grillenbach
Hagen
Windhof
Theinstetten
Reitering
Berging
Rossberg
Reitern
Scharlreit
Marienhöhe
Einsiedelei
Donaudorf
Donau
Persenbeug
Schloss
map 27
37
39
Weins
Burgstall
Im Brand
Am Reiter
Am Garten
Knogl
Priel
Fürholz
Doberg
Holzian
Eichberg
Infang
Rottenhof
Rosenbichl
Forsthub
Rehberg
Loja
Gottsdorf
Auf der Scheibe
Hagsdorf
Ybbs
B 36
B 3
B 25
B 1
A 1

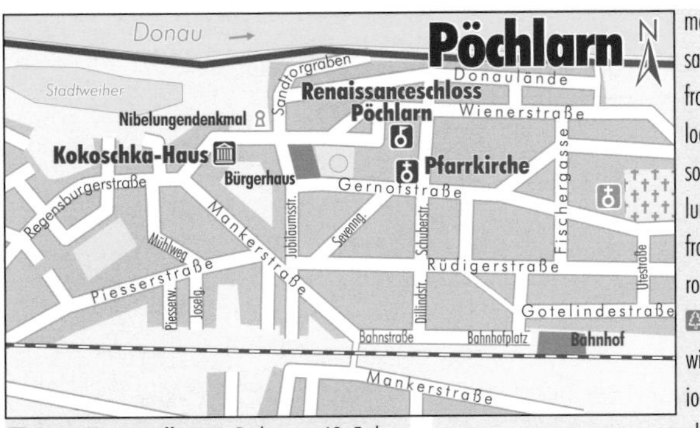

Franz Knapp collection, Rüdigerstr. 63. Etchings, watercolors and prints by the local artist.

Maria Himmelfahrt church. Built 1389-1429 and renovated in the baroque style in 1766. The church's exterior is marked by inlaid grave memorials and Roman stones. The interior features good paintings by Martin Johann Schmidt (Kremser-Schmidt).

Welserturm. Built in 1484, the tower originally served as part of fortifications against Matthias Corvinus of Hungary. Later is was used by salt traders. Today it houses a city museum and exhibitions between May-Oct.

Nibelungen memorial, Donaulände. Monument with 16 mosaic coats of arms from important locations from the song of the Nibelungen, ranging from Worms to Verona to Esztergom.

Schlosspark, with cultural pavilion and centuries-old trees

Pichler, Eisenstr. 2, ✆ 2456

The Danube bicycle tour continues along the right bank of the river to Melk 6 kilometers away ~ the imposing Benedictine abbey dominates views downriver ~ just before the power station the trail turns away from the river and then bends to the left on a service road ~ 300 meter past the power station entrance the trail returns to the river bank and continues to the ship landing ~ at the landing the trail turns to the right, crosses the Melk river and arrives in the town of **Melk**.

Cross **Kremser Straße** to reach the **town's center** ~ you can turn left at the main square to enter the pedestrian zone ~ the bicycle route to the monastery leads past the church and further to the right on **Bahnstraße** ~ at the next intersection turn left in **Abt Karl Straße.** The train station is straight ahead ~ turn left from Abt Karl Straße onto **Jakob Prandtauer Straße** ~ cross **Wiener Straße** and go left up a steep path to the monastery ~ when leaving the monastery, turn right on Wiener Straße and follow it to the pedestrian zone.

Melk **≈km 2036 R**

Postal code: 3390; Telephone area code: 02752

Tourist information, Babenbergerstr. 1, ✆ 52307410

Bicycle shed and lockers, Abbe-Stadler-Gasse, right extension of the pedestrian area.

Benedictine abbey, ✆ 555232. Open: Palm Sunday-3 Nov, May-Sept, 9-18. This grand baroque complex was built under the direction of Jakob Prandtauer 1702-38 on the site of an earlier monastery. The ceiling frescos of the marble chamber, and the 100,000-volume library are two of the reasons Melk is one of the best-known abbeys in Europe.

Peter and Paul abbey church. The baroque church from the first half of the 18th century encloses an unequaled interior decorated with frescos by J.M. Rottmayr. The 64 meter dome is graced by paintings by Troger, an impressive

Pöchlarn – Nibelungen monument

39
40
38
Artstetten
Eichberg
Ferdinand-Museum
Trennegg
Hasling
Hausäcker
Erlanghofholz
Unterbierbaum
Reuter Feld
Obersteinbach
Pargatstetten
Grubholz
Reitern
Im Aschern
Hilmanger
Obererla
Unterthalheim
Ziegelstadl
Langäcker
Kundles
Wolfseck
Angerwiese
Hirschensprung
Untererla
Maria Taferl
Oberthalheim
Wimm
Schlossäcker
Heideck
Tonberg
Grub
Im Graben
Rindfleischberg
Klosterberg
Grammern
Wallfahrtskirche
Kogel
Saulackenberg
Toberl
Zinn
Auratsberg
Hinterbrühl
Krummnußbaum
-an der Donauuferbahn
Steinwand
Rotenberg
Klein-Pöchlarn
Friesenegg
Marbach
Kracking
Autenberg
Großer Mühlberg
Bauernfeld
Granz
Wört
Am Rechen
Oskar-Kokoschka-Geburtshaus
Wallenbach
Krummnußbaum
Annastift
Pöchlarn
Kirchbühel
Loja
Donau
Diedersdorf
Neuda
Brunn
Ornding
Hinterleiten
Kellerhäuser
Grießgrub
Neustift
Golling
Neupöchlarn
Steinwand
Säusenstein
Hühnerberg
map 28
B3
B1
A1

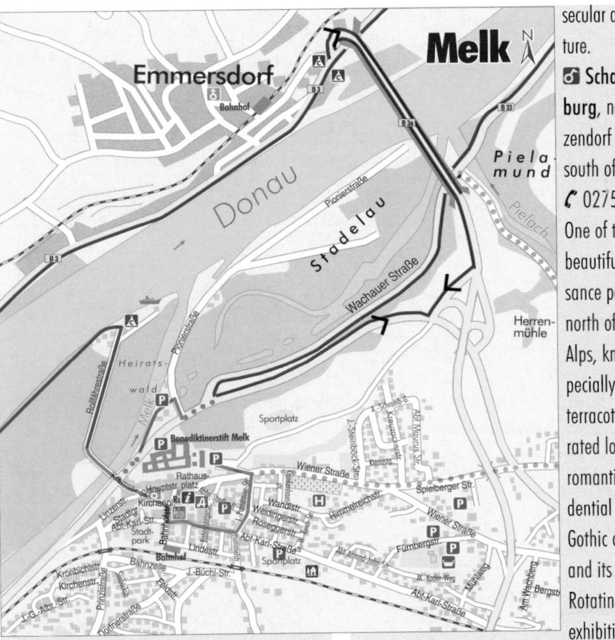

arrangement of columns, open spaces, canopies and clever lighting.

Rathausplatz. Adjacent to the former Lebzelterhaus (1657), includes examples of medieval secular architecture.

Schallaburg, near Anzendorf (5.5 km south of Melk), ✆ 02754/6317. One of the most beautiful Renaissance palaces north of the Alps, known especially for its terracotta-decorated loggia, the romantic residential wing, its Gothic chapel and its gardens. Rotating large exhibitions.

The ***Benedictine Abbey at Melk*** *marks the beginnings of the beautiful Wachau, one of the most romantic wine-growing regions in Austria, and offers a rare interplay of natural and manmade beauty.*

After centuries of mixed fortunes, the abbey at Melk enjoyed a glorious heyday starting in the early 18th century, under the Abbot Berthold Dietmayer. Dietmayer and the St. Pölten builder Jacob Prandtauer were an ideally suited pair, and combined to rebuild the abbey as an expression of newfound optimism and power following the Ottoman wars and the success of the counter reformation.

Benediktinerstift Melk

Tip: The **Danube bicycle** trail continues along the river flood plain to the left of motorized traffic. If you wish to stay on the right bank, turn left on **Wiener Straße** after the petrol station. To reach the left bank Danube bicycle route follow the busy road up the slope and then turn left onto the Danube river bridge. Tourists who wish to avoid some of the traffic and the uphill road can take **Wachauer Straße** to the bridge and then carry their bicycles up the stairs. On the northern bank the Danube bicycle route continues along the river into the famous Wachau region.

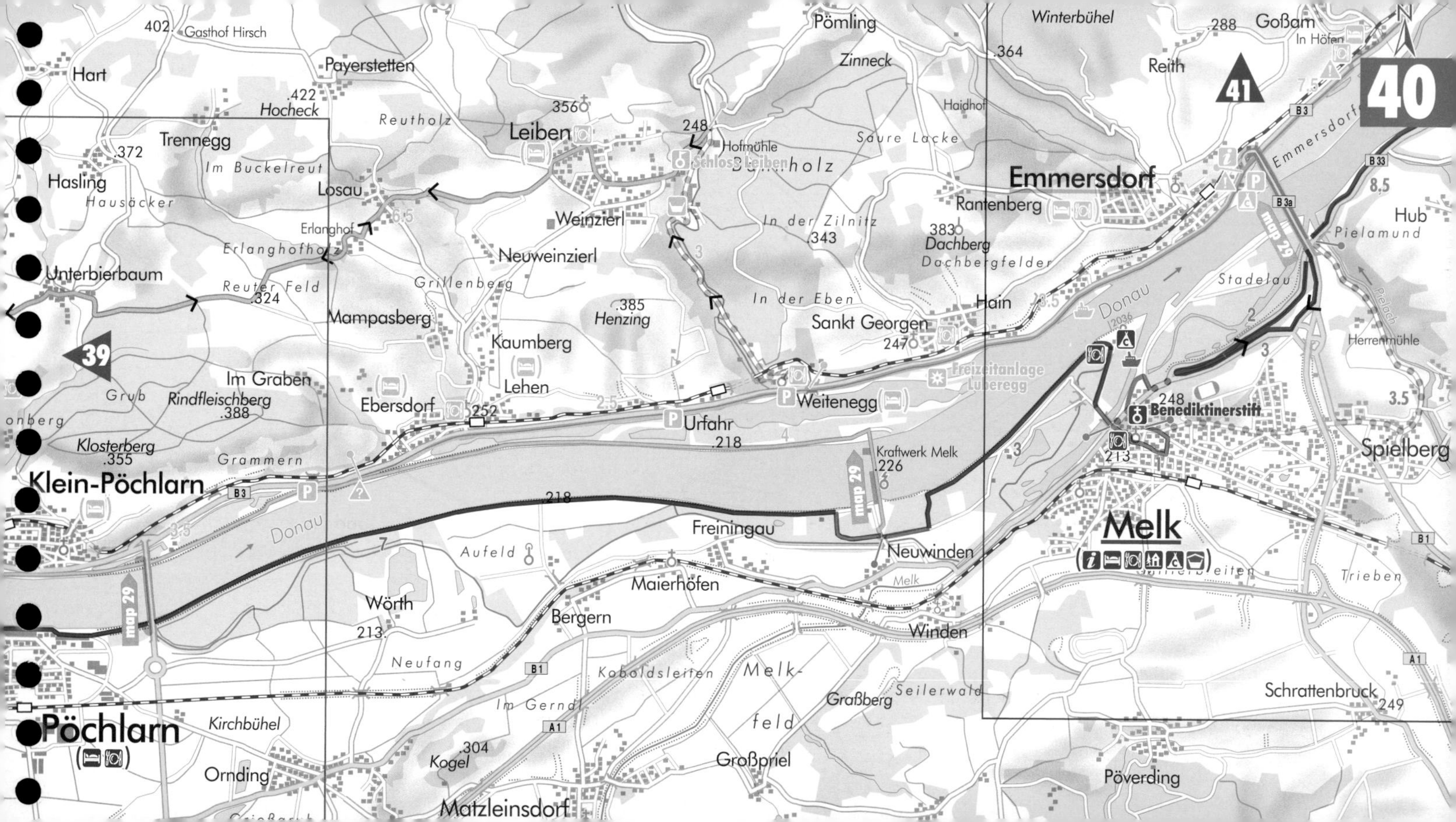
40
41
39
Hart
Payerstetten
Pömling
Zinneck
Winterbühel
Goßam
In Höfen
Reith
Hocheck
Gasthof Hirsch
Leiben
Schloss Leiben
Hofmühle
Haidhof
Saure Lacke
Trennegg
Im Buckelreut
Hasling
Hausäcker
Losau
Reutholz
Weinzierl
Emmersdorf
Rantenberg
In der Zilnitz
Dachberg
Dachbergfelder
Erlanghof
Erlanghofholz
Neuweinzierl
Grillenberg
Unterbierbaum
Reuter Feld
Mampasberg
Henzing
Kaumberg
In der Eben
Sankt Georgen
Hain
Stadelau
Pielamund
Hub
Pielach
Herrenmühle
Im Graben
Grub
Rindfleischberg
Lehen
Ebersdorf
Freizeitanlage Luberegg
Weitenegg
Urfahr
Benediktinerstift
Klosterberg
Grammern
Kraftwerk Melk
Spielberg
Klein-Pöchlarn
Donau
Freiningau
Neuwinden
Melk
Aufeld
Maierhöfen
Trieben
Wörth
Bergern
Winden
Neufang
Koboldsleiten
Melk-feld
Seilerwald
Graßberg
Schrattenbruck
Im Gerndl
Kirchbühel
Pöchlarn
Orning
Kogel
Großpriel
Pöverding
Matzleinsdorf
map 29
B 1
B 3
B 33
B 3a
A 1

Melk to Vienna along the left bank 121 km

Many bicycle tourists will regard the final stage to Vienna as the highlight of the tour. The Wachau – one of Austria's best-known wine-growing regions – offers some of the most beautiful landscapes along the entire Danube River. A centuries-old tradition of producing wines has turned the steep south-facing slopes into terraced "stairs to the heavens," and give the valley its distinctive appearance. Downstream from Krems, the Danube valley then spreads into the expansive flood plains of the Tullner meadows, before reaching the Wiener Pforte. A few kilometers later the tour ends in Vienna, Austria's charming capital city.

The route from Melk to Altenwörth follows quiet country lanes and bicycle trails. Between Altenwörth and Tulln the Danube bicycle route exists only on the southern bank, before returning to the northern side at Tulln.

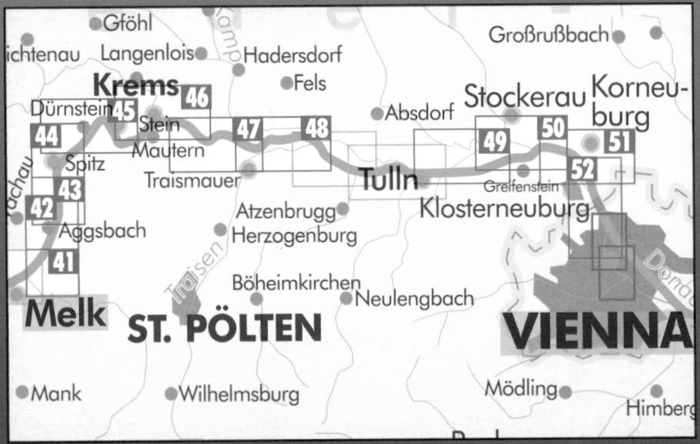

Melk to Spitz on the northern bank 20 km

Aggsbach Markt

On the northern bank, ride under the Danube bridge between Emmersdorf and Melk and proceed along the bicycle trail next to the road ~ after the Schallemmersdorf sign cross Uferstraße ~ and continue on the service lane on the left side between the road and the railroad ~ at Grimsing the route departs briefly from the main road ~ before returning to the main road 1.5 kilometers later. The route continues on the narrow bicycle lane which runs between the road and the railroad ~ in Aggsbach Markt bear left on Dorfstraße.

Aggsbach Markt ≈km 2027 L

Postal code: 3641;
Telephone area code: 02712

- **Town office**, ✆ 214
- **13th century late Romanesque church**
- **Hubhof amusement park**, ✆ 241, 4 km towards Maria Laach/Jauerling (altitude 293 meters, follow the dwarves). Open: Easter to early-Sept, Mon-Sun 10-17, Sept and Oct by request. Fairytale path, fairytale parade, outdoor dinosaur park, live animal enclosure and playground.

After Aggsbach Markt continue down the bicycle lane along the Bundesstraße. Parts of the trail are quite narrow ~ across the river from the ruin on the southern bank turn left from

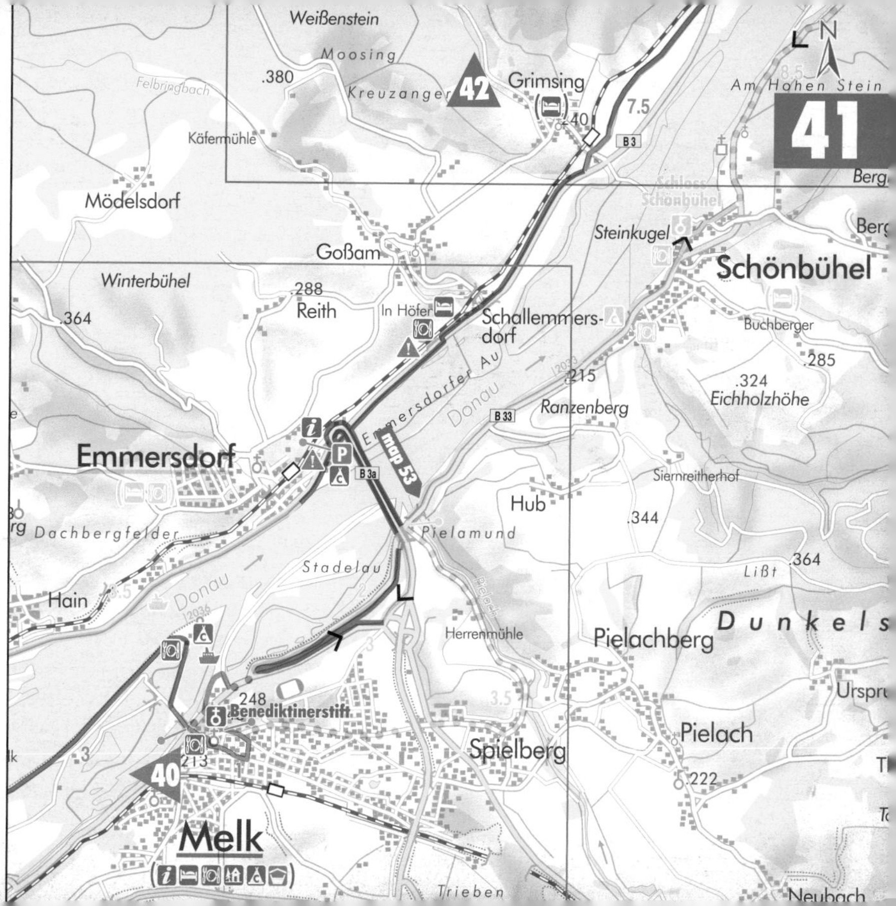

Monument where the Willendorf Venus was found

the riverfront road towards Groisbach ⁓ stay to the right of the railroad and enter Willendorf.

Tip: To reach the Venus museum and the site where the Venus of Willendorf was found turn left at the chapel. To visit the discovery site, a monument and exposed layers of excavation take the footpath on the right after the underpass for the railroad. A replica of the statue can be seen from the route through Willendorf.

Willendorf ≈km **2024 L**

Postal code: 3641; Telephone area code: 02712

Aggsbach Markt town office, ✆ 214

Stone age museum, Willendorf No. 4, ✆ 328. Open: Early May-mid Oct, Sat 14-15:30, Sun/Hol 10-11:30 and 14-15:30 and by appointment.

When the Danube river railroad was being built in 1908, workers found an 11-centimeter fertility figure in the ice-age loess near Willendorf. The limestone figure of a fat naked female caused a sensation, and is regarded as an expression of female fertility, or a symbol of "magna mater." The ***Venus of Willendorf*** *is regarded as the most aesthetically accomplished of more than 130 Paleolithic (old stone age) objects that have been found between southern France and Siberia.*

The next village is **Schwallenbach** ⁓ proceed along a quiet lane through the vineyards ⁓ to the main road which runs along a bicycle trail ⁓ pass beneath the **Hinterhaus ruins** and reach the town of Spitz in the heart of the Wachau ⁓ turn left at the first intersection and then right before reaching the railroad ⁓ at the next intersection go straight ⁓ the crossing street leads to the ferry (right turn) or to the center of town (left) under the railroad ⁓ if you go left, take the right onto **Bahnhofstraße**, and then left to **Kirchplatz**.

Spitz

Spitz a. d. Donau ≈km **2019 L**

Postal code: 3620; Telephone area code: 02713

Tourism association, ✆ 2363

Ferry to Arnsdorf. Open: April-Sept, Mon-Fri 6-21, Sat/Sun/Hol 7-21, Oct, March, Mon-Fri 6-19,Sat 7-19, Sun/Hol 8-19.

Erlauhof castle with shipping museum, Erlahof, ✆ 2246. Open: April-Oct, Mon-Sat 10-12 and 14-16, Sun 10-12 and 13-17. Exhibits and information about Danube shipping since Roman times, with special attention given to rafters and river travel.

St. Mauritius parish church, Marktplatz. The late-gothic lower structure from the 14th/15th centuries with a stately tower that is 100 years

Spitz a. d. Donau

older. Interior mostly late-gothic architecture with baroque features like an altar by Kremser Schmidt (1799).

- **Lower castle.** A walled-up loggia, bay window and coat of arms are what is left of the 14th to 16th century structure.
- **Old Rathaus**. Part of a cluster of Gothic structures, including the Bürgerspital (hospital, from 1400), with a picturesque courtyard. Somewhat diminished through construction of the railroad.
- **Hinterhaus ruin**. Built in the 13th century on a rough outcropping, and extended in the 16th century with round towers, well-preserved ruin includes a large Romanesque keep, a Gothic yard, and Renaissance battlements.
- **Red Gate**. Distinctive gate built of quarried stone which for generations has provided a frame for romantic views of the Wachau landscape.

*Markt **Spitz**, population 2,000, lies at the foot of the **Tausendeimerberg** (thousand pails mountain), which is so named because the hill allegedly produces one thousand pails of wine (56,000 liters) in a good year.*

Spitz to Krems — *19 km*

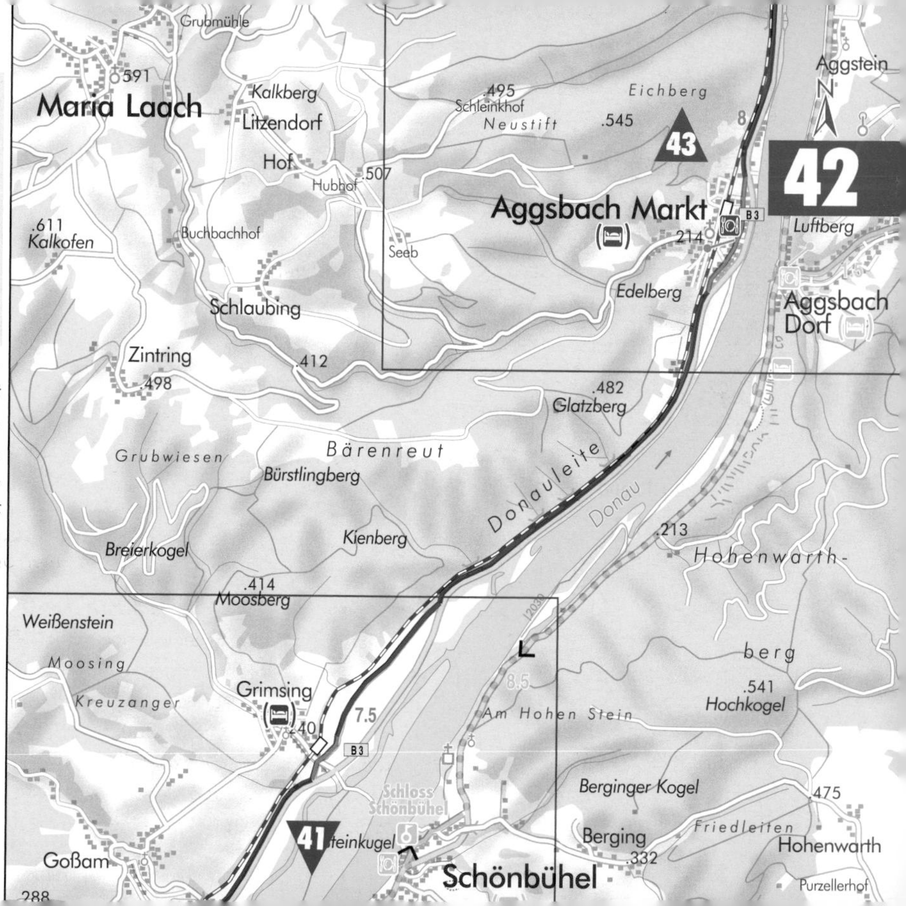

From Kirchplatz take **Marktstraße**, then turn left on **Kremser Straße** and proceed parallel to the Danube's shoreline ~ after the Hotel Mariandl (named after a popular film set in the

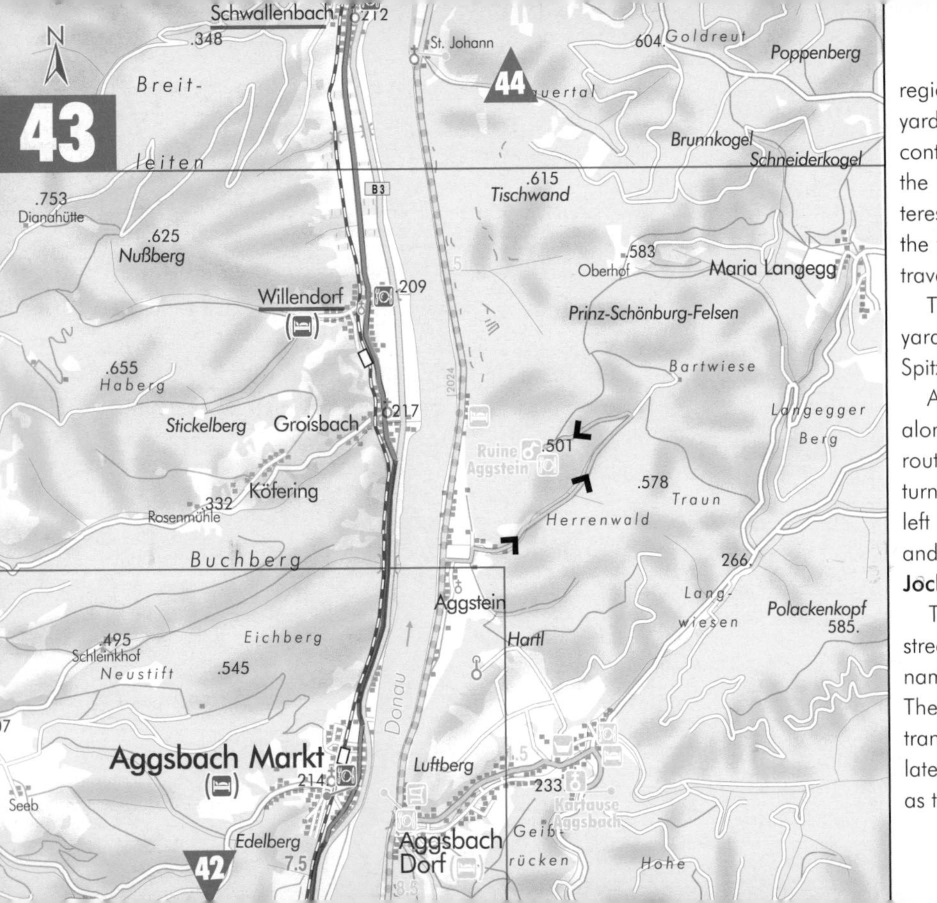

region) and return to the vineyards ~ cross the railroad and continue the tour to the left of the Bundesstraße ~ at the interesting **St. Michael** church the trail returns to very lightly-traveled side streets.

The Wachau's best vineyards are located between Spitz and Dürnstein.

After the panoramic path along the Donaubreiten the route reaches **Wösendorf** ~ turn right at the church ~ turn left at the next crossing street and follow the side street past **Joching**.

The small Ritzlingbach stream is said to have lent its name to Riesling white wine. The local grape was then transplanted to the Rhine and later returned to the Wachau as the Rheinriesling.

Wine in the Wachau

The woods on the south-facing slopes of the Wachau were already cleared and planted with vines by the time of Charlemagne. Today the vineyards still provide a striking element in the landscape of what may be the Danube's most temperate region. The wine industry has survived despite some heavy blows: a period of bad weather in the middle ages and the upheavals of the 30 Years War led to the decay of many vineyards. During the reign of Maria Theresa some wine cellars were even turned over to vinegar production. In 1890 the American phylloxera grape louse devastated the Wachau's vines.

Today the Wachau once again produces wines that are coveted throughout the world.

Especially the white wines, which find excellent nutrients in the local loess soil, have a good reputation among connoisseurs. Four of the best-known wines are the following:

Green Veltliner: *A young and spicy table wine, dry to semi-dry. Austria's most important wine.*

Rheinriesling: *a noble fruity wine which originally came from the Wachau and is prized for its fine bouquet.*

Müller Thurgau: *Austria's second most important white wine, fresh and lively, with intense fruit flavors.*

Neuburger: *A milder, more full-bodied wine.*

"Sturm" *(storm) is the name given to the cloudy grape "most" that is produced in the first weeks of the fermentation process and drunk mainly in the fall. After November 11, "most" is regarded as one of the "Heurigen" – the young, current wines. "Heurige" is also the name of the shops in which vintners sell their own wines.*

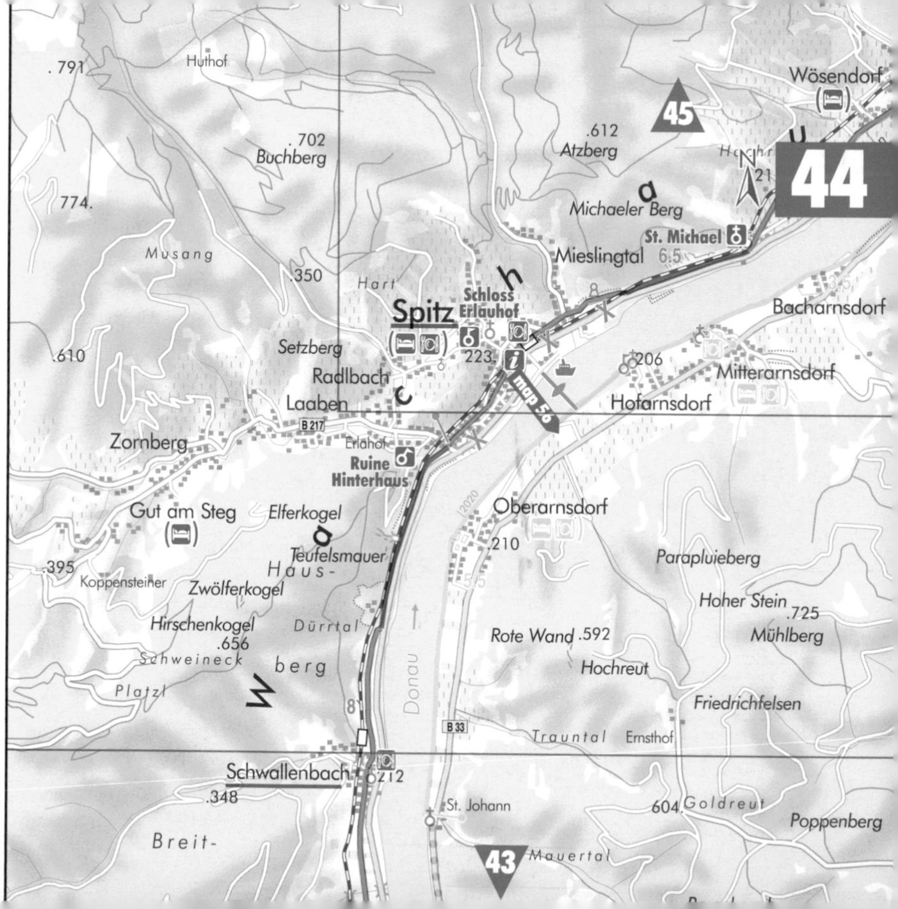

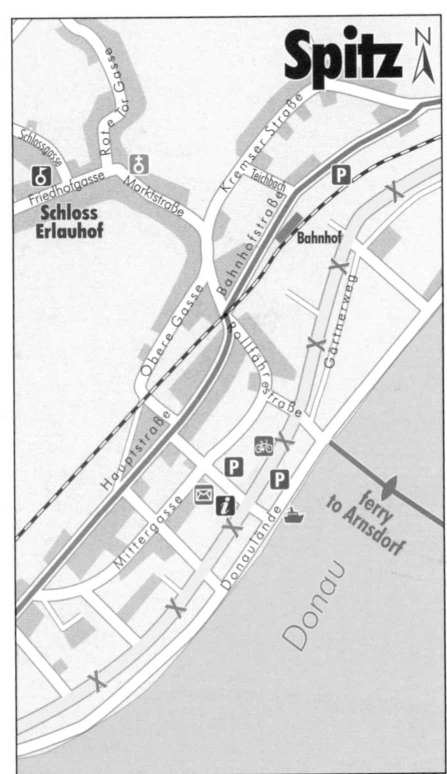

After riding through the pleasant vineyards the route reaches another of the Wachau's highlights – the town of Weißenkirchen ⁓ turn right at the main junction to reach the ferry, or stay left to reach Dürnstein and Krems ⁓ turn right just after the railroad crossing ⁓ continue through the village to the right from the church, past the Wachau museum.

Weißenkirchen ≈km **2013 L**

Postal code: 3610; Telephone area code: 02715

Town office, ✆ 2232, Information about rooms at the ship station, ✆ 2600

Ferry: Mon-Fri 9-12 and 13:30-18:30, Sat/Sun/Hol 9-18:30.

Wachau museum, Teisenhoferhof, ✆ 2268. Open: April-Oct, Tues-Sun 10-17. Part of the museum shows tools and equipment used by vintners, and a historic wine-press. Other exhibits include works by the painters of the Wachau, artists including Jakob Alt, Johann Nepomuk or Martin Johann (Kremser) Schmidt.

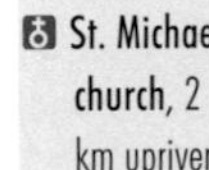

St. Michael church, 2 km upriver. The Gothic main church dates to around 1500, while the old parish building goes back another half a millennium, and is regarded as the oldest in the Wachau. The remarkable 7 rabbits on the presbytery's roof probably depict a hunt, but other fabulous explanations have also been proposed.

Teisenhoferhof, or Schützenhof, market. An especially pretty arcaded courtyard in the Renaissance style dates to the second half of the 15th century. Seat of the Lower Austrian Wine Academy.

Maria Himmelfahrt church, Kirchplatz. The earliest parts of the church, which is situated above the town and surrounded by mostly-intact fortifications, were built around 1400. The interior combines late-gothic and baroque elements.

Weißenkirchen

From the church in Weißenkirchen, the route proceeds down the Donauterrasse ⁓ and out of town past a pretty row of houses with several wine sampling and selling shops (Heurigenschenke) ⁓ after the railroad crossing ride along the bicycle trail to the left of the street ⁓ turn left after one kilometer ⁓ onto a farm lane through the "Frauen-

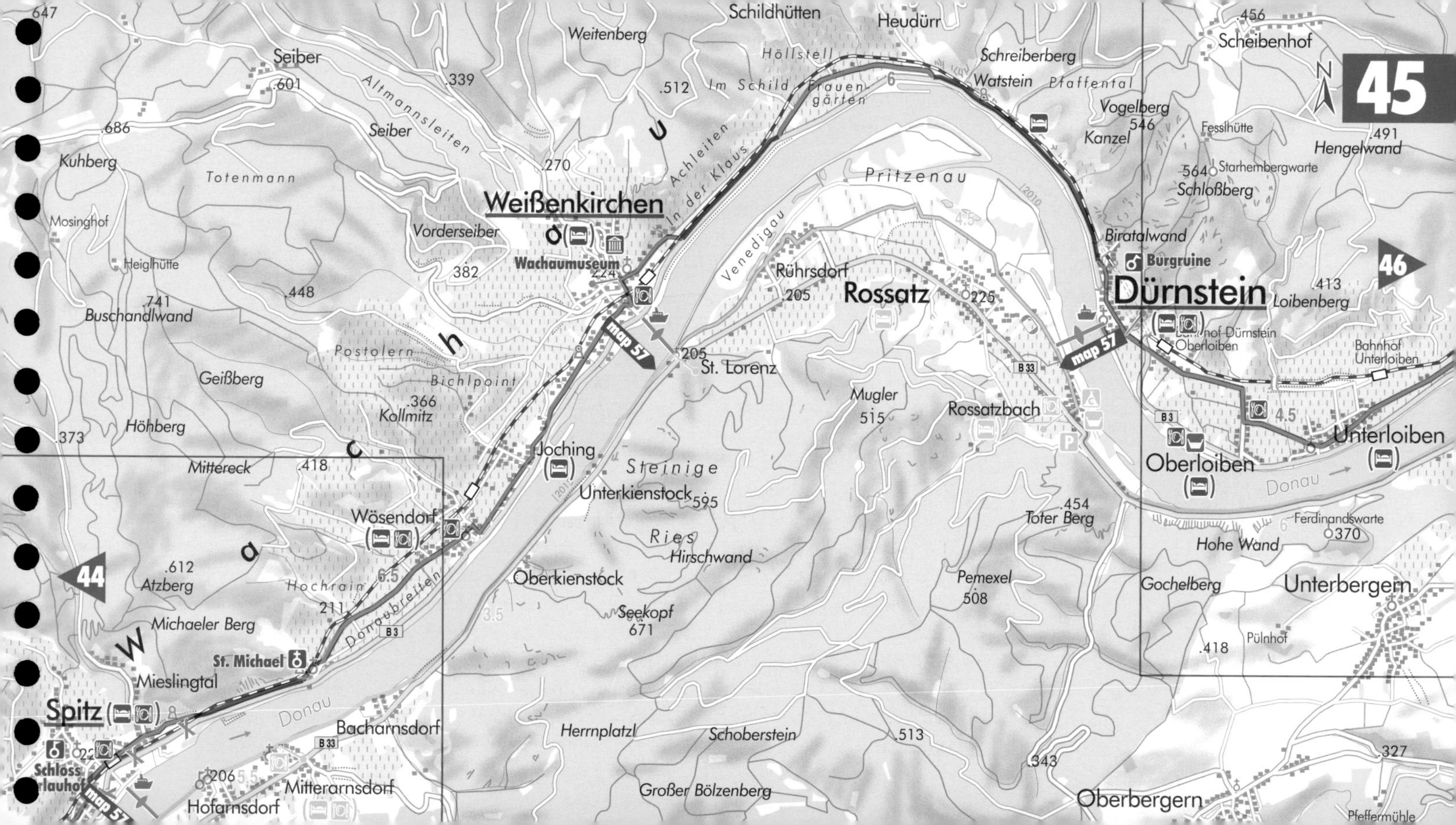
45
44
46
Schildhütten
Heudürr
Scheibenhof
Weitenberg
Seiber
Höllstell
Schreiberberg
Watstein
Pfaffental
Im Schild
Frauengärten
Altmannsleiten
Vogelberg
546
Kanzel
Fesslhütte
Hengelwand
Kuhberg
Totenmann
Achleiten
In der Klaus
Pritzenau
Starhembergwarte
Schloßberg
Weißenkirchen
Mosinghof
Vorderseiber
Venedigau
Biratalwand
Burgruine
Wachaumuseum
Heiglhütte
Rührsdorf
Rossatz
Dürnstein
Loibenberg
Buschandlwand
Bahnhof Dürnstein Oberloiben
Bahnhof Unterloiben
map 57
Postolern
St. Lorenz
Bichlpoint
Geißberg
Mugler
515
Kollmitz
Rossatzbach
Unterloiben
Höhberg
Joching
Mittereck
Steinige
Oberloiben
Unterkienstock
Donau
Toter Berg
Ferdinandswarte
Wösendorf
Ries
Hirschwand
Hohe Wand
Atzberg
Hochrain
Oberkienstock
Pemexel
508
Gochelberg
Unterbergern
Donaubreiten
Michaeler Berg
Seekopf
671
Pülnhof
St. Michael
Mieslingtal
Spitz
Bacharnsdorf
Herrnplatzl
Schoberstein
Schloss Erlauhof
Mitterarnsdorf
Hofarnsdorf
Großer Bölzenberg
Oberbergern
Pfeffermühle

gärten." The extensive terraced vineyards are dotted with small huts used by the vintners. ~ The route continues on a bicycle trail along the main road.

The next station on the Danube bicycle tour is Dürnstein, with the romantically-situated ***ruins of Dürnstein castle*** *above the picturesque town. It is the Wachau's most famous location. England's King Richard the Lionhearted was held hostage, for a king's ransom, in the castle in the 12th century.*

At the sign marking the edge of Dürnstein turn from the bicycle lane onto a side street. The main road passes through a tunnel. ~ The route ascends a small rise and passes under the castle ruins and straight through the historic old town. The prettiest views of Dürnstein are from the beach along the Danube.

Dürnstein ≈km **2009 L**

Postal code: 3601; Telephone area code: 02711

- **Town office, Rathaus,** ✆ 219, Info 200
- **Rossatz-Dürnstein ferry** ✆ 02714/6355. Open: 22-24 April, 10-18; 29 April-June, 10-18; July, Aug, 10-19, Sept-8 Oct, 10-18, 14 & 15 Oct 10-17.
- **Donauschifffahrt** Oberleitner-Fischer OEG, Rossatzbach 40, ✆ 02714/6355. Open: May-Oct charter trips in the Wachau and "Dürnstein at Night" Danube river tours. Every Mon at 21:30 from 5 June to 28 Aug. Departs from Donaupromenade Dürnstein.
- **Dürnstein** castle. Built in the 12th century. Main building and chapel from the High Middle Ages were later incorporated into the larger castle. Richard the Lionhearted was held here in the winter of 1192-93 as he returned from the crusades.
- **Dürnstein Abbey,** ✆ 375. Open: April-Oct, Mon-Sun 9-18. Guided tours every hour on the hour. Augustine monastery established in 1410 and renovated in the baroque style by important period artists in 1710-33. The courtyard counts as especially beautiful.
- **Maria Himmelfahrt abbey church.** A masterpiece of Austrian baroque architecture, with its blue-and-white tower (1733), is famous for its harmony with the surrounding landscape.
- **Kellerschlössl,** ✆ 371. East of the town. Built 1714, with stucco interiors and ceiling frescos presumably by J. Prandtauer. 800 meters of tunnels for storing the wine harvest.

Dürnstein

Depart Dürnstein through the town gate and ride straight across the main road ~ or turn right at the gate to reach the **ferry to Rossatz** and the outdoor pool further downstream ~ the northern bank route proceeds along a narrow lane through vineyards and apricot orchards ~ pass the French memorial (1805) and follow the road as it winds to the right ~ then turn left into the vineyards.

In Unterloiben pass the church on the left ~ through the town and past the Rieslingschurl, a favorite meeting point and photo setting.

About 20 meters past the Rieslingschurl there is a cliff marked with an odd inscription: ***I. Kyselak****. That was the name of a travel-happy Biedermeier fellow who made a bet with friends that he would make himself known throughout the kingdom in the course of three years of travel. Armed with paint and a paint-brush, he scrawled his name in countless unlikely places throughout the land, and won his bet within a year-and-a-half. According to one anecdote, the early graffiti artist was summoned to the Kaiser to explain his actions. After he had chastized and dismissed Kyselak, the Kaiser was stunned to discover that Kyselak had managed to leave his name on the Kaiser's own desk.*

On the other side of the river, the Göttweig monastery dominates the landscape from its hilltop location ~ the left bank route passes a large vineyard and returns to the bicycle trail next to the main road. A roadside marker announces you are departing the Wachau.

Tip: At Förthof the main route leaves the road and leads to the ramp to the Danube bridge to Mautern. A side-trip to the Göttweig monastery starts in the town of Mautern (see page 122).

The next town on the northern bank is Stein ~ ride through the town on a side street parallel to the main road. The enticing Steiner Landstraße behind the Linzer Tor is open to traffic only from the opposite direction.

Tip: We recommend you dismount and wander through the romantic streets and alleys by foot.

Stein a. d. Donau ≈km 2003 L

Postal code: 3504; Telephone area code: 02732

Austropa Tourism office, Undstr. 6, ✆ 82676

St. Nikolaus parish church, Steiner Landstraße. The 3-nave church dates from the 15th century. Ceiling frescos and altar paintings by Martin Johann (Kremser) Schmidt were retained during a re-gothicization of the church in 1901.

Minorites church, Minoritenplatz. The 3-nave pillar-basilica is among the earliest arched-constructions built by the German mendicant order (1264). Noteworthy: The 14th century frescos. Today the church serves as a gallery for modern art projects.

Steiner Landstraße. The well-preserved old buildings and the small open squares decorated with baroque statues and columns give the street its special charm.

Former **Frauenbergkirche**, above the St. Nikolaus parish. Built in 1380. The tower has a large network of arches. Renovated as a war memorial in 1963.

Stein a. d. Donau

Kunstmeile, Kunsthalle and Karikaturmuseum/Deix Haus. The Kunsthalle offers an attractive art program year-round. The Museum of Caricature is Austria's first museum for satire, caricature and political art. Includes an evolving exhibition of works by Manfred Deix.

The riverfront road between Stein and Krems is relatively wide, with bicycle lanes in both directions ~ the two towns have virtually grown together, and the center of Krems is not

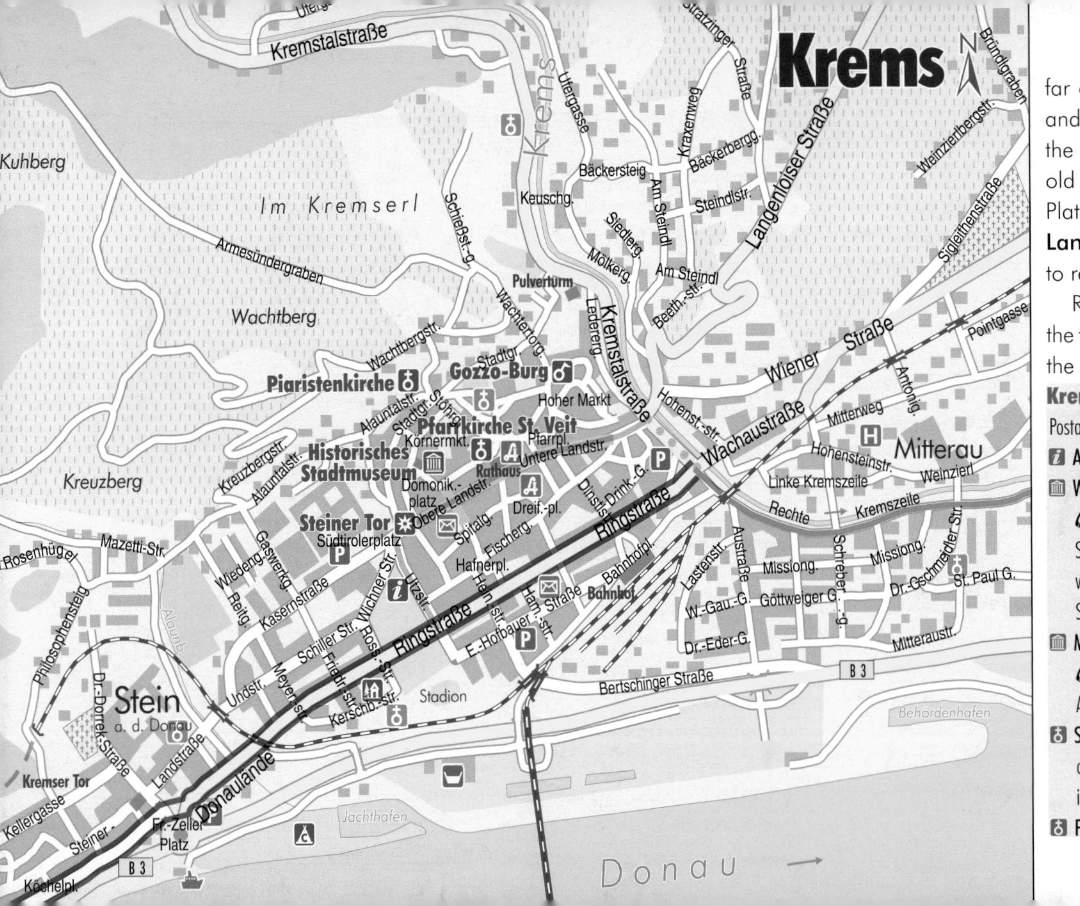

far away ~ ride through the railroad underpass and up Ringstraße past the youth hostel ~ after the city park turn left on **Utzstraße** to reach the old city center. Utzstraße leads to the Südtiroler Platz and the pedestrian zone ~ go down **Obere Landstraße** to the Krems river and then turn right to return to the Danube bicycle trail.

Ringstraße leads straight through the town, past the train station ~ turn right in **Austraße** just before the Krems river to continue the tour downstream.

Krems **≈km 2002 L**

Postal code: 3500; Telephone area code: 02732

- **Austropa Tourism office**, Undstr. 6, ✆ 82676
- **Weinstadt museum**, former Dominican church, Körnermarkt 14, ✆ 801567 and 572. Open: 8 March to late Nov, Tues-Sun 10-18. Subjects: Archaeological collections, folklore and objects related to winemaking, medieval art and works by the baroque painter M. J. Schmidt. Large parts of the former abbey are open to the public.
- **Motorcycle museum**, Egelsee (2 km northwest), Ziegelofeng. 1, ✆ 41428. Open: Mon-Sun 9-17. Private collection with (mostly Austrian) motorcycles and related items representing 8 decades.
- **St. Veit parish church**, Pfarrplatz. Along with the Göttweig abbey church, one of the earliest baroque churches in Austria. Completed in 1630, by Cypriano Biasino.
- **Piaristen church**, Frauenbergplatz. Built 1475-1515 under the

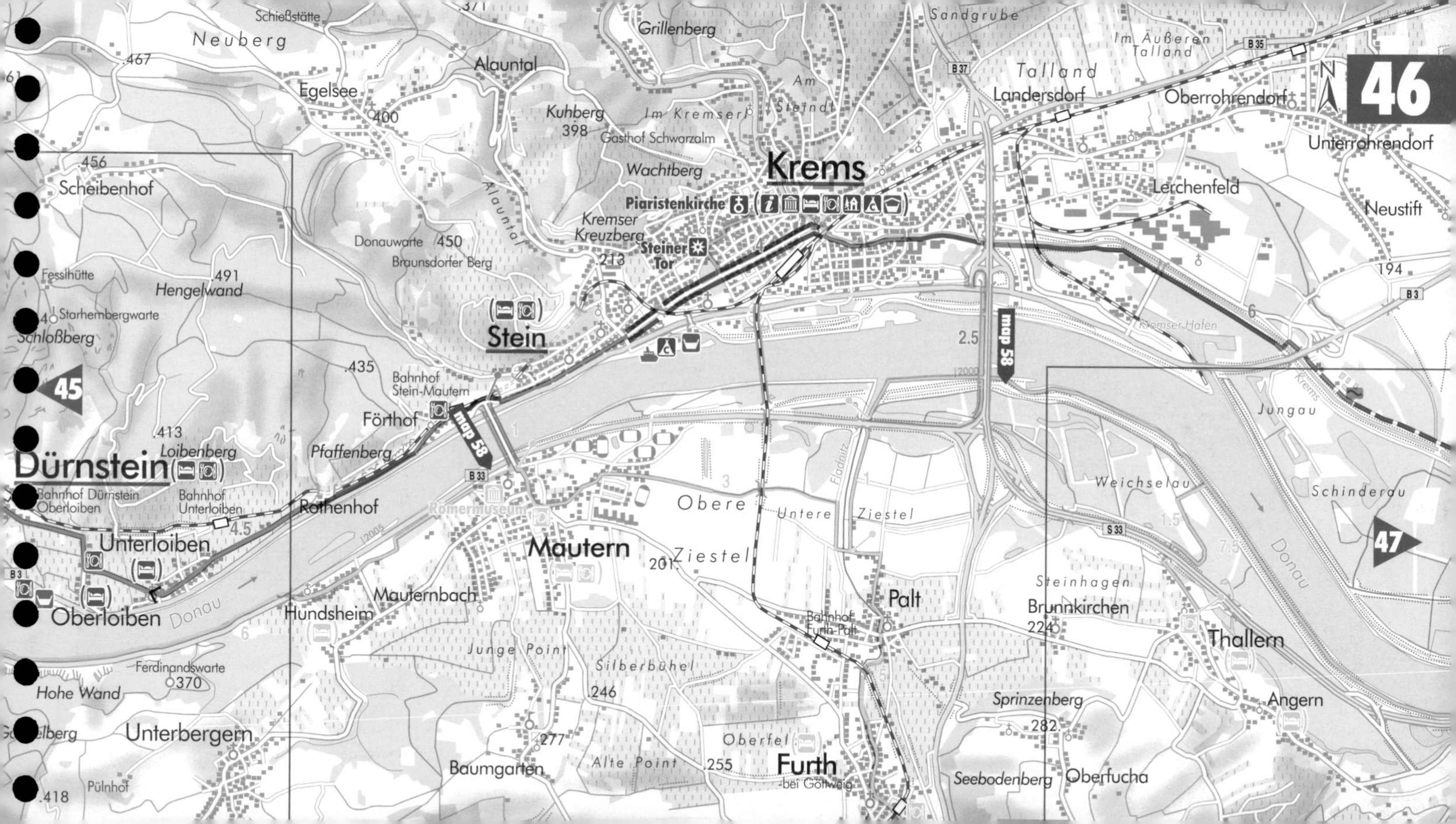
46
Krems
Stein
Dürnstein
Mautern
Furth
-bei Göttweig
Palt
Thallern
Unterloiben
Oberloiben
Unterbergern
Neuberg
Alauntal
Egelsee
Grillenberg
Landersdorf
Oberrohrendorf
Unterrohrendorf
Lerchenfeld
Neustift
Scheibenhof
Hengelwand
Schloßberg
Loibenberg
Förthof
Rothenhof
Mauternbach
Hundsheim
Brunnkirchen
Angern
Oberfucha
Baumgarten
Piaristenkirche
Steiner Tor
Bahnhof Stein-Mautern
Bahnhof Dürnstein Oberloiben
Bahnhof Unterloiben
Bahnhof Furth-Palt
Römermuseum
Donau
map 58
45
47

Krems a. d. Donau

by the German mendicant order. Since the monastery was closed (1785), the buildings have served as a button factory, grain silo and theater. Since 1891 site of the WEINSTADTmuseum.

Gozzo Burg – former Stadtpalais, Hoher Markt. Built 1260-70 in the style of an Italian city palace by Judge Gozzo, the wealthy magistrate and citizen of Krems. The especially beautiful hall makes this the most significant secular structure of the period in Austria.

Rathaus, Pfarrplatz. Presented to the city in 1453 by Ulrich von Dachsberg. The entrance hall features Renaissance pillars from 1549. The noteworthy bay-window with rich relief coats of arm and ornamentation dates from the same time.

influence of Viennese architectural trends, with a handsome stairs and a 3-nave main hall. As in the Viennese style, the pillars are decorated with statues. All altar paintings by Martin Johann Schmidt.

Bürgerspitalkirche (hospital church), Obere Landstraße. Built 1470 with inward-turned buttresses. Sweeping windows and the intricate iron doors of the Gothic sacramental niche.

Former **Dominican church**, Dominikanerplatz. The basilica complex was completed in 1265 and is one of the earliest arched structures built

Town houses, Untere and Obere Landstraße/Körnermarkt/Margarethenstraße. The city's appearance is determined mainly by 16th century structures with their bay windows, reliefs and Sgraffiti on the facades.

Steiner Tor (gate), west end of the city. Built 1480 with 4 Gothic towers, baroque additions 1754. One of Krems' old city gates, today the town's best-known landmark.

Kapuzinerkloster Und, Undstraße. Construction of the complex began in 1614. Center point is the small domed church. Fresco by Daniel Gran (1756).

Grafenegg Palace, 10 km east, ✆ 02735/2205-22. Open: Tues, Thur 13-17, Sat/Sun/Hol 10-17. The most significant Romanesque palace in Austria, surrounded by an English garden.

Krems is regarded as the oldest city in Lower Austria. The town's unique character is shaped by the confusion of baroque town houses with Renaissance courtyards, Gothic bay-windows and chapels nestled into a maze of narrow medieval streets and alleys that crisscross the old city center. The Steiner Tor is the town's best-known landmark, with its tall baroque tower surrounded by pointed-little medieval spires. The Piaristenkirche, the most beautiful of Krems' churches, is on the Wachtberg above the city. The roofed wooden Piaristen stairs lead to the Gothic church and its main altar by Martin Johann Schmidt.

Krems and its perfectly-preserved old city also has a reputation for innovation, with numerous advanced scientific facilities and creative projects.

Tip: Krems is an excellent springboard for other bicycle tours in regions to the north, which are described in the ***bikeline* bicycle touring books "Kamptal"** and **"Waldviertel"**, and the "**Radkarte Kamptal" (bicycle map)**. These are available in German.

Signs for the Danube bicycle tour route lead to the Danube river bridge ~ after the railroad underpass stay left at **Austraße** and proceed down **Rechte Kremszeile**.

Tip: There is a bicycle lane across the bridge, with which one can switch to the southern bank of the river. The marked route goes to the right and across the bridge (see page 124).

Krems to Altenwörth on the northern bank 22.5 km

Ignore the Danube bicycle tour signs and proceed under the main road ~ after 300 meters the route leaves the street and continues on a hiking/biking path next to the Krems river ~ pass the chemicals plant ~ cross the Krems just before the next highway underpass because the street on the other side is in better condition ~ follow the Krems another 2.5 kilometers and cross the river again as you pass Theiß ~ follow a long S-curve along a path which is better, but still has plenty of potholes ~ return to the Danube towpath after 700 meters and three bridges over flood-plain streams.

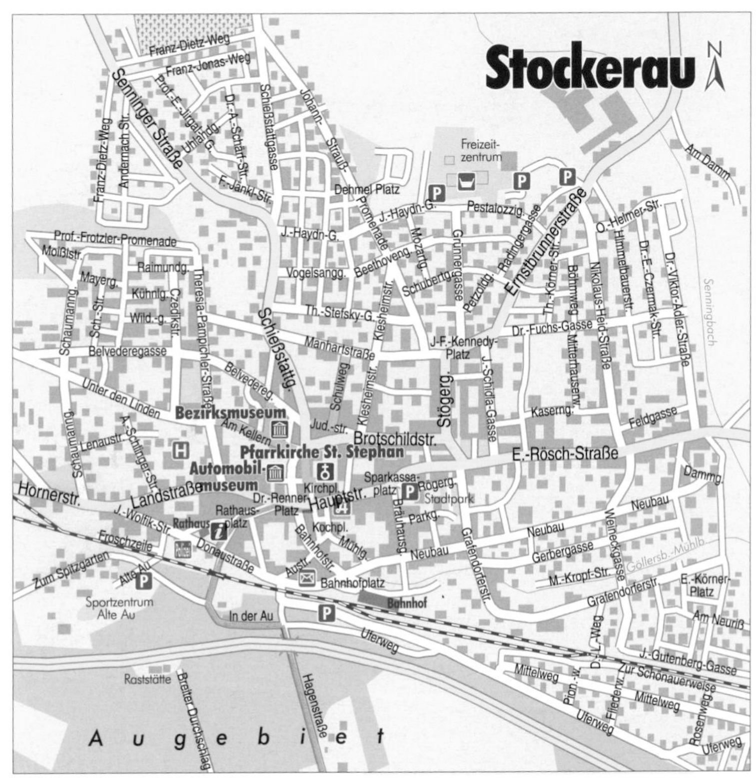

The towpath offers a smooth asphalt surface for fast and easy kilometers to the Altenwörth power station.

Tip: Bicycle tourists in search of nourishment in pleasant surroundings might consider a short detour to Theiß.

Altenwörth

Postal code: 3474; Telephone area code: 02279

- **Tourism association**, Donaulände 39
- **Kamptal bicycle route.** The well-built bicycle trail into the picturesque and culturally interesting Kamptal connects to Altenwörth. Details about the route can be found in *bikeline's* **"Radwandern in Kamptal," the Kamptal region cycling map, and the Waldviertel bicycle atlas** (available in German).

Tip: There is no bicycle route along the northern bank between Altenwörth and Tulln. The southern bank route is described on pages 126 to 130, maps 61 and 62.

The bicycle route crosses the power station dam. Enter through the door next to the main gate. It is unlocked during the day.

Tip: At other times use the speaker phone to ask the attendant to open the gate.

Tulln to Vienna on the northern bank — *38.5 km*

Return to the northern bank on the bridge at Tulln and turn right. Ride through a vacation colony and return to the riverbank ~ proceed down the smoothly-paved towpath ~ to the power station at Greifenstein ~ turn away from the shoreline before reaching the dam ~ and turn right on the wide service road.

Tip: Turn left on the service road if you wish to visit Stockerau. Ride over the Krumpenwasser stream and after 500 meters turn left on a forest path.

48
Hinter dem Kamp
Scheiben
Mehrsiedel
Holzgasse
Lämmerweide
St. Johann
Untere Kammerwiesen
Kamp
Marktfuhrhaufen
Totenlacke
Sandlau
Spitalau
Gigging
Obere Kammerwiesen
Traismauerin Kamp
Großes Neureut
Krieau
Altenwörth
Große Au
47
Krems
Dammboden
Stiftskalblsaum
Kalbsaumlacke
1985
Donau
Kalblsaum
Blankhaufen
Anschütt
Donaukraftwerk Altenwörth
Donau
Obere Placken
Mitterhaufen
Traisen
Gassnerhaus
Mitterau
Hosenhaufen
Roßauerl
Traisen
continue on page 126 map 61
Schweizergrund
Hanslhaufen
Jagdhaus Großer Grund
Sitzenberger Au
Gemeindeau
61
St. Georgen
Schweizerhof
Großer Grund
Saurierpark
Mitterteile
Binteile
Rittersfeld
Romau
Untere Krautau
Auwiesen
Heidengründe
Obere Krautau
Donaufeld
Frauendorf
Traismauer
Stollhofen
Preuwitz
Seefeld
Mitterndorf
B 43
Hilpersdorf
Maria Ponsee
Venusberg

49
50
48
Perzendorf
Neumühle
Zaina
Trübensee
Das Ganze Land
Neuschüttl
Grubau
Forsthaus
Binderau
Binderau
Gemeindeau
Gemeindeau
Obere Kohlstätt
Rustenschacher
Donau
Donau
Egon-Schiele-Museum
Minoriten-
kirche
St. Stephan
Bahnhof
Tulln-Stadt
Bahnhof
Tulln
Tulln
Rafelswörth
Oberaigen
Langenlebarn
Unteraigen
Bahnhof
Langenlebarn
Wipfing
Weinhartshof
Muckendorf
Zeiselmauer
Bahnhof
Zeiselmauer-Königstetten
Wolfpassing

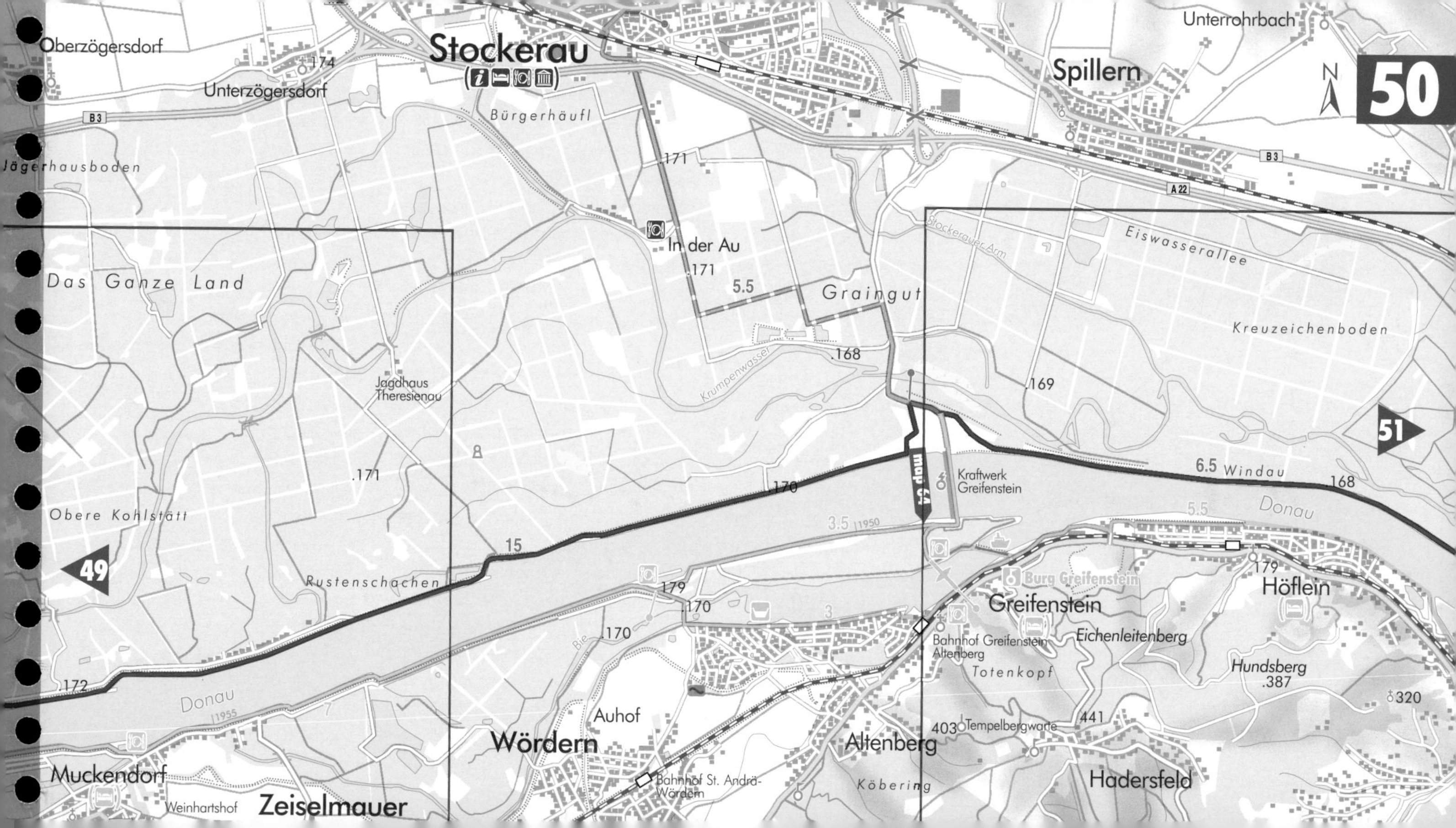
50
51
49
Stockerau
Oberzögersdorf
Unterzögersdorf
174
B3
Bürgerhäufl
Spillern
Unterrohrbach
A 22
Jägerhausboden
171
In der Au
171
5.5
Graingut
Stockerauer Arm
Eiswasserallee
Kreuzeichenboden
Das Ganze Land
Krumpenwasser
168
169
Jagdhaus Theresienau
171
170
map 64
Kraftwerk Greifenstein
6.5
Windau
168
Donau
5.5
3.5
1950
Obere Kohlstätt
15
Rustenschachen
179
170
3
Burg Greifenstein
Greifenstein
179
Höflein
170
Bahnhof Greifenstein Altenberg
Eichenleitenberg
Totenkopf
Hundsberg
387
320
172
Donau
1955
Auhof
403
Tempelbergwarte
441
Wördern
Altenberg
Hadersfeld
Muckendorf
Bahnhof St. Andrä-Wördern
Köbering
Weinhartshof
Zeiselmauer

Burg Kreuzenstein

Follow the signs through the environmentally-protected flood plain ("Au") and reach Stockerau in 4 kilometers.

Stockerau L

Postal code: 2000; Telephone area code: 02266

Town office, Rathaus, ✆ 695.

District museum, Belvederschlössl, ✆ 65188. Open: Sat 15-17, Sun/Hol 9-11. City and local history, plus exhibits on the poet Nikolaus Lenau, who lived in Stockerau 1818-22.

Automobile museum, Jubiläumshalle, ✆ 64564. Open: Sat 15-18, Sun/Hol 10-12 and 14-17.

Rathaus, Rathausplatz. The former Puchheim palace is a stately 17th century baroque construction drafted by Fischer von Erlach d. J.

St. Stephan parish church, Kirchenplatz. The 88 meter tower is the tallest steeple in Lower Austria, built 1725. The early-classical church has a cross-shaped main nave.

Stockerau nature preserve, between Krumpenwasser and the Autobahn. Since construction of the Greifenstein power station, the flood plains can hold water only times of high-water. The various dry and damp flood-plain areas support at least 27 swamp and water plants that are on the red list of endangered plants.

On the northern bank, at the power station gate after the fork to Stockerau.

Tip: The Greifenstein power station may be crossed to reach the southern bank. See page 132. The gate to the dam is open until dark. On the southern bank, take the first left to reach the ferry, which operates between 9 and 21 o'clock and docks near the center of Greifenstein. The terrace restaurant is a pleasant place to wait for the ferry, or cross the old arm of the Danube on the new bridge and reach Greifenstein.

On the northern bank, ride past the power plant entrance and rejoin the towpath just after the road curves right ~ proceed straight ahead towards Korneuburg ~ the Danube slowly turns southward ~ across from a beach on the right bank, the bicycle route turns left into a woods ~ after crossing two small tributaries turn right ~ and then left and over another narrow bridge ~ turn right before the street passes under the Autobahn and cross a pair of tracks ~ or proceed straight under the Autobahn and then under the railroad if you wish to visit Korneuburg ~ and follow bicycle trails along the main road.

Korneuburg ≈km **1943 L**

Postal code: 2100; Telephone area code: 02262

Tourist information, ✆ 770700

Ship landing, Donaulände/corner of Kanalstraße. Passenger ship cruises between Vienna and Dürnstein, May-Oct every Sunday, board in Korneuburg at 9:30. Information in tourism office.

Ferry, Korneuburg-Klosterneuburg, ✆ 0663/011135. March-3 Nov, Mon-Fri after 6:30, Sat/Sun/Hol from 8 until sunset.

Culture center, Dr. Max Burckhard Ring 11, ✆ 72553. Open: Sat 14-17, every first Sunday of the month, 9-12. Building opened in 1908. Contains exhibits from prehistoric to contemporary cultures.

Rathaus, Hauptpl. The neo-gothic building was built 1894-96 and seamlessly incorporates the medieval city tower. Noteworthy: the magnificent ceiling, restored wooden staircases and hearing rooms.

Augustine church. A former monastery church built 1745-48 with grand rococo altar and a painted faux architecture with a depiction of Christ's last meal, by F. A. Maulpertsch (1770).

Kreuzenstein castle, 5 km northwest. Originally destroyed by the Swedish armies, it was

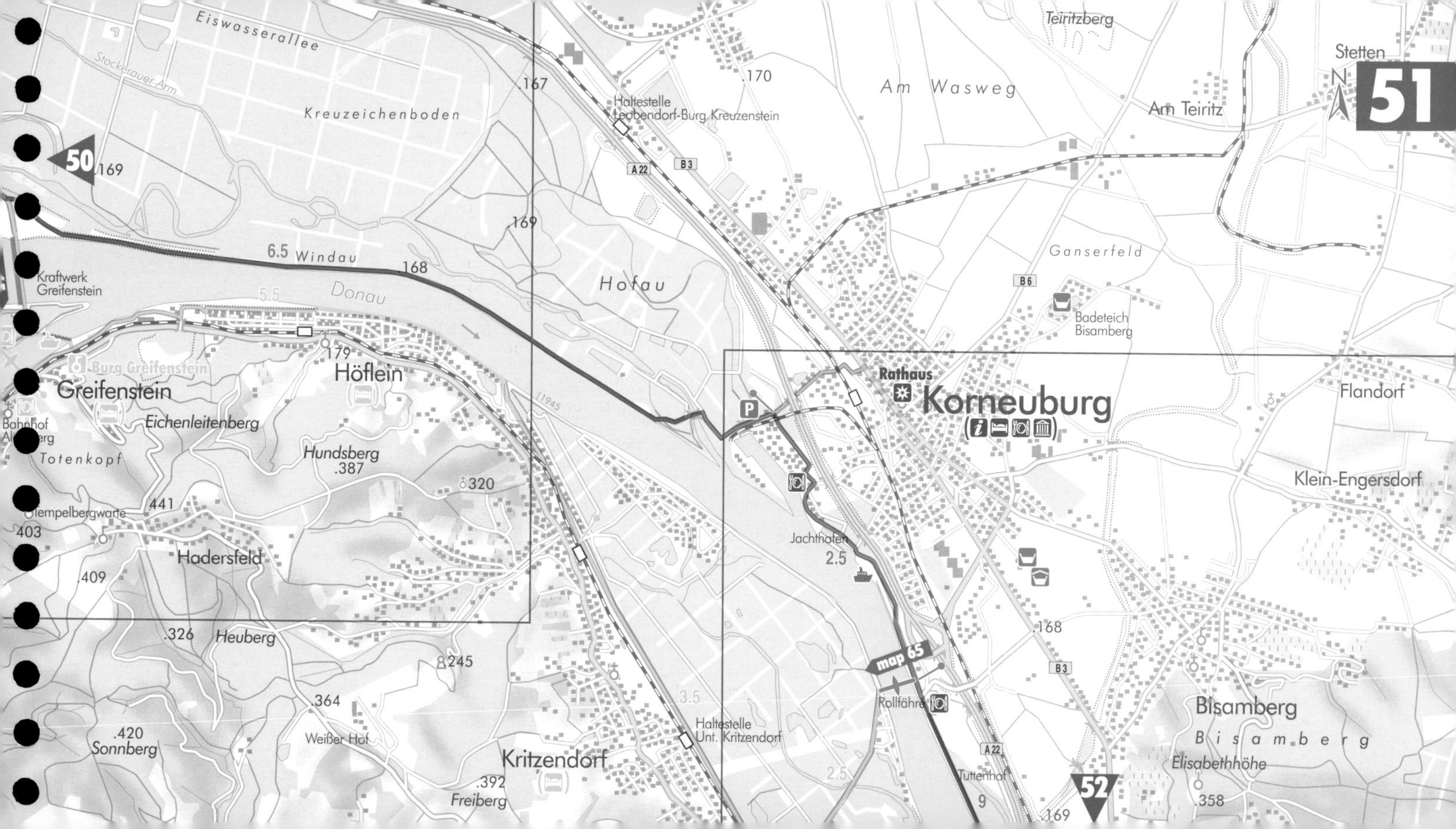

51
50
52
map 65
Eiswasserallee
Stockerauer Arm
Kreuzeichenboden
.169
.167
.170
Haltestelle
Leobendorf-Burg Kreuzenstein
A 22
B 3
Teiritzberg
Am Wasweg
Stetten
Am Teiritz
.169
6.5 Windau
.168
Kraftwerk
Greifenstein
5.5
Donau
Hofau
Ganserfeld
B 6
Badeteich
Bisamberg
179
Burg Greifenstein
Höflein
Greifenstein
Bahnhof
Totenkopf
Eichenleitenberg
Hundsberg
.387
320
441
Tempelbergwarte
403
Hadersfeld
.409
1945
Rathaus
Korneuburg
Flandorf
Klein-Engersdorf
Jachthafen
2.5
.168
B 3
.326
Heuberg
245
.364
.420
Sonnberg
Weißer Hof
Kritzendorf
.392
Freiberg
3.5
Haltestelle
Unt. Kritzendorf
2.5
Rollfähre
A 22
Tuttenhof
9
.169
Bisamberg
Bisamberg
Elisabethhöhe
.358

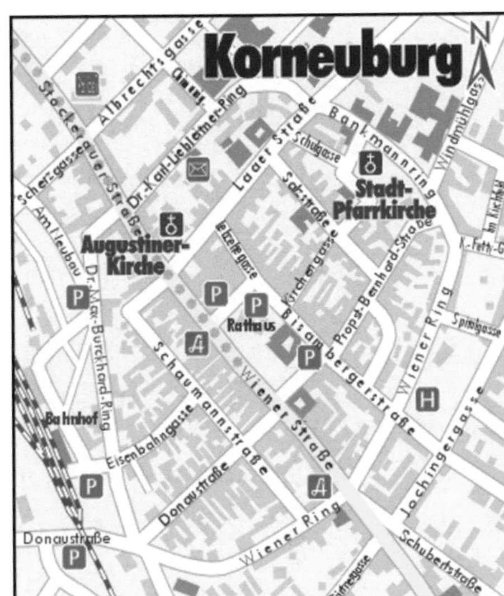

rebuilt as a typical 15th century castle by Graf Wilczek in 1879, using original parts and components collected from throughout Europe.

Rat catcher's well. A beautiful well built in 1898 by the Viennese sculptor Emanuel Pendl. Depicts a rat catcher who is part of the folklore of the city of Korneuburg.

Bicycle rental, Hauptbahnhof, ☎ 72467

The wide path continues towards Vienna parallel with the Autobahn before veering off to the right ~ and left around a quaint old wharf-settlement.

Tip: After 1.5 kilometers through the industrial area the route reaches the ferry to Klosterneuburg (Open: March-Nov, Mon-Fri 6:30 to sunset, Sat/Sun/Hol 8 to sunset), another opportunity to cross to the other side of the river. The southern route then follows a wide asphalt road 2.5 kilometers through the woods to the train station Klosterneuburg-Kierling (see page 134).

On the left bank, continue down the shoreline of the Danube ~ ride onto the towpath 500 meters past the Korneuburg ferry, at the Tuttendörfl inn ~ pass the river locks at which the Neue Donau (New Danube) begins ~ for the following 9 kilometers to the Reichsbrücke in Vienna, we recommend following the various paths down the Donauinsel (island).

The Reichsbrücke is just after the Donauturm (tower), where the United Nations city is also taking shape ~ at the Reichsbrücke you can either board the U-Bahn (subway) or take the bicycle path over the bridge into the center of Vienna.

Tip: The "**Radatlas Wien**" **bicycle guide from *bikeline*** is an excellent guide for getting around the city of Vienna by bike, with maps in a scale of 1:15,000 (available in German). The Danube bicycle route does not end in Vienna, but continues to Bratislava, the capital of the Republic of Slovakia, and

Budapest, Hungary. This stretch is covered in the ***bikeline* volume "Donau Radweg, Teil 3: Wien-Budapest"** (available in German).

Follow the bicycle path along **Lassallestraße** to the **Praterstern**, where one can consider a visit to the world-famous Prater park and its giant Ferris-wheel ~ proceed down Praterstraße to the **Urania** ~ where you connect with the bicycle beltway ("Ring-Rund-Radweg") ~ the Ring is a bicycle route that encircles the old city and connects some of the most important sights in Vienna.

Rathaus
Korneuburg
A 22
2.5
51
B 3
.168
Klein-Engersdorf
Rollfähre
map 66
Tuttenhof
.169
Bisamberg
B i s a m b e r g
Elisabethhöhe
.358
.336
Veitsberg
Falkenberg
3.5
1940
Magdalenenhof
308
Langenzersdorf
Lahnerberg
Stift Klosterneuburg
B 14
.167
B 3
Klosterneuburg
9
Strebersdorf
Neue Donau
A 22
Industriezentrum
Haltestelle Strebersdorf
Donau
Josefinnenhütte
Leopoldsberg
425
Sulzwiese
Kahlenberg
484
Schwarzlackenau
Josefsdorf
Kahlenbergerdorf
1935
.295
Burgstall
Jedlesee
Krapfenwald
VIENNA
N u ß b e r g
.377
Cobenzl
Nußdorf
city map
N
Sievering
Heiligenstadt
Grinzing
52

Melk to Vienna along the right bank 121 km

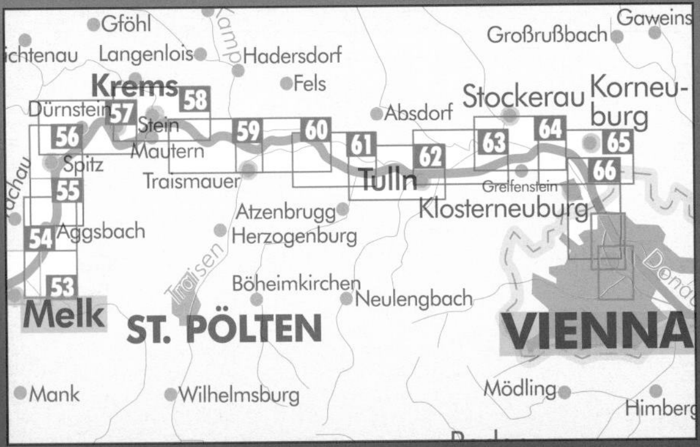

Turning downstream from the Benedictine Abbey at Melk, the Danube bicycle route enters Austria's best-know wine producing region, the Wachau. The river valley is especially beautiful in the spring, when the apricot orchards blossom. The route passes under the ruins of the castle at Aggstein and past the valley's little jewels: Spitz, Weißenkirchen and Dürnstein. The Wachau region ends just before the old city of Krems, where the Danube enters the expansive flatlands of the Tulln plain. The river narrows again once more upstream from Vienna, where it passes the "Wiener Pforte" (gate) at the feet of the Viennese woods before flowing past Klosterneuburg and into Austria's capital city, Vienna.

The route down the southern, or right, bank mostly follows bicycle trails and quiet country lanes and side streets. The only stretch on more heavily trafficked roads, without bicycle lanes, is between Melk and Arnsdorf. The only steep climbs are on the side-trips to the ruins at Aggstein and to the Göttweig monastery.

Schönbühel castle

Melk to Krems **35 km**

Take **Wachauer Straße out of** Melk and underneath the Danube river bridge towards Schönbühel ~ after about 2.5 kilometers on a bicycle lane come to Schönbühel and the palace of the same name ~ cross the road at the Schönhühel Amtshaus ~ and continue on the right side of the B 33 uphill towards Aggsbach-Dorf.

Schönbühel **≈km 2032 R**

Postal code: 3392;
Telephone area code: 02752

Town office, ✆ 8619

St. Rosalia parish church, Servite monastery. A simple, single-nave construction built with the monastery 1666-74. The Peregrin chapel on the side was added in 1737, and contains a dome with a fresco by Johann Bergl (1767).

Schönbühel castle. The complex dates back to the 12th century. The rectangular buildings visible today were built 1819-21. Private property, closed to the public.

About 100 meters after the Schönbühel cemetery the bicycle route uses the forest path on the right side ~ cross a road as the route passes the driveway to the island ~ then take the towpath to the former ship landing at Aggsbach-Dorf.

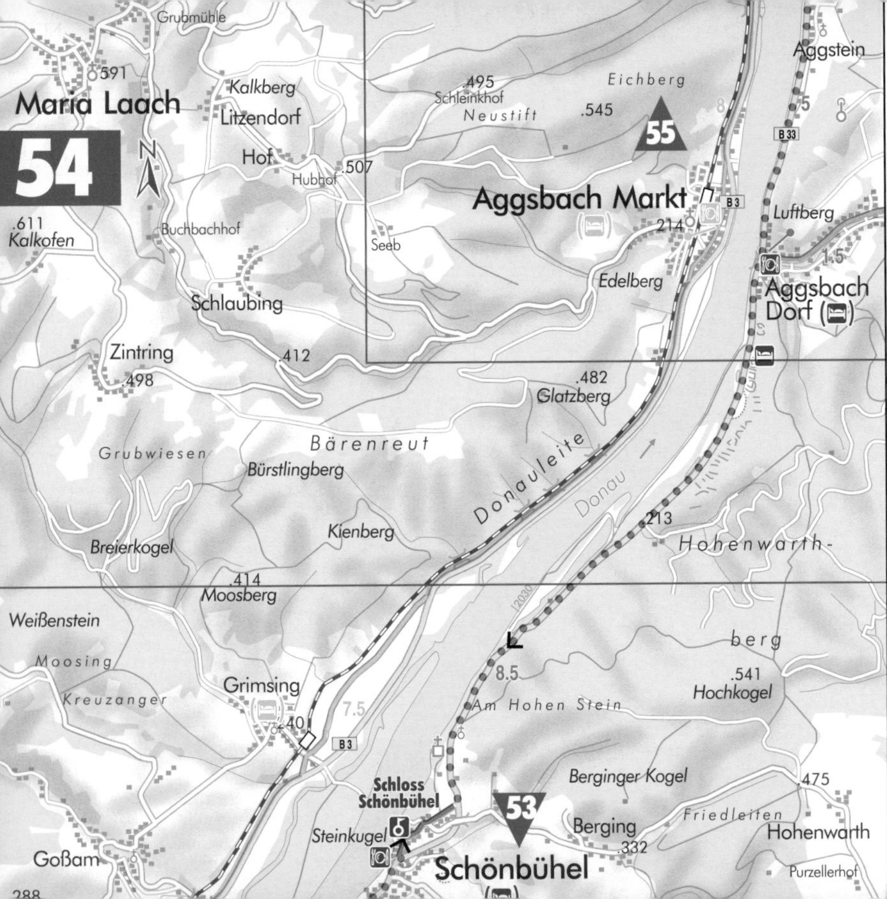

Tip: The Aggsbach Cartusian monastery is a 1.5 kilometer detour up the Wolfensteinbach (creek). 500 meters past the ship landing turn right and ride up the little valley to the next larger fork in the road. Turn right to reach the monastery. There is a public outdoor pool 50 meters to the left of the fork.

Aggsbach-Dorf ≈km **2027 R**

Postal code: 3642; Telephone area code: 02753

Town office, ✆ 8269 or ✆ 8006

Former Cartusian monastery, 2 km east. Established in 1380 by Heidenreich von Maissau of Austria, with 12 Cartusian monks. Joseph II closed the monastery in 1782 following its decline during the Reformation. The parish and its monastery and production facilities date from the 16th and 17th centuries.

Cartusian Maria Himmelfahrt church. The narrow single-nave church was consecrated in 1392. Noteworthy the figured keystone, the baroque pulpit with the four evangelists and the altar paintings (17the century).

A short distance downstream from **Aggsbach-Dorf**, the bicycle route enters **Aggstein**, where the famous castle dominates views of the river from afar.

Tip: The steep forest path to the castle includes grades of up to 20 percent, where even the strongest cyclists dismount and push. The 2 kilometer detour is nevertheless strongly recommended for all who love old castles and spectacular views. The view from the 300 meter plateau extends deep into the Wachau and as far as the Alps. (Open: April-Oct,

Mon-Sun 8-18, with a pleasant castle restaurant.)

Aggstein castle was established in the 13th century. Devastated by the Turks, it was rebuilt in 1606 by Anna von Polheim. One 15th century owner, Scheck von Wald, added a gruesome chapter to the castle's legacy: It is said he hung a heavy cable across the river, extorted extreme tolls from ships and forced his captives to leap from the high rocks. Today four courtyards, a main parapet, the dungeon with an 8-meters deep starvation pit, the kitchen and the old chapel are still intact.

Continue down the river from Aggstein ⁓ turn left to the riverside path after 3.5 kilometers, at the St. Johann church ⁓ the Hinterhaus ruin can be seen on the left side of the river.

Arnsdorf ≈km 2018 R

Ride past **Oberarnsdorf** and to the **ferry to Spitz** (Open: April-Sept, as needed between 6-21, Sat/Sun 7-21) ⁓ the towpath leads past orchards with countless apricot trees and offers a glorious view across the river to Spitz and the vineyards rising up the opposite slopes ⁓ the next town is **Mitterarnsdorf**, a charming wine village.

Tip: Wine growers offering samples can be recognized on the "ausg'steckten" bushes next to the road.

The tour continues downstream towards Rossatz ⁓ after 3.5 kilometers reach **St. Lorenz**, where a **ferry runs across the river to Weißenkirchen** (Open: Mon-Sun 9-12 and 13:30-18:30, Sat/Sun/Hol 9-18:30) ⁓ proceed down the right bank through quiet

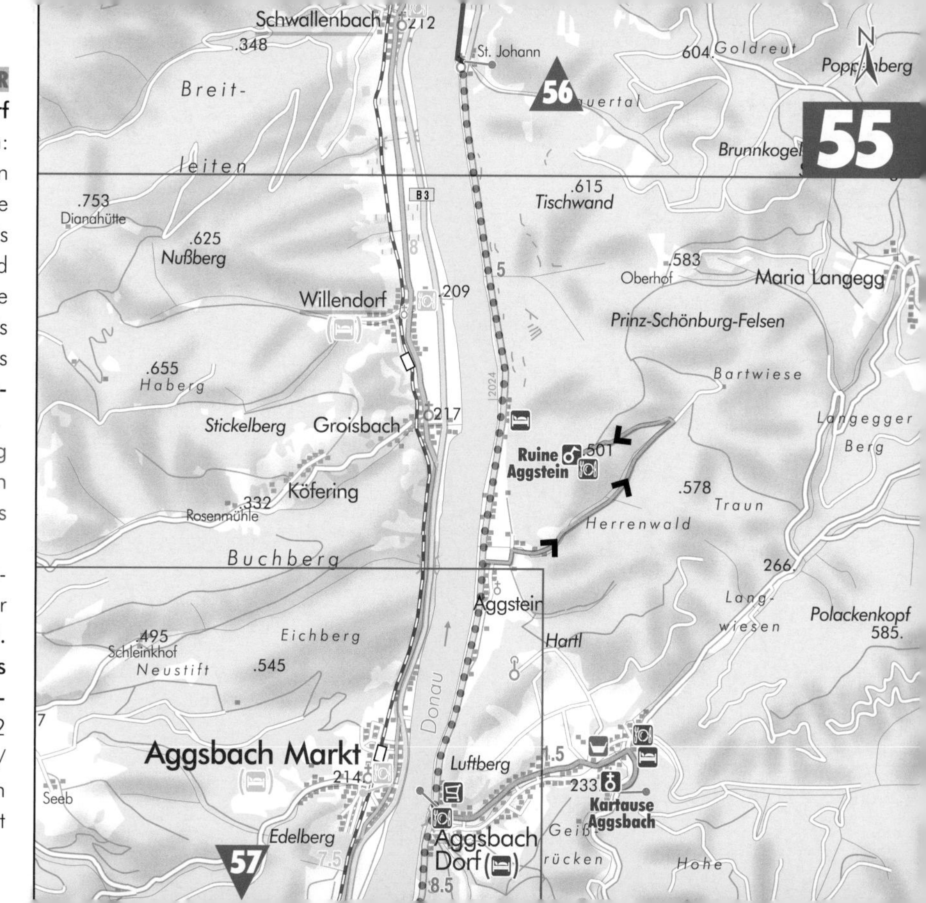

farm lanes and paved side streets ~ in Rührsdorf take **Dorfstraße** through the village ~ and stay left at the next fork in the road and then through an S-curve and then around to the right to reach **Rossatz.**

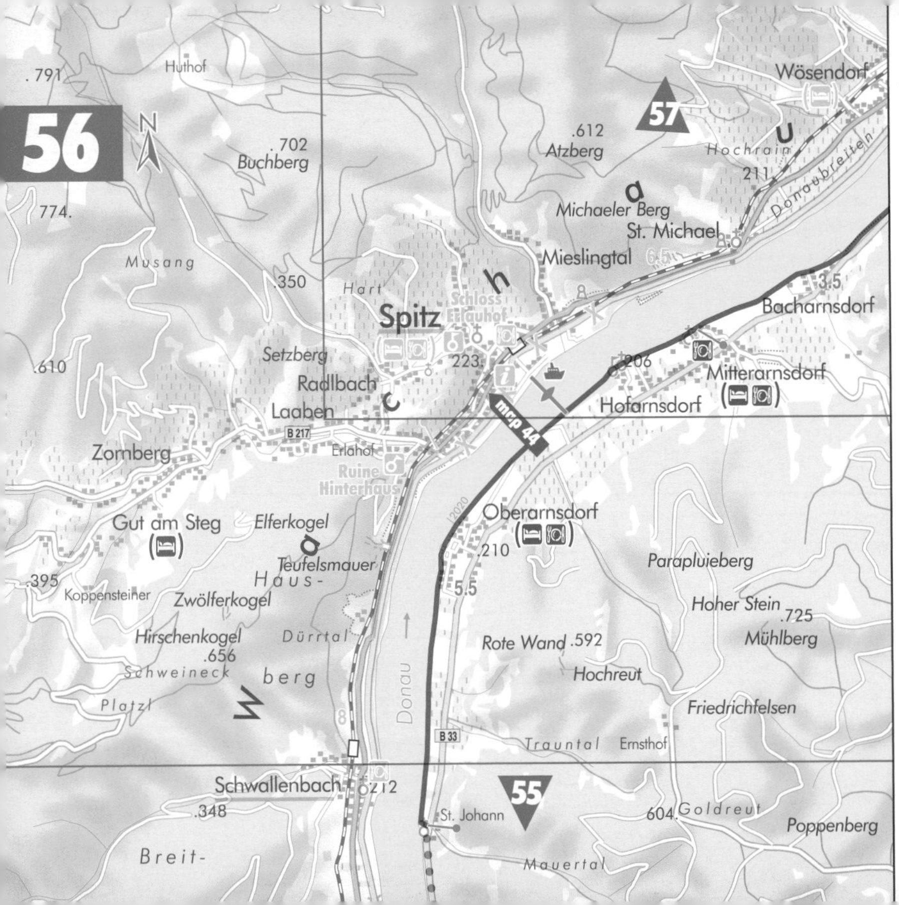

Ruine Aggstein

Rossatz ≈km **2010 R**

Postal code: 3602; Telephone area code: 02714

⛴ **Donauschifffahrt Wachau**, Rossatzbach 40, ✆ 6355. Open: 13 April-27 Oct charter trips between Melk and Krems.

⛴ **Ferry**: 2-17 April, Sat/Sun/Hol 10-18, 18-29 April, Mon-Sun 10-18, 30 April-25 Sept, 9-20, 26 Sept-16 Oct, 10-18, 17 Oct-30 Oct, Sat/Sun/Hol 10-18.

The route passes to the left of Rossatz and reaches the river at the campground, where the **bicycle ferry to Dürnstein** docks ~ on the other side of the Danube, the ruins of Dürnstein castle tower over what is probably the most famous location in the Wachau ~ pass the ferry and ride down the narrow lane past the Römerhof and after 300 meters follow the signs on the pavement to the right to the

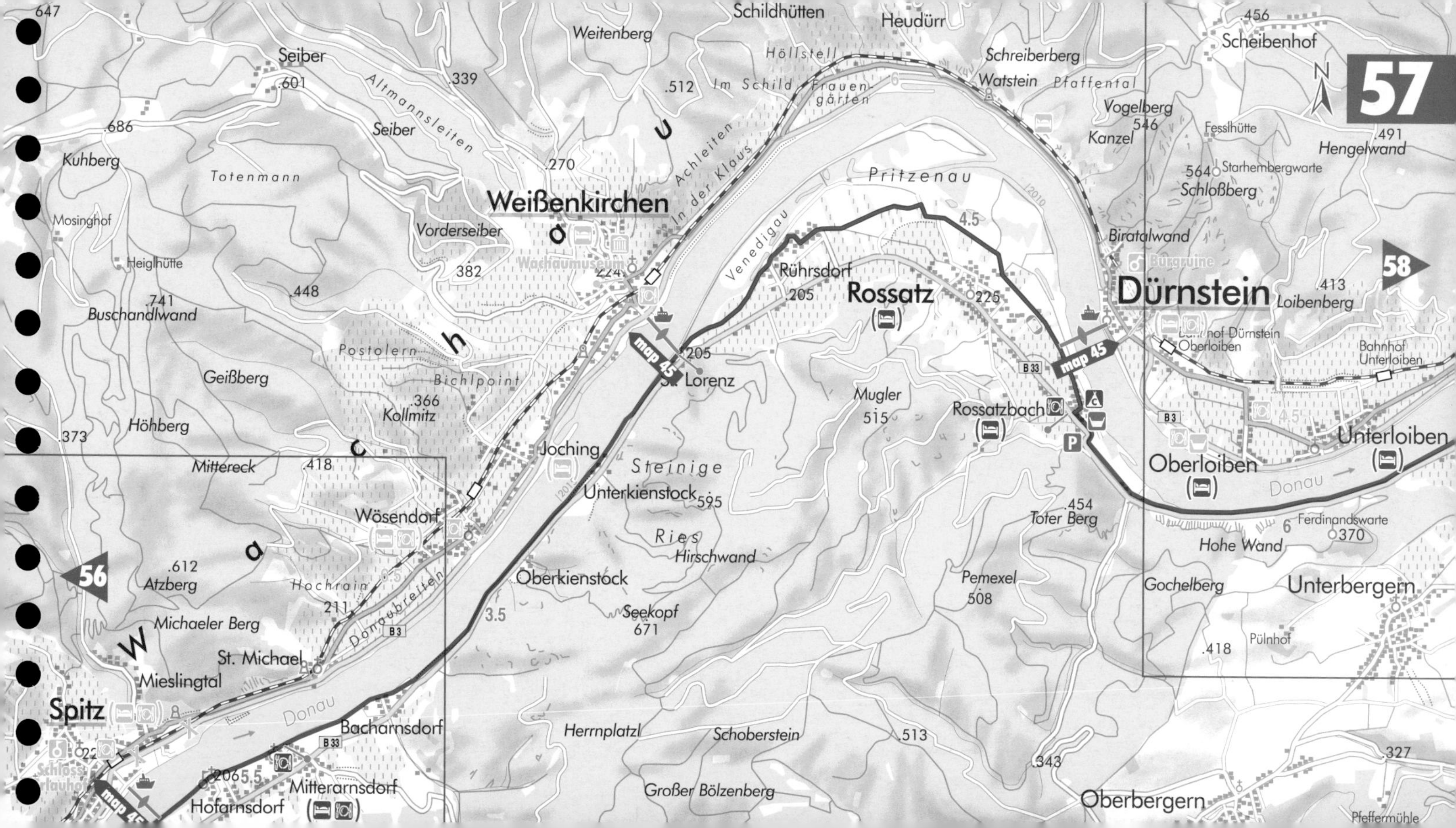
57
56
58
Weißenkirchen
Dürnstein
Rossatz
Spitz
Wachau
Donau
Schildhütten
Heudürr
Scheibenhof
Weitenberg
Seiber
Höllstell
Schreiberberg
Watstein
Pfaffental
Altmannsleiten
Im Schild
Frauengärten
Vogelberg
Kanzel
Fesslhütte
Hengelwand
Kuhberg
Totenmann
Achleiten
In der Klaus
Pritzenau
Starhembergwarte
Schloßberg
Mosinghof
Vorderseiber
Venedigau
Biratalwand
Heiglhütte
Wachaumuseum
Rührsdorf
Burgruine
Loibenberg
Buschandlwand
Postolern
St. Lorenz
Bahnhof Dürnstein
Oberloiben
Bahnhof Unterloiben
Geißberg
Bichlpoint
Mugler
Kollmitz
Rossatzbach
Höhberg
Joching
Unterloiben
Mittereck
Steinige
Unterkienstock
Oberloiben
Wösendorf
Toter Berg
Ferdinandswarte
Ries
Hirschwand
Hohe Wand
Atzberg
Hochrain
Oberkienstock
Pemexel
Gochelberg
Unterbergern
Michaeler Berg
Donaubreiten
Seekopf
St. Michael
Pülnhof
Mieslingtal
Bacharnsdorf
Herrnplatzl
Schoberstein
Schloss Spitz
Mitterarnsdorf
Großer Bölzenberg
Hofarnsdorf
Oberbergern
Pfeffermühle
map 45
B 3
B 33

Rossatz-Arnsdorf

main road ~ turn left towards Mautern ~ and proceed on the bicycle path next to the main road for 3.5 kilometers to Hundsheim, where the bicycle route takes the first possible right turn in the village.

Ride through **Hundsheim** and take the farm lane through the vineyards ~ soon the route again approaches the main road ~ ride across the parking lot at the Römerhalle to reach the Danube river bridge.

Tip: Cross the Danube now if you wish to visit Krems. If you want to continue directly towards Tulln, stay on the right bank and head downstream. This is also the junction where the side-trip to the imposing Göttweig monastery begins. Turn right at the bridge and ride into the center of Mautern.

Mautern **≈km 2003.5 R**

Postal code: 3512;

Telephone area code: 02732

Town office, Rathauspl. 1, ✆ 83151

Roman museum, Schlossg. 12, ✆ 81155. Open: April-Oct, Weds-Sun 10-12, Fri, Sat 16-18, city tours available if requested in advance. Especially noteworthy are Roman wall paintings discovered in the region, plus a large number of prehistoric artifacts and Romanesque and Gothic frescos.

St. Stephan parish church. The Gothic church with polygonal choir dates to around 1400 and is especially noted for the stations of the cross paintings by Martin Johann Schmidt (1770).

Former **Margarethe chapel**, Frauenhofgasse. Documented mention as early as 1083. Built along a Roman city wall, a single-nave Romanesque structure with a square choir.

Town houses, St. Pöltner Straße/Kremser Straße. The intact row of massive Renaissance houses with portals, rounded bay-windows and entrance halls was mostly built in the 16th century.

Schloss. The four-winged building includes 15th century Renaissance elements and once served as administrative offices of the Passau bishopric.

Janaburg. A 16th century building with a Renaissance fountain in the courtyard.

Ride past the Roman hall and the palace on Kremser Straße into the center ~ turn left on **St. Pöltener Straße past the** Rathausplatz and continue to Südtiroler Platz ~ turn left to the Hotel Wagner-Bacher and then turn right on **Grüne Weg** ~ pass the Raabkaserne and head out of town towards Mautern ~ after the railroad turn right at the embankment along the Fladnitz river ~ cross the river at the next bridge.

Tip: Now you must decide whether to turn left and return to the Danube and the southern bank route or make the side-trip to the Göttweig abbey, in which case you turn right and continue upstream along the Fladnitz.

To Göttweig abbey 10 km

Ride under the main road ~ and about one kilometer up the Fladnitz ~ turn left where the bridge crosses the Fladnitz ~ and turn right at the next intersection ~ you reach the village of **Palt** ~ turn right after the church and then left on the second path ~ a pleasant trail follows the course of the Fladnitz to Furth near Göttweig.

The route leaves the river at the church and goes off to the left ~ and begins to go uphill after the railroad underpass ~ turn right after about one kilometer and up the steeper wooded road to the top of the hill

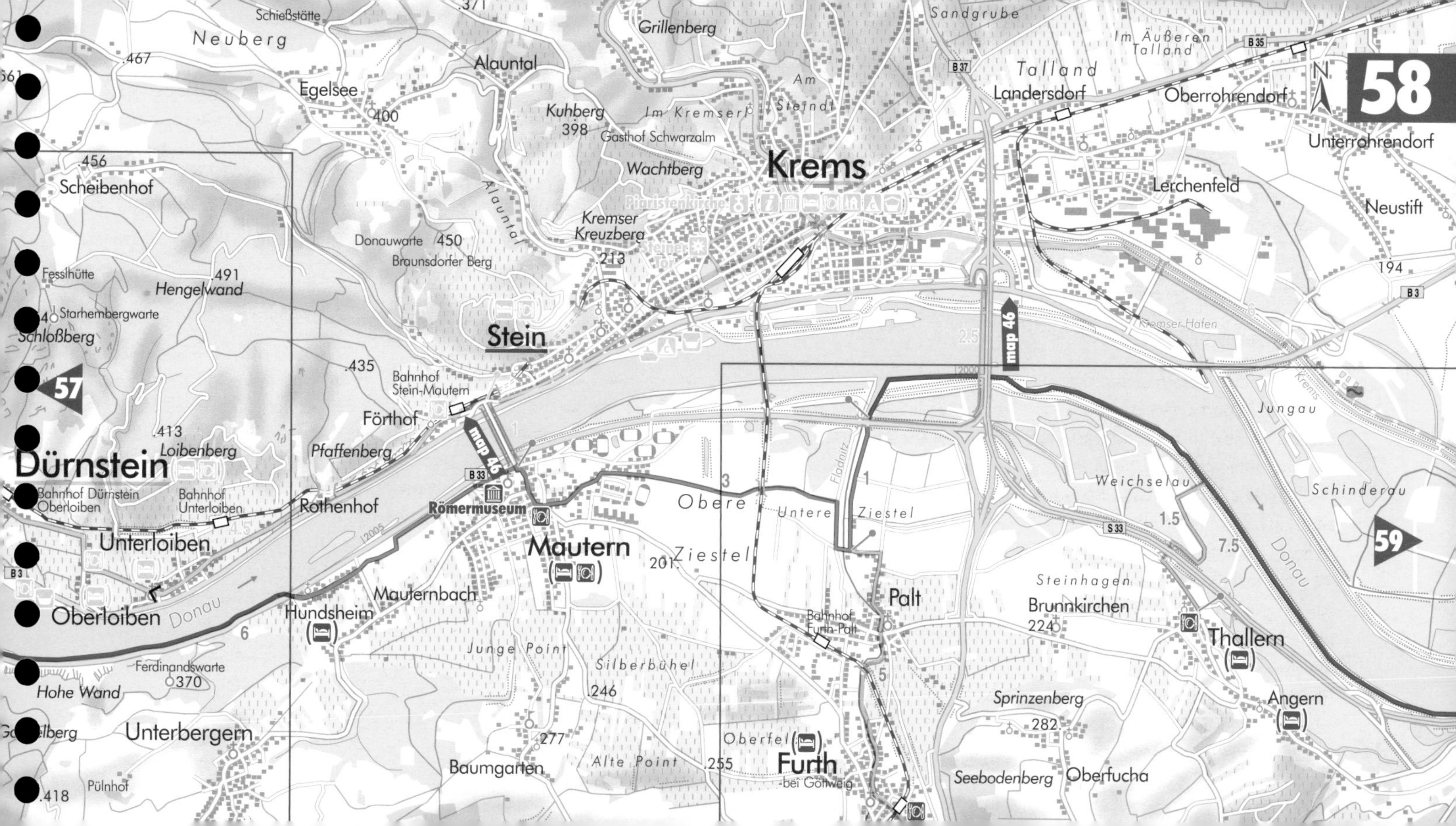
58
Krems
Stein
Dürnstein
Mautern
Furth
-bei Göttweig
Neuberg
Schießstätte
Alauntal
Egelsee
Grillenberg
Kuhberg
398
Gasthof Schwarzalm
Wachtberg
Im Kremserl
Am Steindl
Sandgrube
Im Äußeren Talland
Talland
Landersdorf
Oberrohrendorf
Unterrohrendorf
Lerchenfeld
Neustift
194
Scheibenhof
.456
.467
Donauwarte 450
Braunsdorfer Berg
Kremser Kreuzberg
.213
Piaristenkirche
Steiner Tor
Fesslhütte
.491
Hengelwand
Starhembergwarte
Schloßberg
57
.435
Bahnhof Stein-Mautern
Förthof
Pfaffenberg
.413
Loibenberg
Bahnhof Dürnstein Oberloiben
Bahnhof Unterloiben
Rothenhof
Römermuseum
Unterloiben
Oberloiben
Donau
Hundsheim
Mauternbach
Ziestel
201.
Obere
Untere Ziestel
Palt
Bahnhof Furth-Palt
Weichselau
Schinderau
Jungau
Kremser Hafen
Krems
59
Steinhagen
Brunnkirchen
224
Thallern
Angern
Sprinzenberg
.282.
Seebodenberg
Oberfucha
Oberfel
Junge Point
Silberbühel
.246
Alte Point
.255
.277
Baumgarten
Ferdinandswarte
370
Hohe Wand
Unterbergern
Pülnhof
.418
map 46
B 33
B 37
B 35
B 3
S 33
Fladnitz

Göttweig Benedictine abbey

and the abbey ~ the terraces offer excellent views into the Danube river valley, and a café where the bicycle tourist can rest and recover from the climb up the hill.

Furth bei Göttweig **R**

Postal code: 3511; Telephone area code: 02732

- **Information, town office**, Untere Landstr. 17, ✆ 84622
- **Göttweig Benedictine abbey**, ✆ 85581-231. Open: 21 March-15 Nov, restaurant open daily, guided tours Mon-Sun at 11 and 15. The magnificent abbey complex was built (in part) according to plans drafted by Hildebrandt in Göttweig's early 18th century baroque heyday. Especially noteworthy: the design of the western gate, the Kaiser steps, the library (furnished in 1770), the Altmannsaal and the art collection with medieval valuables.
- **Maria Himmelfahrt abbey church**. Hildebrandt's plans included a large domed church, though changes were made during construction 1750-65. The church with its 2-tower front forms the center of the abbey. Exquisite interior decoration. The crypt includes a stone sculpture of St. Altmann, an important work from about 1540.
- **Weingut Unger (vineyard)**, Kircheng. 14, ✆ 85895. Open: Mon, Wed, Thur, Fri 8:30-12 and 13-18, Sat 9-12:30. Serves and sells wine. Wine cellar tours with tasting in the abbey cellars by appointment.

Roll down from Göttweig and follow the Fladnitz back to the Danube river route.

Ride along the Fladnitz towards the Danube ~ pass under the Bundesstraße.

Tip: To cross the river to Krems, turn right after passing under the Bundesstraße and take the bicycle lane across the bridge (see page 106).

Krems to Altenwörth power station *25.5 km*

The Danube river bicycle route hugs the river shoreline downriver from the Fladnitz ~ ride under the Danube river bridge and around the harbor, where an odd sign warns of mooring lines from ships ~ after one kilometer, at the house, ride up to the embankment crown for a better view of the scenery.

After 4 kilometers ride past the **Bertholdstein ruins** to a bicycle rest area with fast-food stand and the opportunity to branch off to **Hollenburg**. The town is behind the Autobahn at the foot of the highest elevation in the region, the Schiffbergs.

Hollenburg **≈km 1994 R**

Postal code: 3506; Telephone area code: 02739

- **Parish church**. 3-nave pillar basilica with characteristic west tower and a noted Gothic Madonna from around 1420.

After **Hollenburg** the path downriver enters an increasingly flat and open landscape.

Tip: After 6 kilometers the route passes an inn where the tourist faces another choice: Either continue down the river or take the Schubert bike trail through the Tulln plain. This detour visits the places where Franz Schubert spent his summers. The posted tour is 14 kilometers longer than the Danube route and mostly follows quiet country lanes. The nearby town of Traismauer is worth a visit even if you do not continue down the Schubert tour.

59
58
60
Palt
Bahnhof Furth-Palt
Brunnkirchen
Steinhagen
Weichselau
Thallern
Angern
Glockenberg
Sprinzenberg
Seebodenberg
Oberfucha
Furth bei Göttweig
Aigen
Stift Göttweig
Grünberg
Tiefenfucha
Panholz
Goldbühel
Kleinwien
Predigtstuhl
Krustetten
Paudorf
Hungerfeld
Pammerhof
Höbenbach
Riedlermühle
Adalbertrast
Eichholz
Stauden
Runde Heide
In der Tränk
Ried
Neusiedl
Nußdorf
Parapluiberg
Franzhausen
Spatzenberg
Hollenburger Wald
Wagram
Schiffberg
Hollenburg
Kleedorf
Ruine Bertholdstein
Hopfengrund
Riedhaufenau
Schinderau
Jungau
Theiß
Theißer Au
Weidacker
Donaudorf
Herzogenburgerin
Neureut
KW Theiß
Tratwegerin
Obere Kammerwiesen
Hinter dem Kamp
Wurmsaumlacke
Wuemsaum
Steinplanen
Stiftskalblsaum
Donau
Fischerlacke
Mittersaum
Gassnerhaus
Würbelmühle
St. Georgen
Saurierpark
Rittersfeld
Romau
Fischerei
Traismauer
Venusberg
B 33
S 33
B 43

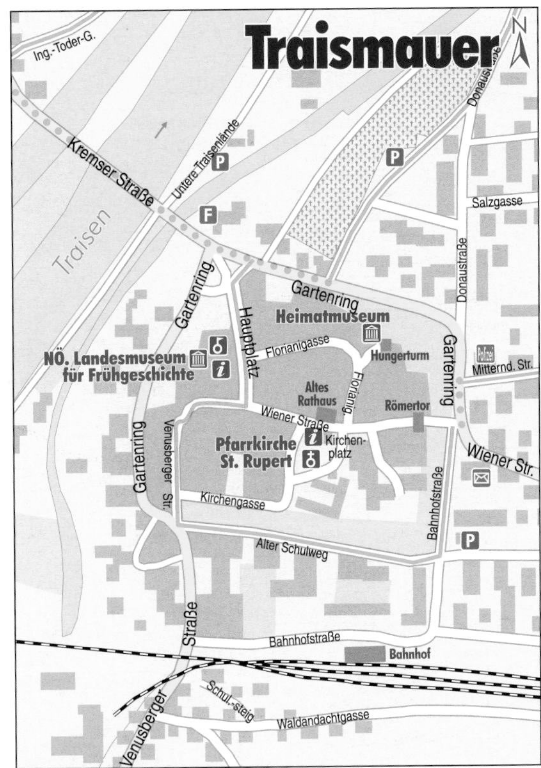

Traismauer

Postal code: 3133; Telephone area code: 02783

Information office, Schloss, ✆ 8555

Lower Austria State Museum for Prehistory, Hauptpl. 1, ✆ 8555. Open: April-Oct, Tues-Sun 9-17. Documents the first millennium AD with archaeological finds.

Saurierpark (dinosaur park), Traisen flood plain north of Traismauer, ✆ 20020. Open: 23 March-1 Nov, Mon-Sun 9-18. A 2.5-hectare wilderness populated with life-sized representations of the some of the best-known dinosaurs.

Palace, Hauptplatz. The original castle at the site is mentioned in the Nibelungenlied. Used as administrative offices by the Salzburg archbishops and rebuilt in the 16th century. "Kulturzyklus" (culture events) from April-Oct.

St. Rupert parish church, Kirchenplatz. Includes 13th century remnants of the original late-Romanesque church. The late-Gothic reconstruction included a period archwork. The interior decorations are from the 18th century.

The **Danube bicycle route** continues down the southern bank from the **inn near Traismauer** ~ after 7 kilometers it veers away from the river just before the locks at the **Altenwörth power station** ~ curve to left at the Traisen river and proceed to a bridge ~ turn right over the small river, or turn left to cross the dam and reach the northern bank of the Danube and the town of Altenwörth.

Altenwörth power station to Tulln 20.5 km

After crossing the Traisen make the sharp left turn ~ and follow the tributary to where it meets the Danube.

Two power generating stations now dominate the landscape as the route proceeds downstream: the thermal plant at Dürnrohr and the never-completed nuclear power plant at Zwentendorf. In the background the northern fringes of the Wienerwald can be seen.

After 1.5 kilometers the route turns to the right and onto an unpaved trail through a shady flood-plain woods ~ cross a narrow bridge ~ and take the paved trail to the left, past the power plant ~ the trail joins the power plant service road as far as a bridge ~ turn left onto the towpath ~ just before kilometer 1975 a road to the campground and the center of **Zwentendorf** branches off to the right. The main route continues straight down the Danube.

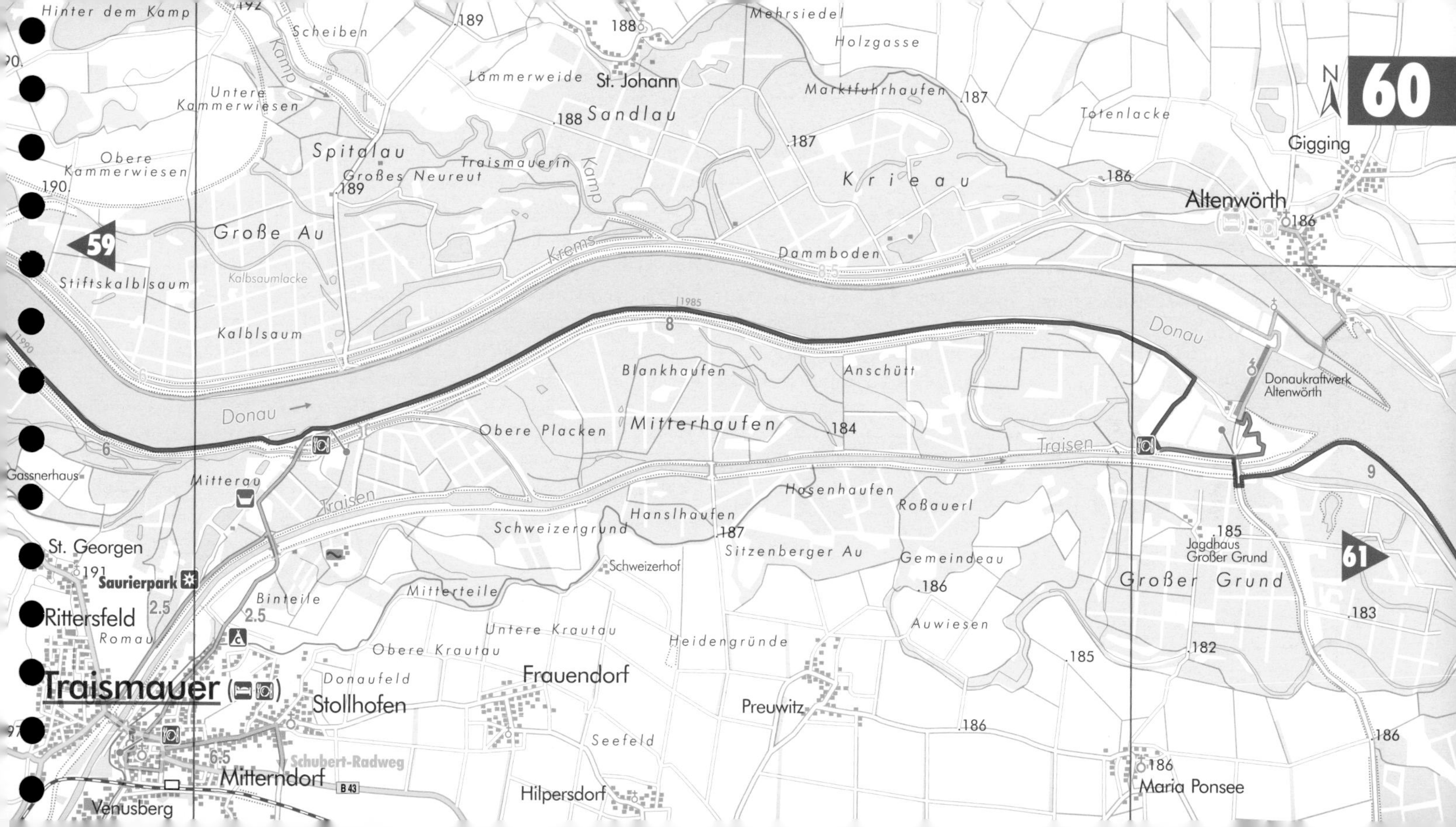

60
Hinter dem Kamp
Scheiben
.189
188
Mehrsiedel
Holzgasse
Kamp
Lämmerweide
St. Johann
Marktfuhrhaufen
.187
Untere
Kammerwiesen
.188
Sandlau
Totenlacke
.187
Gigging
Obere
Kammerwiesen
Spitalau
Traismauerin
Kamp
Großes Neureut
.189
Krieau
.186
190.
Altenwörth
186
59
Große Au
Krems
Dammboden
Kalbsaumlacke
Stiftskalblsaum
8.5
1985
Kalblsaum
8
Donau
1990
Blankhaufen
Anschütt
Donaukraftwerk
Altenwörth
6
Donau
Obere Placken
Mitterhaufen
.184
Traisen
6
Gassnerhaus
Mitterau
9
Traisen
Hasenhaufen
Roßauerl
Hanslhaufen
Schweizergrund
.187
.185
Jagdhaus
Großer Grund
St. Georgen
Sitzenberger Au
61
191
Schweizerhof
Gemeindeau
Saurierpark
Mitterteile
.186
Großer Grund
Binteile
2.5
2.5
Rittersfeld
.183
Romau
Untere Krautau
Auwiesen
Obere Krautau
Heidengründe
.182
.185
Traismauer
Donaufeld
Frauendorf
Stollhofen
Preuwitz
.186
186
Seefeld
6.5
Schubert-Radweg
186
Mitterndorf
B 43
Maria Ponsee
Hilpersdorf
Venusberg

Zwentendorf ≈km **1974 R**

Postal code: 3435; Telephone area code: 02277

Town office, ✆ 2209-0

Zwentendorf nuclear power plant. Austria's only nuclear power plant never went into operation. Closed as a result of a voter referendum forced by Austrian environmentalists in 1979.

"Schiffer" and "Schopper"

Navigation of the Danube began with "naufahren" – the art of guiding heavy, freight-loaded flat-bottom barges downriver on the Danube's current. Most of these ships never returned to their harbors of origin, and instead landed with the "plättenschinder" who chopped them into firewood. But first they had to survive the journey downstream with its many hazards. Many merchants even unloaded their cargoes and transported them overland past the dangerous narrows in the Greiner Struden.

A growing commerce in grains and wine from eastern regions created a demand for transports upriver, in which the barges where hauled against the current by teams of horses. The arduous trip from Vienna to Linz took more than 3 weeks; and another 8 days to reach Passau from Linz.

The craftsmen who built the vessels that plied the Danube were called "schopper." Every river develops its own kinds of vessels. The Danube's boat and barges originally consisted of various simple "plätten" and "mutzen." Then came the "gamsen" that were used especially on the Inn river to haul gravel before being sent downriver to the "plättenschinder" when they were too worn out for heavy loads. Around 1850 the Danube's most elegant type of ship was developed, the sleek "siebner."

Turn right at the concrete block where the unpaved trail ends after **Zwentendorf** ~ then left towards **Kleinschönbichl** ~ pass the village and the pleasure boat harbor ~ turn right before the Perschlingbach ~ take the first bridge over the stream and proceed along the bicycle trail that follows the road to **Pischelsdorf** ~ turn left under the large linden tree at the end of the village, or proceed straight if you wish refreshment from the village inn.

Pischelsdorf

The bicycle route circles around Pischelsdorf ~ stay left along the woods ~ then cross a small stream and ride down a paved ribbon of trail ~ after about 2 kilometers the trail ends at a main road that leads into the village of **Langenschönbichl** ~ at the other end of the village turn left towards **Kronau** ~ and follow the lightly-traveled lane through the fields into Kronau.

At the **B 19** junction proceed straight under the bridge ~ and then up the dike and over the Große Tulln river ~ turn left and follow the Große Tulln to the Danube and ride into the "garden city" of Tulln.

Tip: The small harbor is a good place from which to start a tour through Tulln. Turn right on Klosterweg, which leads past the museum to the main square. The Egon Schiele Museum is directly adjacent to the Donaulände.

Tip: The ***bikeline* bicycle atlas "Weinviertel"** (available in German) describes other tours through the region of that name. S-Bahn trains to Vienna depart from Tulln train station.

Tulln ≈km **1963 R**

Postal code: 3430; Telephone area code: 02272

Tourism information, ✆ 65836

Egon Schiele Museum, Donaulände 28, ✆ 64570. Open: Tues-Sun 10-18. More than 100 works by Egon Schiele on display in the former city jail. Includes "View of Klosterneuburg across snow-covered vineyards" (1907). Exhibits and information about Schiele's life and times.

61
Altenwörth
In den Weidäckern
Hochau
Seewiesen
Harraßäcker
Donaukraftwerk
Altenwörth
Donau
Traisen
Mistbutten
Jagdhaus
Eleonorenhain
Brennten
Utzenlaa
Bergau
Rondellenwasser
Kälberau
Gegenau
Kranawettenau
Michaelergrund
Jagdhaus
Großer Grund
Großer Grund
Eisteich
60
Rabischwasser
ehemaliges
Kernkraftwerk
Mühlhäufl
Brunnader
Plackenwasser
Roßwörthaufen
Maria Ponsee
Jagdhaus
Plackenhaus
Kaindorf
Bärndorf
Placken
Goldwascher
Buttendorf
Zwentendorf
Donau
Kleinschönbichl
Erpersdorf
62
Geschirrwasser
Dürnrohr
Donau-Chemie
Umspannwerk-Dürnrohr
Perschling
Pischelsdorf
Langenschönbichl
B3

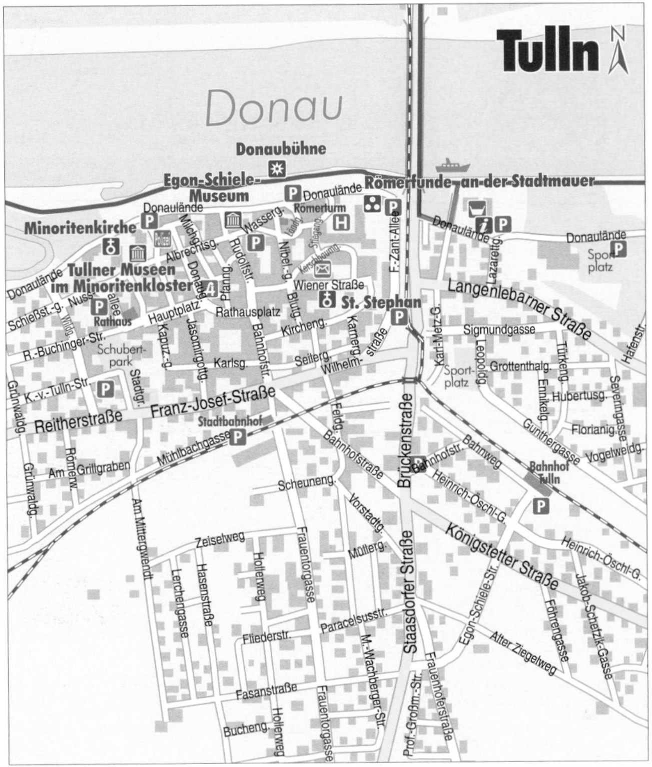

Tulln

Roman museum, Marc Aurel Park 1b, ✆ 65922. Open: Tues-Sun 10-18. Original artifacts and exhibits about military and civilian life in the Roman encampment "Comagenis" between about 90-488 AD.

Tulln museums in the Minorite monastery, Minoritenplatz 1, ✆ 61915. Includes exhibits on the city, life on the river, geology, fire defense and the Austrian sugar museum.

St. Stephan church, Wiener Straße. The 12th century church is especially noteworthy for its Romanesque west-portal, decorated with statutes (probably the 12 apostles) set into niches around the round arches. The most valuable interior elements come from closed monasteries like the Cartusian abbey at Gaming.

Karner – Dreikönigskapelle, next to St. Stephan. The most beautiful example of this typically Austrian structure, combines late-Romanesque and early Gothic elements (13th century).

Minorite church, Minoritenplatz. The abbey church was built 1732-39, with stylistically unified interior decoration and excellent altar statuary, baroque crypt and an old hermitage with walls decorated with shells, stones and bones.

Tulln

Roman tower at the Donaulände. A tower from the Roman cavalry fort Comagna is one of the oldest surviving structures in Austria.

City center. Dominated by single-story country houses, many with medieval elements.

Aubad

Tip: The Danube bicycle route on the northern bank can be reached by crossing the Danube river bridge from Tulln. See page 108, map 49 for a description. Turn right from the

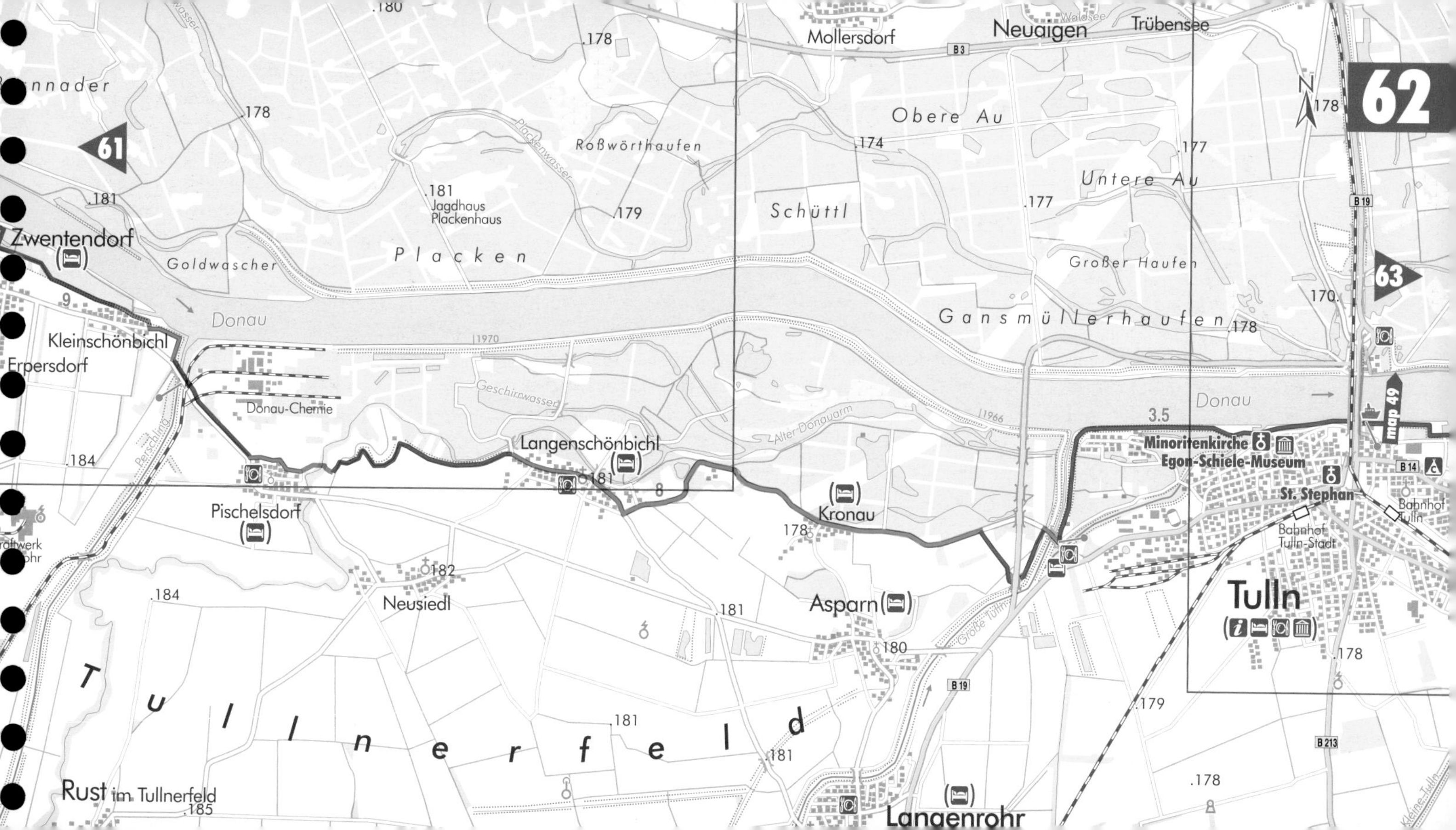

62
61
63
map 49
Zwentendorf
Kleinschönbichl
Erpersdorf
Donau-Chemie
Donau
Goldwascher
Placken
Jagdhaus Plackenhaus
Roßwörthaufen
Plackenwasser
Schüttl
Obere Au
Untere Au
Großer Haufen
Gansmüllerhaufen
Mollersdorf
Neuaigen
Trübensee
B 3
B 19
B 14
B 213
Geschirrwasser
Alter Donauarm
Langenschönbichl
Pischelsdorf
Kraftwerk
Perschling
Neusiedl
Kronau
Asparn
Minoritenkirche
Egon-Schiele-Museum
St. Stephan
Bahnhof Tulln
Bahnhof Tulln-Stadt
Tulln
Große Tulln
Kleine Tulln
Tullnerfeld
Rust im Tullnerfeld
Langenrohr

southern bank route and go up the ramp to the bridge, which has a narrow bicycle lane across the river.

Tulln to Vienna on the southern bank 38 km

From the Danube promenade in **Tulln** follow the towpath to the Danube river bridge ~ ride under the bridge and follow the shoreline towards Greifenstein about 15 kilometers downstream ~ the **Aubad** public swimming lake is on the right just past the harbor ~ the Danube becomes wider and ever more lake-like as it approaches the next power station.

After about 3 kilometers pass through **Langenlebarn** ~ and along a vacation colony near **Muckendorf** ~ the silhouette of **Kreuzenstein** castle comes into view ~ arrive at the **Greifenstein power station** after another 4 kilometers.

Tip: At a yacht harbor about 2 kilometers before the power station a road branches off to the right. Straight ahead the route stays on the river, north of an old arm of the Danube. It is possible until sundown to cross the Danube on the power station dam (after dark use the speakerphone to ask the attendant to open the gate). The road to the right leads south around the old arm of the river and to the town of Greifenstein (see page 108).

Take the right at the yacht harbor, cross the stream that feeds the old arm and turn left ~ and proceed on the towpath to the **old harbor** and the **beach** ~ pass the ferry landing and ride to the town of Greifenstein.

On the main route, turn right in front of the power station and reach the **Gasthaus Jarosch** ~ pass the ferry landing on the northern side of the old arm of the Danube ~ and cross the body of water on a new bridge ~ on the **Greifenstein** side the town is to the right while the main route continues downstream to the left.

The old castle Greifenstein is perched above the village's pretty houses, which include the first villas done in the "Viennese country house style."

Greifenstein ≈km 1949 R

Postal code: 3422; Telephone area code: 02242

- **Greifenstein town office**, Hauptstr. 43, ✆ 32231 or St. Andrä-Wördern government office, ✆ 31300.
- **Power station ferry:** Mon-Sun, 9-21 as needed.
- **Castle.** Rebuilt in the 19th century by Prince Johann Lichtenstein, on the remains of an older fortification, as a typical small castle with walls, keep and main hall. Restaurant.

The route from Greifenstein continues down the river between the shoreline and the railroad ~ turn left at the first junction and return to the towpath ~ at the edge of **Höflein** the route makes a small detour and comes back to the shoreline ~ return to the towpath after the fork in the town ~ and ride a short piece along the Danube as it starts to turn south and enter the **Wiener Pforte**. The route follows the railroad, away from the river.

Kritzendorf

At the **Kritzendorf train station** either turn right into the town or straight on towards Klosterneuburg ~ after 3.5 kilometers arrive at the **Klosterneuburg-Kierling train station** and turn left over the Klosterneuburger Durchstich (canal).

Do not miss the opportunity to visit the impressive monastery complex in Klosterneuburg before setting off on the final kilometers into Vienna. The abbey dominates the town nestled between the woods of the Kahlenberges and the Leopoldsberges and the Viennese Hausbergen.

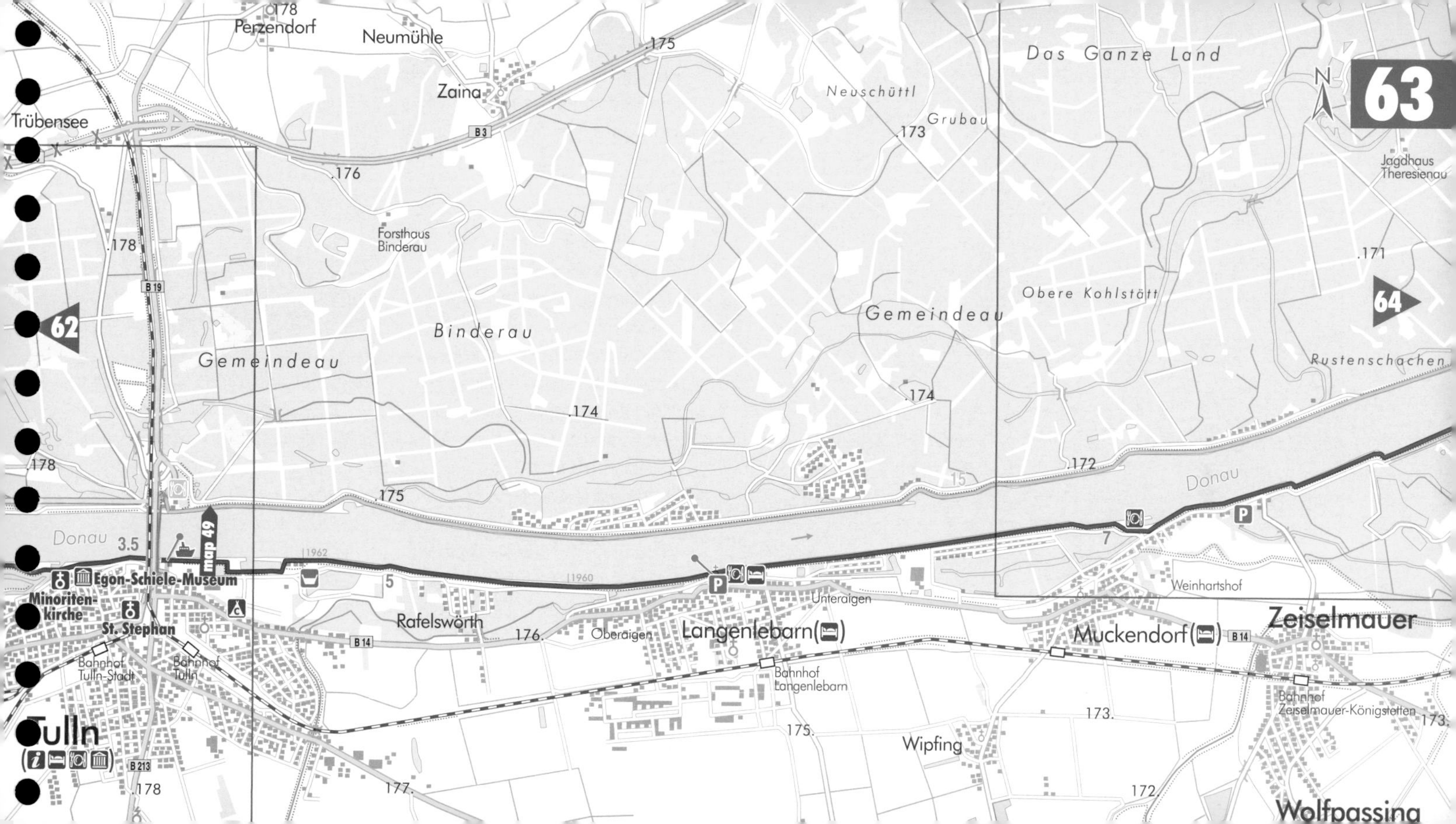
63
Perzendorf
Neumühle
Zaina
Trübensee
Das Ganze Land
Neuschüttl
Grubau
Jagdhaus Theresienau
Forsthaus Binderau
Binderau
Gemeindeau
Gemeindeau
Obere Kohlstätt
Rustenschachen
62
64
Donau
Donau
map 49
Egon-Schiele-Museum
Minoritenkirche
St. Stephan
Bahnhof Tulln-Stadt
Bahnhof Tulln
Tulln
Rafelswörth
Oberaigen
Unteraigen
Langenlebarn
Bahnhof Langenlebarn
Weinhartshof
Muckendorf
Zeiselmauer
Bahnhof Zeiselmauer-Königstetten
Wipfing
Wolfpassing
B3
B19
B14
B14
B213

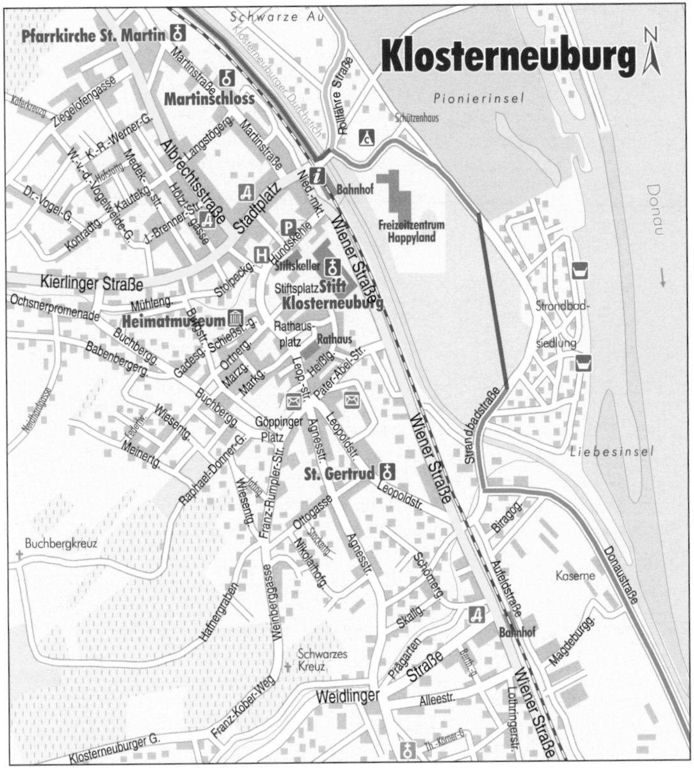

Through the underpass at the train station and to Niedermarkt ~ take **Hundskehle** directly to the Rathausplatz and the abbey.

Klosterneuburg ≈km 1940 R

Postal code: 3400; Telephone area code 02243

Information and guest service, Donaupark Camping, In der Au, ✆ 32038

Abbey museum, Stiftspl. 1, ✆ 411154. Open: May-Nov, Tues-Sun 10-17. Gothic painted panels and sculptures, Renaissance bronzes, ivory and small figures from the 10th through the 19th centuries. Among the artists represented: Rueland Frueauf the Younger, Rudolf v. Alt and Egon Schiele.

Essl collection of contemporary art, An der Donau-Au 1. Open: Tues-Sun 10-19, Wed 10-21. Austria's largest private art collection, with 3,200 m² exhibition space and sculpture garden.

Archaeological museum. Underneath St. Martin church, Martinstr. 38. Open: Sun 10-12 and by appointment. Documents 1,000 years of church history. The oldest traces at the site are from a Frankish wooden church from around

Klosterneuburg

900. Also noteworthy: a late-Gothic baptismal.

Mährisch-Schlesisches museum, Schießstattg. 2. Open: Tues 10-16, Sat 14-17, Sun 10-13. Collections largely from the eastern Sudetenland and Beskidenland, showing religious life and customs.

Klosterneuburg abbey, Stiftspl. 1, ✆ 411212. Guided tours: Mon-Sun 10-17. Medieval monastery building. Built starting in 1108 on the site of a Roman fort and extensively expanded from the 15th to the 19th centuries. Open only for guided tours. The impressive baroque new buildings were built 1730-55 under Karl VI and

64
Stockerau
Oberzögersdorf
Unterzögersdorf
174
B3
Bürgerhäufl
Unterrohrbach
Spillern
A 22
ägerhausboden
.171
In der Au
.171
5.5
Graingut
Stockerauer Arm
Eiswasserallee
Kreuzeichenboden
Das Ganze Land
Krumpenwasser
.168
.169
Jagdhaus
Theresienau
65
.171
map 50
Kraftwerk
Greifenstein
6.5
Windau
.168
.170
Donau
5.5
3.5
(1950
Obere Kohlstätt
15
63
Rustenschachen
179
.170
3
Burg Greifenstein
Greifenstein
179
Höflein
.170
Bahnhof Greifenstein
Altenberg
Eichenleitenberg
Totenkopf
Hundsberg
.387
.172
Donau
(1955
7
320
Auhof
441
403
Tempelbergwarte
Wördern
Altenberg
Muckendorf
Bahnhof St. Andrä-
Wördern
Köbering
Hadersfeld
Weinhartshof
Zeiselmauer

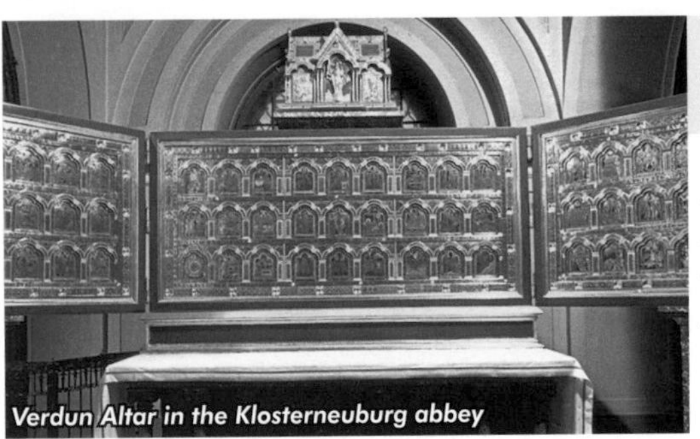
Verdun Altar in the Klosterneuburg abbey

The interior features 16 over-sized gold-plated wooden statues.

were intended to embody the unity of church and empire. Growing secularization of society ended the project prematurely. Guided tours include the Kaiser chamber with outstanding stuccowork and the Gobelin chamber.

♁ **Unsere Liebe Frau (Our Dear Lady) abbey church**. Romanesque structure from 1114-36. The interior dates from the 18th century. The famous Verdun Altar, perhaps the most impressive enamel work of the Middle Ages consists of 51 panels with biblical images and can be found in the Leopold chapel.

♁ **St. Martin parish church**, Martinstr. 38. The old parish building dates to the 11th century.

The House of Babenberg moved its palace from Melk to Klosterneuburg in 1106, before the dynasty extended its influence into the Danube's Viennese plain, which was still controlled by Hungary and the Slavs. Even after Vienna became the Babenberg capital, Klosterneuburg remained important as the Kaiser's retreat. After the Turkish wars, Donato Felice d'Allio erected a abbey palace modeled after the Spanish Escorial.

After the **Klosterneuburg-Kierling train station** cross the Klosterneuburg Durchstich (canal) ~ immediately turn right towards the Schützenhaus, where bicycle tourists coming from the northern bank route arrive from Korneuburg ~ follow the moderately-traveled road around the recreation center ~ and stay right as you pass the beach colony, or go left if you wish to visit the outdoor public pool ~ cross the Klosterneuburg Durchstich again and then the Weidlingbach ~ turn left on Donaustraße and return to the riverfront.

The Danube bicycle route passes to the left of the ***Kahlenberg*** *and the* ***Leopoldsberg****, the southern exposures of which are covered with Vienna's vineyards. The fine wines from these hills can be tasted at the famous "Heurigen" in Grinzing, Nußdorf or Kahlenbergerdorf. Wine is also produced on the left flank of the Pforte, on the* ***Bisamberg*** *across the river.*

Take **Donaustraße** through the commercial area and come to the Vienna city limits ~ turn left on **Kuchelauer Hafenstraße** and proceed under the railroad towards Kahlenbergerdorf, a wine-producing town with Heurigen and romantic small bridges.

Kahlenbergerdorf R

The route turns onto the bicycle path that runs to the left of the railroad ~ from this point on the route into the center of Vienna is virtually impossible to lose ~ ride through a park and for a short time along the Danube ~ to where the route leaves the river's main stream and follows the Danube canal towards the old city ~ take the tunnel under the railroad at **Nußdorf,** before the shipping locks.

The bicycle route passes a small rise where the Austrian art nouveau architect Otto Wagner built the works that block the Danube canal. Then downhill and left before the railroad underpass ~ signs for the bicycle route now name the Urania, an education center, as the route's destination ~ follow the "Donau-

65
64
66
map 51
Eiswasserallee
Stockerauer Arm
Kreuzeichenboden
.169
.167
.170
Teiritzberg
Stetten
Am Wasweg
Am Teiritz
Haltestelle
Leobendorf-Burg Kreuzenstein
A 22
B 3
6.5
Windau
.168
Kraftwerk
Greifenstein
5.5
Donau
Hofau
Ganserfeld
B 6
Badeteich
Bisamberg
Burg Greifenstein
179
Höflein
Greifenstein
Rathaus
Korneuburg
Flandorf
Eichenleitenberg
Totenkopf
Hundsberg
.387
320
Klein-Engersdorf
441
403
Hadersfeld
Jachthafen
2.5
.409
.168
.326
Heuberg
245
B 3
Rollfähre
.364
3.5
Haltestelle
Unt. Kritzendorf
Bisamberg
.420
Sonnberg
Weißer Hof
Kritzendorf
Bisamberg
A 22
Elisabethhöhe
2.5
Tuttenhof
.392
Freiberg
.358
.169

View towards Vienna

ceed straight on the bicycle trail along Praterstraße as far as Praterstern. You can continue either on Prater Hauptallee or Lasallestraße towards the river. The Danube bicycle route from Vienna to Budapest is described in "**Donau Radweg, Teil 3" from *bikeline*** (available in German).

kanal Radweg" under numerous bridges ~ on the right note the colorful garbage incinerator that the artist and architect Friedensreich Hundertwasser attempted to make more aesthetically interesting.

Tip: The city becomes increasingly dense and soon the bicycle tourist must decide how to continue (refer also to the left-bank descriptions). To stay on the Danube bicycle route and continue towards Bratislava, take the Aspernbrücke across the Danube canal and pro-

If you wish to proceed into the center of Vienna, continue along the Danube canal ~ after the **Rossauer Kaserne** you can turn onto **Schottenring** and follow the Vienna "Ring Rund Radweg" which makes a complete circuit through the city center.

Vienna's **Westbahnhof train station** can best be reached from the Ring ~ at the Kunsthistorische Museum (art history museum) take the bicycle trail next to **Babenbergerstraße** and then to **Mariahilfer Straße**, Vienna's busy shopping avenue ~ the street has no bicycle lanes or paths, and plenty of city traffic, but the speed limit is just 30 km/h and it leads straight to the train station.

Tip: If you wish to avoid some of the heavy traffic on the **Mariahilfer Straße**, turn right on **Stiftgasse** and then left on **Lindengasse**, which leads to the **Gürtel**. Turn left on the Gürtel bicycle trail and follow it to the train station. The most comfortable way to reach the train station is with the U-3 subway line, which may be used with bicycles at the times shown below.

Vienna ≈km **1929**

Telephone area code: 01

- **Viennese tourism association**, 1025 Vienna, ✆ 24555
- **Tourist Info Vienna**, 1, Albertinaplatz/corner of Maysedergasse
  Hotel reservations: 24555
- **Bike & U-Bahn (subway)**. Mon-Fri 9-15 and after 18:30, Sat after 9, Sun/Hol all day. A half-price ticket must be purchased for the bicycle. Enter subway cars only at doors marked with the bicycle symbol. On the U 6 line only in cars with low floors.
- **Bike & Schnellbahn (commuter trains)**. Mon-Fri 9-15 and after 18:30, Sat after 9, Sun/Hol all day. Bicycles may be brought on board all trains that are shown in the schedules with a bicycle symbol. In Vienna's central zone (Zone 100) it is necessary to purchase a half-price ticket for the bicycle. For all other trains purchase a bicycle day-ticket.
- **Guided bicycle tours: Pedal Power Tours**, Ausstellungsstr. 3, ✆ 7297234 and **Vienna-Bike**, Wasag. 28/2/5, ✆ 3191258. Discovery rides through Vienna.
- **Wien-Karte (Vienna ticket)**, 72-hour ticket valid for all forms of public transportation, includes discounts to many museums and other sights. Available from Tourist Information offices, many hotels and ticket-offices at larger U-bahn stations.
- **Albertina**, Albertinapl. 1, ✆ 53483510. Open:

Rathaus
Korneuburg
Klein-Engersdorf
A 22
B 3
.168
65
map 52
Rollfähre
Tuttenhof
.169
2.5
3.5
Bisamberg
B i s a m b e r g
Veitsberg
Elisabethhöhe
.358
.336
Falkenberg
Magdalenenhof
308
Langenzersdorf
Lahnerberg
1940
Stift Klosterneuburg
B 14
Klosterneuburg
.167
B 3
Strebersdorf
Neue Donau
A 22
Industriezentrum
Haltestelle Strebersdorf
Donau
Josefinnenhütte
Leopoldsberg
425
Kahlenberg
484
Sulzwiese
Schwarzlackenau
Josefsdorf
Kahlenbergerdorf
1935
Donauinsel
Jedlesee
.295
Burgstall
VIENNA
Krapfenwald
Nußberg
.377
Cobenzl
Nußdorf
city map
N
Sievering
Heiligenstadt
Grinzing
Donaukanal
66

daily 10-18, Wed 10-21. One of the world's most important museums. Artists represented range from Michelangelo to Rubens, Dürer to Picasso. Special exhibitions. Archives include more than 60,000 drawings and about 1 million printed pages from the late Gothic period to the present.

Kunsthistorisches (art history) Museum, 1, Maria-Theresien-Platz, ✆ 525240. Open: Tues-Sun 10-18, Thur 10-21. One of the most renowned art collections in the world. The core collection includes works by Dürer, Rubens, Titian, and Bruegel the older (largest Bruegel collection in the world). Also noteworthy: the Egyptian/Oriental collection, antiquity collections and numismatics collection.

Naturhistorisches(natural history) Museum, 1, Maria-Theresien-Platz, ✆ 521770. Open: Wed-Mon 9-18. Includes minerals, rare uncut diamonds and meteorites, a fossil collection and 15,000 skeletons (including dinosaurs). Prehistoric items include the original "Willendorf Venus" (see page xxx) and anthropological items from the early-Paleolithic period to the present.

Österreichisches Museum für angewandte Kunst (applied arts) (MAK), 1, Stubenring 5, ✆ 711360. Open: Tues-Sun 10-18, Thur 10-21. East-Asian and Islamic art, library, glass and ceramics, metalworks, Viennese workshops, collections of furniture, textiles and rugs.

Jüdisches Museum der Stadt Wien (City of Vienna Jewish Museum), 1, Dorotheerg. 11, ✆ 5350431. Open: Sun-Fri 10-18, Thur 10-21. Opened 50 years after the end of World War II. Changing exhibitions illustrate Jewish cultural history, art, literature and photography.

Museum für Völkerkunde (ethnology), 1, Neue Burg/Heldenplatz, ✆ 534300. Open: Wed-Mon 10-16. In addition to permanent exhibits like Kaiser Maximilian's Mexican collection (which includes the disputed feather headdress of Montezuma), James Cook's polynesian collection and bronzes from Benin.

Österreichische Nationalbibliothek (national library), 1, Josefspl. 1, ✆ 534100. Open: March-Mid May, Mon-Sat 10-14, 15 May-26 Oct, Mon-Sat 10-16, Sun/Hol 10-13. The baroque main hall was created by Fischer von Erlach and son 1723-37. Ceiling painting by Daniel Gran. Holds the 15,000 gold-printed volumes of Prinzen Eugen von Savoyen.

KunstHausWien (Vienna art house), 3, Untere Weißgerberstr. 13, ✆ 7120491. Open: Mon-Sun 10-19. Paintings, architecture, sculptures by Hundertwasser, plus exhibitions featuring other 20th century artists.

Kunsthalle Wien (Vienna art museum), 4, Karlsplatz/Treitlstr. 2, ✆ 521890. Open: Mon-Sun 10-18, Thur 10-20. Rotating exhibitions featuring contemporary art and masterpieces of classic modernism.

Haus der Musik, 1, Selerstätte 30, ✆ 5164851. Open: Mon-Sun 10-22. Thema: All about music, with many things that visitors can try.

Schatzkammer (treasure chamber), 1, Hofburg-Schweizerhof, ✆ 5337931. Open: Wed-Mon 10-18. One of the world's greatest treasure troves, includes the Holy Roman Emperor's crown (c. 962), the Austrian Emperor's crown, the Burgundy treasure and the treasures of the Order of the Golden Fleece.

Österreichische Galerie des 19. und 20. Jhs. (Austrian gallery of the 19th and 20th centuries), 3, Oberes Belvedere, Prinz-Eugen-Str. 27, ✆ 795570. Open: Tues-Sun 10-17. A survey of Austrian painting from Biedermeier through the Ringstraße Period to art nouveau. Large collections of works by Klimt, Schiele and Kokoschka, plus Waldmüller, Romako, Makart, Wotruba and others.

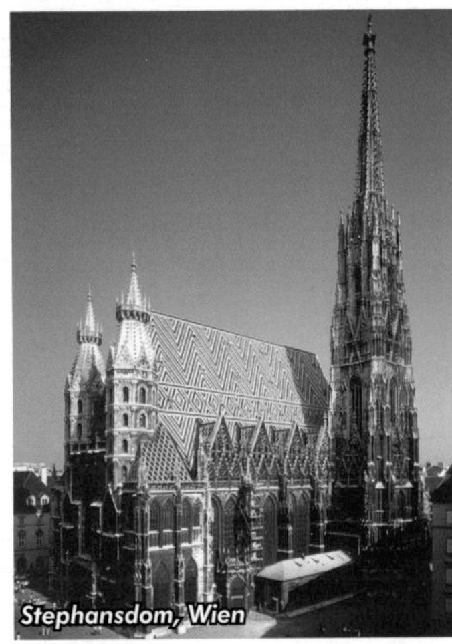
Stephansdom, Wien

Heeresgeschichtliches Museum (military history), 3, Arsenal, Objekt 18, ✆ 795610. Open: Sat-Thur 10-16. Occupies an oriental-classical

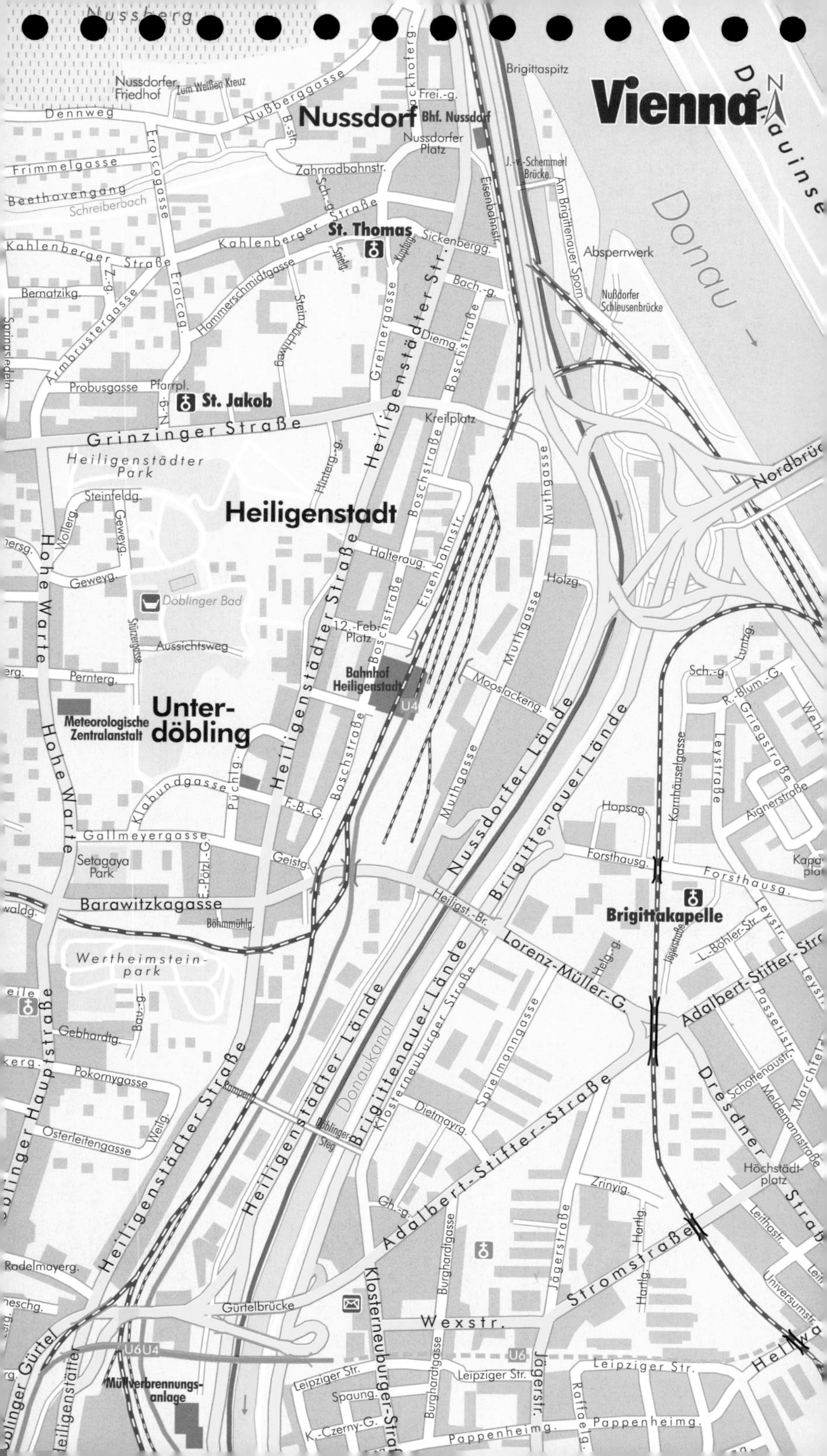

Vienna
N
Donauinsel
Donau
Brigittaspitz
J.-v.-Schemmerl Brücke
Am Brigittenauer Sporn
Absperrwerk
Nußdorfer Schleusenbrücke
Nordbrücke
Nussberg
Nussdorfer Friedhof
Zum Weißen Kreuz
Dennweg
Nußberggasse
Nussdorf
Bhf. Nussdorf
Nussdorfer Platz
Frimmelgasse
Beethovengang
Schreiberbach
Zahnradbahnstr.
Eroicagasse
St. Thomas
Sickenbergg.
Kahlenberger Straße
Bernatzikg.
Armbrustergasse
Hammerschmidtgasse
Steinbüchlweg
Greinergasse
Heiligenstädter Str.
Bach.-g.
Diemg.
Boschstraße
Eisenbahnstr.
Probusgasse
Pfarrpl.
St. Jakob
Grinzinger Straße
Kreilplatz
Heiligenstädter Park
Heiligenstadt
Steinfeldg.
Wollerg.
Geweyg.
Halteraug.
Muthgasse
Holzg.
Döblinger Bad
Stürzergasse
Aussichtsweg
Hohe Warte
Pernterg.
12.-Feb.-Platz
Bahnhof Heiligenstadt
U4
Mooslackeng.
Unter-döbling
Meteorologische Zentralanstalt
Klabundgasse
Püchlg.
F.-B.-G.
Gallmeyergasse
Setagaya Park
Geistg.
Barawitzkagasse
Böhmmühlg.
Heiligst.-Br.
Nussdorfer Lände
Brigittenauer Lände
Wertheimstein-park
Bau-g.
Gebhardtg.
Pokornygasse
Osterleitengasse
Weilg.
Döblinger Hauptstraße
Heiligenstädter Straße
Heiligenstädter Lände
Donaukanal
Döblinger Steg
Klosterneuburger Straße
Dietmayrg.
Spielmanngasse
Lorenz-Müller-G.
Brigittakapelle
Forsthausg.
Hopsag.
Kornhäuselgasse
Leystraße
Griegstraße
Aignerstraße
Adalbert-Stifter-Straße
Dresdner Straße
Höchstädtplatz
Zrinyig.
Hartlg.
Jägerstraße
Burghardtgasse
Stromstraße
Radelmayerg.
Gürtelbrücke
Wexstr.
Döblinger Gürtel
U6 U4
Müllverbrennungs-anlage
Leipziger Str.
Spaung.
K.-Czerny-G.
Pappenheimg.
Raffaelg.
Jägerstr.
U6
Universumstr.
Leithastr.

Rathaus, Wien

building from 1857, which was Vienna's first building planned as a museum. Contains valuable Austrian military items from the 30 Years War to World War I.

Sigmund Freud Museum, 9, Bergg. 19, ✆ 3191596. Open: July-Sept, Mon-Sun 9-18, Oct-June, Mon-Sun 9-16. The founder of psychoanalysis lived here from 1891 until he was forced to leave in 1938.

Salvador Dalí Show, 1, Josefspl. 5, ✆ 5122549. Open: Mon-Sun 10-18.

Secession, 1, Friedrichstr. 12, ✆ 5875307. Open: Tues-Fri 10-18, Sat/Sun/Hol 10-16. Built 1897-98 according to plans by Joseph Olbrich for the "Viennese Secession" group of progressive artists. Rotating exhibitions of modern art plus the 34-meter Beethoven frieze by Gustav Klimt.

Straßenbahnmuseum (tram museum), 3, Erdbergstr. 109, ✆ 790944900. Open: May-4 Oct, Sat/Sun/Hol, 9-16. More than 80 historic vehicles since 1871, plus buses and wagons used in Vienna public transportation.

Uhrenmuseum (clock museum), 1, Schulhof 2, ✆ 5332265. Open: Tues-Sun 9-16:30. More than 3,000 clocks and watches, and all kinds of curiosities.

Theater museum, 1, Lobkowitzpl. 2, ✆ 51288000. Open: Tues-Sun 10-17. The museum includes mainly stage settings, costumes and props as well as photos and drawings.

Lipizzaner museum in the Stallburg, 1, Reitschulg. 2, ✆ 5264184. Open: Mon-Sun 9-18. Paintings and other items about the Spanish Riding School, tours of the stables used by the Vienna's famous Lipizzaner horses.

Prater Ferris-wheel

Museums Quartier Wien (Vienna museum quarter), 7, Museumspl. 1, ✆ 5235881. A spectacular concentration of cultural exhibitions on the edge of old Vienna. The 8th largest museum district in the world.

Stephansdom (cathedral), 1, Stephansplatz, ✆ 515523526. Guided tours: Mon-Sat 10:30 and 15, Sun/Hol 15. Austria's most important Gothic structure and, along with the Prater Ferris-wheel, a Vienna landmark. Noteworthy: the red marble gravestone for Kaiser Frederick III, Anton Pilgram's pulpit (1514/1515), the Viennese "Neustädter Altar" (1447). Guided tours of the extensive catacombs under the cathedral Mon-Sat at 10, 11, 11:30, 14, 14:30, 15:30, 16, 16:30, Sun/Hol 14, 14:30, 15:30, 16, 16:30.

Schloss Schönbrunn (palace), 13, Schönbrunner Schloss-Straße (U-Bahn station), ✆ 81113. Open: April-Oct, Mon-Sun 8:30-17, Nov-March, Mon-Sun 8:30-16:30. Original plans by Fischer von Erlach proposed a palace that would be

Vienna
Augarten
Augartenpalais
Nordwestbahnstraße
Obere Augartenstraße
Untere Augartenstr.
Rembrandtstr.
Taborstraße
Leopoldsgasse
Karmelitermarkt
Karmeliterk.
Große Schiffg.
Obere Donaustraße
Franz-Josefs-Kai
Wettsteinpark
Rossauer Steg
Rossauer Lände
Spittelauer Lände
Brigittenauer Lände
Donaukanal
Klosterneuburger-Straße
Wallensteinstr.
Wallensteinpl.
Jägerstr.
St. Brigitta
Brigittapl.
Hannovermarkt
Hannoverg.
Raffaelg.
Hartlgasse
Leipziger Str.
Pappenheimg.
Wexstr.
Rauscherstraße
Gaußpl.
Porzellang.
Alserbachstr.
Lichtensteinstr.
Lichtenstein Park
Museum Moderner Kunst
Franz Josefs Bahnhof
Nordbergstr.
Althanstr.
Augasse
Universitätszentrum mit Wirtschaftsuniversität
Rossauer Kaserne
Bergg.
Währinger Str.
Türkenstr.
Hörlg.
Deutschmeisterplatz
Maria-Theresien-Str.
Schottenring
Börse
Börsepl.
Wipplingerstr.
Hohenstaufeng.
Schottenstift
Freyung
Herrengasse
Schottentor
Universität
Votivkirche
Votivpark
Rooseveltplatz
Universitätsstr.
Dr.-Karl-Lueger-Ring
Burgtheater
Rathauspark
Reichsratsstr.
Parlament
Volksgarten
Ballhausplatz
Bundeskanzleramt
Minoritenk.
Minoritenplatz
Theseustempel
Alte Hofburg
St. Michael
Kohlmarkt
Graben
St. Peter
Stephansplatz
Stephansdom
Dom- und Diözesanmuseum
Universitätskirche
Dominik.-k.
Postsparkasse
Wollzeile
Schulerstr.
Rotenturmstraße
Fleischmarkt
Schwedenplatz
Hoher Markt
St. Ruprecht
Rupr.-stiege
Morzinplatz
Salztorbr.
Marienbr.
Schwedenbr.
Salzgries
Maria a. Gestade
Altes Rath.
Judenpl.
Concordiaplatz
Rudolfplatz
Tiefer Graben
Am Hof
Kirche am Hof
Renng.
Heinrichsg.
Neutorg.
Vermessungsamt
Franz-Hochedlinger-G.
Bauernfeldplatz
Schlickpl.
Schlickg.

larger and more magnificent than Versailles. Built 1696-1730, with 1,441 rooms and chambers. Served as Habsburg summer residence and venue of the Congress of Vienna.

- **Zoo - Tiergarten Schönnbrunn**, Schlosspark near Hietzinger Tor (U-Bahn), ✆ 87792940. Open: March, Mon-Sun 9-17:30, April 9-18, May-Sept, Mon-Sun 9-18:30, Oct, Feb, 9-17, Nov-Jan, 9-16:30. The world's oldest zoo set in a baroque park, with many innovative ideas for keeping animals.
- **Spanish Riding school**, 1, Hofburg, Innerer Burghof "Morgenarbeit": Sept-mid-Dec, Feb-June, Tues-Sat 10-12. Observe the training of the Lipizzaner horses. No ticket reservations necessary.
- **Ringstraße**. The old city defensive fortifications were demolished 1857-58 and replaced by a beautiful boulevard with buildings that include the Burg theater, Museum of Art History and the Parliament. The bourgeois class also erected a monumental structure, the Palais.
- **Belvedere**, Prinz-Eugen-Straße 27. The palace is regarded as one of the most beautiful baroque structures. Built 1700 by Lukas von Hildebrandt as a summer residence for Prinz Eugen von Savoyen. Includes an elegant terraced garden with cascades and sculptures.
- **Spittelberg**. The neighborhood between Breite Gasse and Stiftgasse provides an example of how an historic (in this case Biedermeier period) area can be preserved and revitalized. Today a popular and lively artists' quarter with flair.
- **Naschmarkt**, Wienzeile between Getreidemarkt and Kettenbrückengasse. Vienna's largest fruit and vegetable market, full of individuality and atmosphere, is the living antithesis of modern supermarkets. Large flea market on Saturdays.
- **Riesenrad (Ferris wheel)** in the Prater. Open: Nov, Dec, Jan, Feb 10-20; March, April & Oct, 10-22, Mai-Sept, 9-24. Built 1896/97 by the engineer Walter Basset, with 61 meter diameter.

Vienna. Monarchs called the city on the Danube their capital for more than 7 centuries, it was the center of an empire and today remains one of Europe's most important cultural centers. How can one briefly describe such a city without resorting to stilted clichés or omitting something important? One way, perhaps, is to look at the city's relationship to the river that feeds it.

Although Vienna lies on the banks of the Danube, which may even have been blue long ago, the city has no historic riverfront, no pleasant promenades along the water and little of a river city's character. Merely the Little Danube, a canal really, flows through the center of the Austrian capital. In the 19th century Vienna sacrificed its direct links to the Danube by digging a ruler-straight canal to bypass the river's winding course and help regulate its flow. Officials at the official opening of the canal in 1875 called it an Austrian engineering marvel. The small Wien river was also banished to a featureless man-made channel.

Are the city and the river irreconcileable opposites? The most recent attempt to manipulate the river and its landscape has, at least, brought the city's residents closer to the Danube. The broad flood plain along the straightened Danube, which for years had been a barren urban wasteland, was excavated for a new channel. The excavated material was piled in the center, creating the long slim Donauinsel (Danube island) which has since become one of Vienna's most popular recreation areas.

Vienna
city centre (I.)
Sigmund-Freud Museum
Rossauer Kaserne
Altes Allgemeines Krankenhaus
Nationalbank
IX.
Votivkirche
Börse
Schottenring
Maria-Theresien-Str.
Währinger Str.
Universitätsstr.
Landesgericht
Universität
Schottenstift
Maria a. Gestade
St. Ruprecht
Altes Rathaus
Kirche a. Hof
Rathaus
Rathauspark
Burgtheater
Theseus Tempel
Bundeskanzleramt
Parlament
Volksgarten
Minoritenkirche
St. Michael
St. Peter
Dom- und Diözesanmuseum
Stephansdom
Universitätskirche
Dominik.-k.
Alte Hofburg
Hofreitschule
Schatzkammer
Nationalbibliothek
Jüd. Museum
Heldenplatz
Neue Hofburg
Burgtor
Volkskundemuseum
Kapuzinergruft
Mechitaristenkirche
Volkstheater
Naturhistor. Museum
Maria Theresia Denkmal
Maria-Theresien-Platz
Kleinstes Haus Wiens
Messepalast
Kunsthistor. Museum
Tabakmuseum
Goethe Denkmal
Burggarten
Staatsoper
Opernring
Kärntner Ring
Westbahnhof
Mariahilfer Str.
Theater an der Wien
Secession
Kunstakademie
Kunsthalle
Südbahnhof
Künstlerhaus
Musikverein
Karlsplatz
Konzerthaus
Kursalon
Johann-Strauß-Denkmal
Stadtpark
Schubert-Denkmal
Bruckner-Denkmal
Museum f. Angew. Kunst
Reg.-gebäude
Urania
Uraniastr.
Franz-Josefs-Kai
Donaukanal
Obere Donaustr.
Untere Donaustr.
Karmeliterkirche
II.
Taborstr.
Praterstraße
Praterstern
BAHNHOF WIEN NORD
Dogenhof
Volksprater
Planetarium
Riesenrad
Pratermuseum
Schweizerhaus
Liliputbahn
Rechnungshof
Kunsthaus Wien
Hundertwasserhaus
Prater
Krankenhaus St. Elisabeth
BAHNHOF WIEN MITTE
Beethovenhaus
Landstraßer Hauptstr.
III.
Rochuspark
Pfarrkirche Peter u. Paul
Schüttelstr.
Erdberger Lände
Weißgerberlände
Ausstellungsstraße
Am Heumarkt
Schubertring
Parkring
Stubenring
Burgring
Dr.-K.-Lueger-Ring
Dr.-K.-Renner-R.
VII.
VIII.

Overnight accommodations

The following list includes hotels (H), hotels garni (Hg), inns (Gh), pensions (P) and private rooms (Pz), as well as youth hostels and campgrounds in the towns along the cycle route. These towns are not listed in alphabetical order, but according to their location along the river.

We have not attempted to list every possible place where visitors can spend the night, and listings should not be construed as any kind of recommendation. The Roman number (I-VI) after the telephone number indicates price range. These fall into six categories, listed below, and do not necessarily reflect the relative comfort and quality available:

I	less than € 15
II	€ 15 to € 23
III	€ 23 to € 30
IV	€ 30 to € 35
V	€ 35 to € 50
VI	more than € 50

These categories are based on the price per person in a double room equipped with shower or bath, with breakfast, unless otherwise indicated. Rooms with bath or shower in the hall are indicated with the symbol ⊠.

Because we wish to expand this list and keep it up-to-date, we welcome any comments, additions or corrections you may have. There is no charge for a listing.

Schärding

H Biedermeier Hof, Passauerstr. 139, ✆ 3064, IV

Passau (D) R

Postal code: D-94032-36; Telephone area code: 0851

ℹ Tourist Information, 94032, Rathausplatz 3 and Bahnhofstr. 36, ✆ 95598-0

H Holiday Inn, 94032, Bahnhofstr. 24, ✆ 5900-0, V-VI

H Weißer Hase, 94032, Ludwigstr. 23, ✆ 92110, VI

H Altstadt-Hotel, 94032, Bräug. 23-29, ✆ 3370, V-VI

H Wilder Mann, 94032, Rathauspl., ✆ 35071, V-VI

H Passauer Wolf, 94032, Rindermarkt 6, ✆ 93151-10, V-VI

H Wienerwald, 94032, Gr. Klingerg. 17, ✆ 33069, III-IV

H Euro Hotel Passau, Neuburger Str. 128, ✆ 98842-0, III-IV

Hg Residenz, 94032, Fritz-Schäffer-Promenade, ✆ 989020, V-VI

Hg König, 94032, Untere Donaulände 1, ✆ 3850, V-VI

Hg Herdegen, 94032, Bahnhofstr. 5, ✆ 955160, IV-V

Hg Spitzberg, 94032, Neuburgerstr. 29, ✆ 955480, IV-V

Hg Deutscher Kaiser, 94032, Bahnhofstr. 30, ✆ 95566-15, IV-V

H Schloss Ort, 94032, Im Ort 11, ✆ 34072, V-VI

H Rotel Inn, 94012, Hbf./ Donaulände, ✆ 95160, II

P Rößner, 94032, Bräug. 19, ✆ 93135-0, III-IV

Gh Blauer Bock, 94032, Höllg. 20, ✆ 34637, III-V

P Gambrinus, 94032, Haibach 20, ✆ 2905, III

Auf der Veste Oberhaus 125, 94034, ✆ 41351

Drei-Flüsse-Camping, Irring (10 km Donau aufwärts), ✆ (08546) 633

Innstadt:

H Am Jesuitenschlössl, 94032, Kapuzinerstr. 32, ✆ 38640-1, V-VI

Hg Vicus, 94032, Johann-Bergler-Str. 2, ✆ 93105-0, IV

P Vilsmeier, 94032, Lindental 28a, ✆ 36313, III

Haidenhof:

H Dreiflüssehof, 94036, Danziger Str. 42/44, ✆ 72040, IV-V

H Best Western, 94036, Neuburger Str. 79, ✆ 9518-0, V-VI

Hg Albrecht, 94036, Kohlbruck 18, ✆ 959960, V

Hg Haidenhof, 94036, Brixener Str. 7, ✆ 95987-0, III

P Gabriele, 94032, Adalbert-Stifter-Str. 12, ✆ 6446, III

Pz Weidinger, Brixener Str. 78, ✆ 51975, II ⊠

Grubweg:

H Burgwald, 94034, Salzweger Str. 9, ✆ 94169-0, IV

P Frickinger, 94034, Christdobl 13, ✆ 41222, III

Gh Rosencafé, 94034, Donaustr. 23, ✆ 42811, II-III

Hals:

Gh Zur Triftsperre, Tirftsperrstr. 15, ✆ 51162, II-III

Gh Zur Brücke, Landrichterstr. 13, ✆ 43475, II

Zeltplatz an der Ilz, 94034, Halserstr. 34, ✆ 41457

Passau-Haibach R

Postal code: 94032; Telephone area code: 0851

Pension Gambrinus, Haibach 20 (south bank), ✆ 2905, III

Kellberg L

Postal code: 94136; Telephone area code: 08501

H Ferienidyll Maxhöhe, Gut Wolfersdorf 1, ✆ 91110

H Lindenhof, Kurpromenade 12, ✆ 8080

Gh Zum Kirchenwirt, St.-Basius-Str. 1, ✆ 8116, II-III

Gh Kernmühle, bei Kellberg (north bank), ✆ 567, II-III

Hinding R

Postal code: 4785; Telephone area code: 07713

ℹ Tourismusverband Freinberg, ✆ 8244

H Faberhof, Hinding 18, ✆ 20975, III-IV
P Pfeiffer, Hinding 46, ✆ 8218, II
Pz Bachl, Hinding 43, ✆ 8202, I-II

Pyrawang R

Postal code: 4092; Telephone area code: 07714
ℹ Gemeindeamt Esternberg, ✆ 6655-10
Pz Holzapfel, Nr. 18, ✆ 6178, I
Pz Unterholzer, Nr. 17, ✆ 6172, I
Pz Grasegger, Nr. 29, ✆ 6170, I
Pz Grassegger, Nr. 12, ✆ 6208, I
Pz Fischer, Nr. 9, ✆ 6504, I
⛺ Camping Fischer, Pyrawang 9, ✆ 6504, April-Okt.

Erlau (D) L

Postal code: 94130; Telephone area code: 08591
Gh Zur Post, Hauptstr. 22, ✆ 91490, II-III
Gh Zum Edlhof, Edlhofstr. 10, ✆ 466, III-IV

Obernzell (D) L

Postal code: 94130; Telephone area code: 08591
ℹ Tourist Information, Marktpl. 42✆ 9116-119
H Fohlenhof, Matzenberger Str. 36, ✆ 9165, V
H Donautal, Passauer Straße. 19, ✆ 939788, II-III
Gh Alte Schiffspost, Marktpl. 1, ✆ 1030, III-V
Gh Zum Freischütz, Bachstr.7, ✆ 1863, II
P Zur Brücke, Bachstr. 13, ✆ 1379, II-III
P Jell, Siedlungsstr. 10, ✆ 1319, II
P Haus Sybill, Max-Moser-Str. 4, ✆ 751,I-II
Pz Nowak, Hameter Str. 41, ✆ 670, III
Pz Buchner, Rechenmacher Weg 4, ✆ 700, III
Pz Juhnke, Krankenhausstr. 10, ✆ 2999, V
Pz Feiler, Hameter Str. 20, ✆ 1836, V

Kasten R

Postal code: 4091; Telephone area code: 07714
ℹ Tourismusverband Vichtenstein, ✆ 8055-0
Gh Pilsl-Wurmsdobler, Kasten 19, ✆ 6502, I-II
Gh Klaffenböck, Kasten 15, ✆ 6505, II
P Donautal, Kasten 22, ✆ 6310-0, II
Bh Schusterbauer, Kasten 3, ✆ 6549, I
Bh Reierbauer, Kasten 8, ✆ 6531, I
Bh Petern, Kasten 13, ✆ 6529, I
⛺ Campingplatz, an der Donau, Gemeindeamt: ✆ 8055

Vichtenstein R

Telephone area code: 07717
Gh Schusta z'Weinbrunn, Wenzelberg 1, ✆ 7586, I

Jochenstein (D) L

Postal code: 94107; Telephone area code: 08591
ℹ Tourist-Information Untergriesbach, ✆ 08593/1066
Gh Kornexl, Am Jochenstein 10, ✆ 1802, I-II
Gh Fesl, Kohlbachmühle 1 (2.5 km outside town), ✆ 320, II-III
⛺ Camping Kohlbachmühle, ✆ 320

Engelhartszell R

Postal code: 4090; Telephone area code: 07717
ℹ Tourismusverband, ✆ 8245 (Sparkasse)
Pz Jausenstation "Zum Jochenstein", Maierhof 17, ✆ 8123, I
H „Zum Goldenen Schiff", Nibelungenstr. 2, ✆ 8009, III-IV
Gh Mühlböck, Marktstr. 35, ✆ 8013, II
Gh Ronthalerhof, Ronthal 2 (3.5 km south east), ✆ 8083, III
Gh Zum Haugstein, Stadl 8, ✆ 7318
Pz Hufschmiede, Nibelungenstr. 11, ✆ 8059, II
Pz Donaublick, Sauwaldstr. 122, ✆ 8172, II
Pz Reiter, Siedlungsstr. 76, ✆ 8131, I
Pz Bernhard, Maierhof/Donau 24, ✆ 8070, I
PZ Hechinger, Stiftstr. 16, ✆ 8088, I
Pz Ecker, Maierhof 31, ✆ 8173, I, II
Pz Familie Landl, Maierhof 8, ✆ 7836, II
Bh Berndl, Stadl 13, ✆ 7136, I
Bh Huber, Nibelungenstr. 40, ✆ 8285, I
Bh Jager a. Bach, Flenkental 7, ✆ 7555, I
Radpension Hl. Antonius, Nibelungenstr. 68, ✆ 20049, II
⛺ Freibad-Camping, ✆ 0664/8708787, Apr.-Okt.

Engelszell R

Gh Engelszeller Stüberl, Engelszell 20, ✆ 8037

Kramesau L

Gh Luger, Kramesau 4, ✆ 07285/507, II

Niederranna L

Postal code: 4085; Telephone area code: 07285
ℹ Marktgemeindeamt Hofkirchen, ✆ 255
Pz Knogler, Nr 31, ✆ 562, I-II
Gh Draxler, Nr 3, ✆ 511, II-III
Pz Leitner, Nr 46, ✆ 519, II
Pz Ecker, Nr. 60, ✆ 516, I
Pz Berger, Nr 7, ✆ 512, I
Gh Ratzenböck, Freizell (3 km downriver), ✆ 226, I
P Pumberger, Au 1 (across from Schlögen), ✆ 6317, II
⛺ Zeltplatz Ratzenböck, Freizell, ✆ 226

Marsbach

Postal code: 4085; Telephone area code: 07285
ℹ Marktgemeindeamt Hofkirchen, ✆ 255
H Falkner, Nr. 2, ✆ 223, V-VI
Gh Pühringer, Nr. 4, ✆ 293, II-III

Dorf

Postal code: 4133; Telephone area code: 07286
Bh Schlagnitweit, Dorf 10 (pick up service), ✆ 7994 or 81161, II
Bh Wögerbauer, Dorf 9, ✆ (8)312, I-II

Niederkappel L

Postal code: 4133; Telephone area code: 07286
ℹ Gemeindeamt, Niederk. 48, ✆ 8555-0
Gh Leitenbauer, Nr. 32, ✆ 8594, III

Grafenau

Gh Gierlinger, Grafenau 17, ✆ 7213, II
Bh Bumberger, Grafenau 3, ✆ 7633, II

Wesenufer R

Postal code: 4085; Telephone area code: 07718
ℹ Tourismusverband Waldkirchen-Wesenufer, 7255
Gh Schütz, Wesenufer 17, ✆ 7208, III
Gh Zum Schiffmeister, Wesenufer 19, ✆ 7220, I-II
Gh Hofer, Ratzling 13, ✆ 7354, II
P Feiken, Wesenufer 65, ✆ 7506, II
Pz Donaubauer, Wesenufer 44, ✆ 7206, I
Bh Viehböck, Wesenufer 15, ✆ 7213, I
⛺ Nibelungen-Camping, Wesenufer 73, ✆ 7589, vom 1. April-30. Sept.

Au

Postal code: 4085; Telephone area code: 07285

Pz/ Zur Fährfrau, Au 1, 6317, II

Haibach-Schlögen R

Postal code: 4083; Telephone area code: 07279

Tourismusverband Haibach-Schlögen, 8235

Gh Pointner, Haibach 4 (pick up service), 8226, III

H Donauschlinge, 8212 od. 8240, III-IV

P Schlögen, 8241, III

Pz Knogler, Moos 2 (3,5 km south, pick up service), 8522, II

Pz Gaisbauer, Linetshub 6 (pick up service), 8245

Bh Niedernhager, Sieberstal 4 (pick up service), 8340, I-II

Bh Wolfartner, Linetshub 3 (pick up sservice), 8359, I-II

Bh Schönhuber, Haibach 61 (pick up service), 8237, I

Bh Pointner, Haibach 15 (pick up service), 8305

Bh Steinbock, Sieberstal 2, (pick up service), 8242

Bh Straßl, Linetshub 2, 8358

Terrassencamping Donauschlinge, 8241, April 1st - Okt 15th

Inzell R

Postal code: 4083; Telephone area code: 07279

Gh Steindl „Zum Hl. Nikolaus", Inzell 6, 8328

P Reisinger E., Inzell 9, 8581, I-II

Bh Reisinger G., Inzell 2, 8715, I-II

Pz Pointner, Inzell 10, 8297, I-II

Camping Steindl, Inzell 6, 8328

Obermühl L

Postal code: 4131; Telephone area code: 07286

Tourismusverband Obermühl-Kirchberg, 7216

Gh Aumüller, Obermühl 13, 7216, II

Gh Bruckwirt, Graben 6, 8321, II-III

Gh Gierlinger, Grafenau 17, 7213, II

Bh Grafenauer Hof, Grafenau 3, 7633, II

Haizing R

Postal code: 4081; Telephone area code: 07273

Pz Martina u. Alois Wolkerstorfer, Haizing 23, 7397

Aschach a.d. Donau R

Postal code: 4082; Telephone area code: 07273

Zimmervermittlung, 7000 o. 6355-13

Gh Aschacher Hof, Ritzbergerstr. 7, 6360, III

Gh Kaiserhof, Kaiserau 1, 6221-0 o. 8775, II-III

Gh Zur Sonne, Kurzwernhartpl. 5, 6308, III

Gh Fischerhof, Oberlandshaag 10, 07233/7412, II-III

Gh Zum Goldenen Hirschen, Reitingerstr. 13, 6247, III

P Köpplmayr, Stiftstr. 1, 6349, III

Pz Kaiser, Himmelreich 6, 8753, I

Pz Rammelmüller, Siernerstr. 72, 8982, I

Pz Ehrengruber, Oberlandshaag 102, I-II

Pz Jonach, Oberlandshaag 58, 7480, I-II

Hartkirchen:

Gh Stadler, Kirchenpl 12, 6367

Pz Knogler, Schmiedstr. 6, 6454, II

Pz Hofer, Kapellenstr. 4, 8119, I-II

Bh Gruber, Vornholz 7, 6651, I

Oberlandshaag L

Postal code: 4101; Telephone area code: 07233

Gh Peterseil „Fischerhof", Nr.10, 7412, II

Pz Leirich, Nr. 58, 7480, I

Pz Ehrengruber, Nr. 102, 7506, I

Unterlandshaag:

Pz Pichler, Unterlandshaag 13, 7466, I

Pz König, Unterlandshaag 12, 7463, II

Feldkirchen an der Donau L

Postal code: 4101; Telephone area code: 07233

Tourismusinformation, Hauptstr. 1, 7190

H TOP-RAD-STOP Faustschlössl, Oberlandshaag 2, 7402

Gh Schloss Mühldorf, Mühldorf 1, 7241, II-III

Gh Danninger, Pesenbach 24, 7273, II

Gh Wögerer, Marktpl. 18, 7223

Pz Hummer, Bad Mühllacken 12, 6843, II

PZ Falkner, Oberlandshaag 103, 7521, II

Pz Sonnleitner, Bad Mühllacken 22, 6683, II

Pz Pichler, Unterlandshaag 13, 7466, I

Pz Lackner, Bad Mühllacken 60, 7281, I

Pz Mayer, Wolfsbach 52, 6787, I-II

Pz Ehrlinger, Wolfsbach 49, 6789, II

Pz Leitner, Weidet 7, 7516, II

Pz Kneidinger, Bad Mühllacken 13, 6844, I

Pz Kneidinger Martina, Schulstr. 8, 6758 o. 0664/3449110

Pz Petermüller, Bad Mühllacken 16, 6686, I-II

Pz Rothbauer, Audorfer Str. 14, 6733, I

Pz Luger, Im Feld 1, 6486, I

Pz Weissenberger Erika, Reicherlweg 1, 7695

Pz Zauner, Lauterbachstr. 2, 6331

Bh Radlbauernhaus, Bergheim 2, 6821, I

Bh König, Unterlandshaag 12, 7463, 20500, II

Bh Rabeder, Bad Mühlacken 18, 6681, I

Bh Hengstschläger, Oberndorf 14, 6671, I

Bh Schöppl, Bad Mühllacken 19, 6688, II

Campingplatz Puchner, Golfplatzstr. 21, near the lakes, 7268 od. 0664/4824900, Mai-Okt.

Goldwörth:

Pz Baumgartner, Ahornw. 19, 07234/82021, II

Pz Satzinger, Donaustr. 2, 07234/2801, I-II

Pz Übermasser, Goldwörther Str. 14, 07234/29172, I-II

Bergheim:

Gustl's Radlbauernhaus, Bergheim 4, 6821, I

Weidet

Postal code: 4101; Telephone area code: 07233

Pz Leitner, Weidet 16, 7516 o. 07234/82713, II

Campingplatz Gruber, Weidet 7 (near the lakes), 7268

Brandstatt R

Postal code: 4070; Telephone area code: 07272

Gh Dieplinger, Brandstatt 4+2, 2324, III

Gh Klingelmayer, Pupping 14, 2427, II

P Webinger, Brandstatt 1, 4279

Fischrest. Dannerbauer, Brandstatt 5, 2471

Eferding R

Postal code: 4070; Telephone area code: 07272
Tourismusverband, 5555-160
H Brummeier, Stadtplatz 31, 2462, V
Gh Zum Goldenen Kreuz, Schmiedstr. 29, 4247-48, II
Gh „Zum Stadtkrug", Stadtplatz 28, 6060, III

Ottensheim L

Postal code: 4100; Telephone area code: 07234
Marktgemeindeamt, 82255-0
H Donauhof, An der Fähre, 83818-0, III
Gh Rodlhof, Rodl 11, 83790, II, Camping allowed
Gh Schwarzer Adler, Marktpl. 19, 82224, III
Gh Zur Post, Linzer Str. 17, 82228, II
Pz Pumberger, Hanriederstr. 14, 82352, II
Pz Hemmelmayr, Sternstr. 9, 83031, I-II
Pz Pumberger, Jörgerstr.7, 82123, II
Pz Brem, Jörgerstr. 6, 84673, II
Pz Brandstätter, Ludlg. 5, 83816, II
Pz Kerschbaummeyr, Birkenweg 5 (pick up service), 84291, II
Pz Mayerhofer, Feldstr. 9, 84687, II
Pz Ruttmann, Hambergstr. 15, 82066, I-II
Pz Schwendtner, Linzer Str. 34, 83115, II
Pz Stallinger, Jungbauernhügel 7, 85063, II
Pz Wolfsteiner, Am Teichfeld 10, 84020, II
Gh Bergmayr, Walding Nr. 9, 82308, III
Camping Hofmühle, Höflein 20 (1.5 km west), 82418

Wilhering L

Postal code: 4073; Telephone area code: 07226
Gemeindeamt, 2255
Gh „Zur Alm", Linzer Str. 32, 2212, III
Gh „Zur Post", Höfer Str. 5, 2214
Gh Bründl, Fallerstr. 28, 2186
Bründl, Fallerstr. 28, 2186

Puchenau L

Postal code: 4040; Telephone area code: 0732
„Zur Hammerschmiede", 22 10 46, II
Pz Kepplinger, Großambergstr. 17, 22 17 59
Pz Bamminger, Schlossholzweg 17, 22 16 86

Linz R

Postal code: 4020; Telephone area code: 070
Tourist-Information, Hauptpl. 1, 7070-1777
Internet: www.linz.at
H Schillerpark, Am Schillerpl., 6950, VI
H City-Hotel, Schillerstr. 52, 652622, VI
H Dom Hotel, Baumbacherstr. 17, 778441, V, VI
H Ebelsberger Hof, Wiener Str. 485, 311733, IV, V
H Novotel, Wankmüllerhofstr. 37, 347281-0, V
H Prielmayerhof, Weißenwolffstr. 33, 7741310, V
H Courtyard by Marriott, Europapl. 2, 6959-0, VI
H Spitzhotel, Fiedlerstr. 6, 7364410, VI
H Steigenberger Maxx, Am Winterhafen 13, 7899-0, V
H Arcotel Nike, Untere Donaulände 9, 7626-0, V, VI
H Drei Mohren, Promenade 17, 772626, V-VI
H Zur Lokomotive, Weingartshofstr. 40 (near train station), 654554/55, IV
H Nibelungenhof, Scharitzerstr. 7 (near train station), 656047, V
H Wolfinger, Hauptplatz 19, 7732910, IV-V
H Kolping, Gesellenhausstr. 5, 661690, IV
H Goldener Adler, Hauptstr. 56, Linz-Urfahr, 731147, IV
H Donautal, Obere Donaulände 105 (vor Linz), 795566, III-IV
Gh Goldener Anker, Hofgasse 5, 771088, III-IV
H Sommerhaus, Julius-Raab-Str. 10 (Katzbach), 2457-376, IV
H Ibis, Kärntnerstr. 18-20(near train station), 69401, IV-V
H Zum Schwarzen Bären, Herrenstr. 9-11, 772477-0, IV-V
H Mühlviertlerhof, Graben 24, 772268, IV
H Haselgraben Stuben, Leonfeldnerstr. 322, 254148, III
H Landgraf, Hauptstr. 12, 700711, III
H Kleinmünchen, Wiener Str. 406, 301313, III-IV
H Wienerwald, Freinbergstr. 18, 777881, II
H Nöserlgut, Landwiedstr. 69, 683326, III
Gh Wilder Mann, Goethestr. 14 (near train station), 656078, III
Gh Goldenes Dachl, Hafnerstr. 27, 775897, II
Gh Rothmayr, St. Margarethen 17 (vor Linz), 774849, III
St. Magdalena, das Bildungszentrum, Schatzweg 177, 253041-0, II
Jugendgästehaus, Stanglhofweg 3, 66 44 34
Landesjugendherberge Lentia 2000, Blütenstr. 23, Linz-Urfahr, 73 70 78
Jutel Linz, Kapuzinerstr. 14, 778777, I
Campingplatz Pichlinger See, Wiener Str. 937, 30 53 14

Steyregg L

Postal code: 4221; Telephone area code: 0732
Stadtgemeindeamt, 640155
H Weißenwolff, Weißenwolffstr.4, 64 00 39-0, IV
P Würzburger, Stadtpl. 20, 640118, II
Pz Buchberger, Weih-Leite 4, 641671, I
Pz Haneder, Dörfl 17, 640724, II
Pz Mayr-Preslmayr, Plesching 1, 244393, II

Windegg:

Pz Osterkorn, Nr. 23, 640197, II
Pz Reisinger, Nr. 24, 641766, II
Pz Käferböck, Nr. 25, 640798, II
Campingplatz Pleschinger See, 247870

Luftenberg-Abwinden L

Postal code: 4222; Telephone area code: 07237
Mostschenke Reiter, Abwinden-Dorf 3, 2455, II
P Bauer in Hof, Abwinden-Dorf 3, 2455-0
Pz Resanka, Abwinden-Dorf 227, 4530, I, II
Pz Janusko, Steining, Fischerweg 9, 2689, I, II

St. Georgen a. d. Gusen L

Postal code: 4222; Telephone area code: 07237
Marktgemeinde, Marktpl. 2, 2255-0
P Kogler, Linzer Str. 28, 2214
P Kram, Wimminger Str. 8, 3302
P Zum Holzwurm, Mauthausener Str. 4, 63131

Langenstein L

Postal code: 4222; Telephone area code: 07237

Rasthaus Langenstein Ost, Hauptstr. 13, ☎ 5251, II

Pz Bindreiter, Hauptstr. 42, ☎ 2212

Pz Primetzhofer, Hackstiegelweg 2, ☎ 4345

Mauthausen L

Postal code: 4310; Telephone area code: 07238

Fremdenverkehrsverband, ☎ 2243

Gh Donauhof, Promenade 30, ☎ 2183, III

P Weindlhof, Kirchenweg 12, ☎ 2641, II

H Mühlviertlerhof, Heindlkai 5, ☎ 2230, III

P Chinarestaurant Lin & Yin, Heindlkai 11, ☎ 2180, III

Gh Zur Traube, Heindlkai 15, ☎ 2023-0, III

Gh Neuhofer, Hinterbergstr. 42 (Bahnhof), ☎ 2245, II

Gh Machlandblick, Oberzirking 4, ☎ 2516, II

Gh Maly, Machlandstr. 1, ☎ 2249, II

Pz Auböck, Haid 3, ☎ 4410, I

Pz Windner, Haid 9, ☎ 2541, I

Pz Freudenthaler, Nelkenweg 3, ☎ 4811, I

Pz Pirklbauer, Ufer-Str. 23, ☎ 4543, I

Pz Großbauer, Albern 23, ☎ 3555, I

Bh Peterseil, Reiferdorf 11, ☎ 2864, I

Bh Walenta, Hinterbergstr. 33, ☎ 2308

Au a. d. Donau L

Postal code: 4331; Telephone area code: 07262

Gh Jägerwirt, Oberer Markt 24, ☎ 58514, III

Gh Stadler, Marktstr. 19, ☎ 58591, I-II

Gh Pühringer, Marktstr. 42, ☎ 58513, II

Pz Froschauer, Marktstr. 28, ☎ 58509, I-II

Pz Waldmann, Gartenweg 3, ☎ 58031

Campinganlage, Hafenstr., ☎ 53090

Naarn L

Postal code: 4331; Telephone area code: 07262

Gemeindeamt, ☎ 58255

Gh Zur Traube, Pergerstr. 4, ☎ 58274, II

Pz Landhaus Hackner, Bäckerfeld 2, ☎ 53806, II

Ruprechtshofen:

Gh Fröschl, Nr. 6, ☎ 58288, I-II

Staffling:

Pz Kastner, Staffling 16, ☎ 57872, II

Asten R

Postal code: 4481; Telephone area code: 07224

Gh Reisinger, Zur Krone, Wienerstr. 6, ☎ 6122, II

Gh Stögmüller, Wienerstr. 13, ☎ 1976, II

Gh Födermayer, Wiener Str. 14, ☎ 6101, II

Astner Stubn, Bahnhofstr. 4, ☎ 6212

St. Florian R

Postal code: 4490; Telephone area code: 07224

Tourismusverband, ☎ 8955

Gh Zur Kanne, Marktpl. 7, ☎ 4288, III-IV

H Erzh. Franz Ferdinand, Marktpl. 13, ☎ 4254-0, IV

Gh Zur Grünen Traube, Tillysburg 14, ☎ 07223/3644, III

Pz Zum Goldenen Pflug, Speiserberg 3, ☎ 4226, II-III

Enns R

Postal code: 4470; Telephone area code: 07223

Tourismusverband, Hauptpl. 1, ☎ 82777

H Lauriacum, Wiener Str. 5-7, ☎ 82315-0, V

H Am Limes, Stadlg. 2b, ☎ 86401, III

H Zum Goldenen Schiff, Hauptpl. 23, ☎ 86086, IV

H/Gh Zum Schwarzen Bären, ☎ 82671

Gh Rosenhof, Bahnhofweg 16, ☎ 85317, III

Gh Binder, Enghagen 17, ☎ 85203, II

Gh Wurdinger, Vilma-Eckl-Pl. 5, ☎ 82866,III

Gh Ennser Pfandlstube, Mauthausnerstr. 37, ☎ 83875, III

Pz Leitner, Schulgraben 4, ☎ 82683 o. 82385-16, II

Pz Rittberger, Mauthausner Str. 11, ☎ 82532, II

Pz Berndl, Stiegengasse, ☎ 82278 oder 85366, II

Pz Lehner, Waldstr. 3, ☎ 83613, I

Ennsdorf-Pyburg: (Postal code: 4482)

Gh Stöckler, Wiener Str. 5, ☎ 82600, II

St. Pantaleon

Postal code: 4303; Telephone area code: 07435

Gh Winklehner, ☎ 7584

Wallsee-Sindelburg R

Postal code: 3313; Telephone area code: 07433

Gemeindeamt Wallsee-Sindelburg, ☎ 2216

Gh Grünling, Wallsee 7, ☎ 2231, II

Gh Sengstbratl, Wallsee 21, ☎ 2203, II

Gh Hehenberger, Sindelburg 29, ☎ 2207, III

Gh Wallseerhof, Schulstr. 49, ☎ 2223, II

Pz Hickersberger, am Donau-Altarm Wallsee, ☎ 2550, II

Pz Feirer, Wallsee 192, ☎ 2569, II

Pz Baumgartner Gertrude, Ufer 7, ☎ 2688, II

Pz Neulinger, Marktpl., ☎ 2238, II

Pz Korner, Ufer 20, ☎ 2843, I

Pz Zur Waldermühle, 2km after Wallsee, ☎ 2786

Mostheuriger Zeillinger, Hofing 93, ☎ 2383

Lampersberger, Witzmannsdorf 45, ☎ 07478/434

Sommerau:

Bh Waser, Sommerau 20, ☎ 2786, I

Mitterkirchen L

Postal code: 4343; Telephone area code: 07269

Marktgemeindeamt, ☎ 8255-0

Gh Häuserer, Mitterkirchen 10, ☎ 8325, II

Bh Moser, Mitterkirchen 27, ☎ 8311, II

Bh Gusenbauer, Hofstetten1, ☎ 7838, II

Bh Langeder, Mitterk. 26, ☎ 83130, II

Camping Mairhofer, beim Weisching lake, ☎ 8258

Wörth:

Pz Heiml, Wörth 13, ☎ 8250, I

Hörstorf:

Gh Stadlbauer, Hörstorf 4, ☎ 8322, II

Pz Stemmer, Hörstorf 6, ☎ 8187, I-II

Pz Frei, Hörstorf 43, ☎ 8219

Hütting:

Bh Buhri, Hütting 33, ☎ 8314, II

Baumgartenberg

Postal code: 4342; Telephone area code: 07269

Marktgemeindeamt Baumgartenberg, ☎ 2550

Gh Zum Klosterwirt, Nr. 3, ☎ 210

Mettensdorf L

Marktgemeindeamt Baumgartenberg, ☎ 2550

Gh Lettner, Untermühle, Mettensdorf 1, ✆ 281, I-II
Bh Lettner, Schneckenreitsberg 1 (near Klam), ✆ 7195, I
Radler-Camping Lettner, Mettensdorf 1, ✆ 281

Klam L

Postal code: 4352; Telephone area code: 07269
Gemeindeamt, Klam 43, ✆ 7255
Gh Fraundorfer, Klam 1, ✆ 7206, II
Pz Lettner, Klam 10, ✆ 7238, II

Ardagger Markt R

Postal code: 3321; Telephone area code: 07479
Gemeindeamt, ✆ 7312-0
Gh Zum Schatzkastl, Markt 120, ✆ 7500, III
Gh Zur Donaubrücke, Tiefenbach 49, ✆ 6119, III
Pz Pressl, Markt 29, ✆ 7445, II
Pz Kneissl, Markt 3, ✆ 6182, II

Stift Ardagger:

Gh Stiftstaverne, Nr. 3, ✆ 6565, IV
Pz Brandstetter, Nr. 7, ✆ 7393, I

Grein a. d. Donau L

Postal code: 4360; Telephone area code: 07268
Tourismusverband, ✆ 7055
Gh Zur Traube, Greinburgstr. 6, ✆ 312, III
H Goldenes Kreuz, Stadtpl. 8, ✆ 316, IV
Gh Binderalm, Herdmann 4 (pick up service), ✆ 434, III
P Faltinger, Kaiser-Fried.-Str. 1, ✆ 374, II
P Temper, Jubiläumsstr. 36, ✆ 209, I-II
Pz Hametner, Brucknerstr. 19, ✆ 386, I-II
Pz Kloibhofer, Brucknerstr. 1, ✆ 378, II
Pz Eder, Jubiläumsstr. 38, ✆ 410, I-II
Pz Prinz, Brucknerstr. 11, ✆ 7918, II
P Martha, Hauptstr.12, ✆ 345, II-III
P Regina, Klosterg. 4, ✆ 275, II
P Tirol, Spitzfeldstr. 16, ✆ 256, II
Pz Lumesberger, Großgraben 13, ✆ 7256, II
Pz Schlossgangl, Großgraben 3, ✆ 7308, II
Pz Pauckner, Großgraben 1, ✆ 7550, II
Pz Oberzaucher, Fadingerstr. 11, ✆ 495, I
Bh Wurzergut, Herdmann 10 (pick up service), ✆ 456, II
Campingplatz beim Hafen, ✆ 21230, 1. Mai bis 31. Okt.

St. Nikola L

Postal code: 4381; Postal code: Telephone area code: 07268
Gemeindeamt, ✆ 8155
H Zur Post, Nr. 31 , ✆ 8140-0, III
Bh Wörthbauer, Struden 26, ✆ 8025, I

Sarmingstein

P Strudengauhof, Sarmingstein 13, ✆ 8302, II
P Monika, Sarmingstein 11, ✆ 8232
P Schiffmeisterhaus, Sarmingstein 7, ✆ 8294

Hössgang-Freyenstein R

Postal code: 3323; Telephone area code: 07471
Gh „Zur Ruine Freyenstein", Nr. 8, ✆ 2272, II

Willersbach-Hengstberg

Pz Wiesinger, Hengstberg 11, ✆ 07412/53739, II

Weins-Isperdorf L

Postal code: 3683; Telephone area code: 07414
Gh Donaublick, Isperdf. 3, ✆ 7228
Gh „Zur Bahn", Weins 36, ✆ 203, III

Ybbs a. d. Donau R

Postal code: 3370; Telephone area code: 07412
Tourist Information, ✆ 55233
Gh „Zum Braunen Hirschen", Rathausg. 9, ✆ 52245, III
Gh Lindenhof, Stauwerkstr. 45, ✆ 53003, III
Gh Fischerhaus, Stauwerkstr. 71, ✆ 56435, II-III
Gh Zur Blauen Weintraube, Herreng. 8, ✆ 52498
H Babenbergerhof, Wiener Str. 10, ✆ 54334, IV
Hg Villa Vogelsang, Am Vogelsang, ✆ 54681, III-IV
Gh „Zur Stadt Linz", Stauwerkstr. 29, ✆ 52445, II
Gh „Zum Goldenen Adler", Kircheng. 15, ✆ 52232, II
Pz Weber, Trewaldstr. 13, ✆ 58957, I
Pz Fleischerei Moser, Stauwerkstr. 3, ✆ 52434, II
Bh Glöcklhof, Bergingstr. 10, ✆ 52823, II
Gh Pizzeria Giovanni, Schiffmeisterpl. 6, ✆ 56980
Gh „Florianistubn", Sarling 10a, ✆ 56220, II
Camping-Gasthaus Zur Alm, Oberegging 32 (4 km south), ✆ 52213-0

Säusenstein:

Gh Donaublick, Nr. 42, ✆ 55877, II
Bh Hell, Diedersdorf 3, ✆ 38372, I-II
Bh Zehetgruber, Diedersdorf 6, ✆ 55836, I

Persenbeug-Gottsdorf L

Postal code: 3680; Telephone area code: 07412
Marktgemeindeamt,Rathauspl. 1 ✆ 52206
Gh Zum Weißen Lamm, Hauptstr. 16, ✆ 58930, III
Pz Hochstöger, Pappelstr. 3, ✆ 53515, II
Pz Slawitscheck, Nibelungenstr. 62, ✆ 58955, I-II

Hagsdorf:

Pz Leeb, Hagsdorf 19, ✆ 54718, II

Gottsdorf-Metzling:

Gh Zum Kirchenwirt, Donaustr. 31, ✆ 52772, II
Gh Zum goldenen Groschen, Wachaustr. 57, ✆ 52443, I-II
Gh Donaurast Nimführ, Wachaustr. 28, ✆ 52438, IV
Pz Donaublick, Wachaustr. 91, ✆ 52254, II
Pz Köck, Donaustr. 34, ✆ 52843, I
Pz Pressl, Donaustr. 38, ✆ 53353, I

Loja:

Pz Köfinger, Wachaustr. 101, ✆ 54212, I

Priel

P Porranzl, Harland 263, ✆ 55484

Granz L

Pz Familie Nagl, Granz 36, ✆ 6935

Marbach L

Postal code: 3671; Telephone area code: 07413
Fremdenverkehrsstelle, ✆ 7045
H Nibelungenhof, Donau 10-11, ✆ 227, III
H Wachauerhof, Nr. 43, ✆ 7035, IV-V
Gh Zur schönen Wienerin, Nr. 48, ✆ 7077, III
Konditorei Braun, Wachaustr. 49, ✆ 203, II
Pz Hofmann, Donauuferstr. 44, ✆ 7044, II
Pz Loidhold, Marbach 19, ✆ 343
Camping Marbach, ✆ 0664/5518815

Krummnussbaum a.d. Dub L

Postal code: 3671; Telephone area code: 07413

Gh Zum Alten Richter, Nr. 6, ✆ 355, II

Pz Zeilinger, Nr. 126, ✆ 7610, II

Maria Taferl L

Postal code: 3672; Telephone area code: 07413

ℹ Marktgemeinde, ✆ 7040

H Krone, Nr. 24, ✆ 6355, V (pick up service)

H Kaiserhof, ✆ 6355, V (pick up service)

P Krone Kaiserhof, ✆ 6355, III-IV (pick up service)

H Rose, Nr. 20, ✆ 304, IV-V (pick up service)

H Zum Guten Hirten, Nr. 23, ✆ 377, III (pick up service)

P Traube, Nr. 23, ✆ 377, II (pick up service)

Gh Goldener Löwe, Hauptstr. 6, ✆ 340, II-III (pick up service)

Gh Dobler, Nr. 10, ✆ 221, II

Gh Gressl, Obererla 25, ✆ 372, II

P Regina, Nr. 42, ✆ 266, II (pick up service)

Café Maria Theresia, Maria T. 9, ✆ 7033, II (pick up service)

P Schüller, Nr. 5, ✆ 303, II (pick up service)

Pz Hinterleitner, Maria Taferl 28, ✆ 7839, I

Pz Rameder-Hackl, Maria Taferl 25, ✆ 7039, I

P Weiss, Obererla 49, ✆ 388, II, (pick up service)

Bh Iber, Untererla 8, ✆ 267, I-II, (pick up service)

Thalheim:

Pz Reisinger, Unterthalheim 34, ✆ 66544, I-II

Gh Blumentalhof, Ziegelstadl 3, ✆ 8289, I-II

Artstetten-Pöbring L

Postal code: 3661; Telephone area code: 07413

ℹ Gemeindeamt, Artstetten 8, ✆ 8235

H Schlossgasthof, Nr. 12, ✆ 8303, III

Gh Landstetter, ✆ 8303

Gh Kloihofer, ✆ 8301

Leiben L

Postal code: 3652; Telephone area code: 02752

ℹ Marktgemeinde, ✆ 71287

Gh Traube, Leiben 7, ✆ 71252, II

Pz Kaufmann, ✆ 72352, I

Krummnussbaum R

Postal code: 3375; Telephone area code: 02757

ℹ Gemeindeamt, ✆ 2403

Gh Landgasthof Gutlederer, Haupstr. 26, ✆ 8463

Gh Zur Schlosstaverne, Hauptstr. 36, ✆ 2331

P Jürgen, Bahnhofstr. 5, ✆ 7304, III

P Lechner, Hauptstr. 51, ✆ 7793, I

Kleinpöchlarn L

Postal code: 3660; Telephone area code: 07413

Gh Zum Dorfwirt, Marktpl. 2, ✆ 8420, II

Gh Schauer-Lahmer, Kremser Str. 6, ✆ 8224, II

Gh Zur Fähre, Zur Fähre 6, ✆ 8361, II

P Kammerer, Linzerstr. 8, ✆ 8297, II

⛺ Campingplatz Klein-Pöchlarn, ✆ 8300-10

Ebersdorf L

Postal code: 3652; Telephone area code: 02752

Gh Düregger, Ebersdorf 4, ✆ 71415, III

Gh Gruber, Lehen 6, ✆ 71225, II

Weitenegg:

Gh Gruber, Weitenegg 10, ✆ 71445, II-III

Pöchlarn R

Postal code: 3380; Telephone area code: 02757

ℹ Fremdenverkehrsstelle, ✆ 2310-11

H Moser, Bahnhofpl. 3, ✆ 2448,III-IV

Gh Futtertrögl, Kirchenpl. 2, ✆ 2395, III

Gh Scheichelbauer, Wiener Str. 15, ✆ 2367, II

P „Haus Barbara", Wiener Str. 4, ✆ 2321, II

Pz Kronawetter, Bahnstraße 13, ✆ 4526, I

Pz Schmoll, Rüdigerstr. 28, ✆ 8490, II

Pz Waldbauer, Wiener Str. 36, ✆ 8553 oder 7395, II (July/August only)

⛺ Tent or in the Rudervereinshaus

⛺ Naturfreunde Bootshaus, max. 10 Pers., Tent and emergency camp (Showers, WC)

Melk R

Postal code: 3390; Telephone area code: 02752

ℹ Tourist Information, ✆ 52307-410

H „Zur Post", Linzerstr. 1, ✆ 52345, IV-V

H Stadt Melk, Hauptpl. 1, ✆ 52547, IV-V

H Fürst, Rathauspl. 3, ✆ 52343, IV

H Wachau, Wachberg 157, ✆ 52531-13, III-IV

Café Central, Hauptpl. 10, ✆ 52278, IV-V

Gh Goldener Stern, Sterng. 17, ✆ 52214, II

H Wachauerhof, Wiener Str. 30, ✆ 52235, IV

Gh Goldener Hirsch, Rathauspl. 13, ✆ 52257, II-III

Gh Weißes Lamm, Linzer Str. 7, ✆ 54085, II

Pz Horak, Wiener Str. 82, ✆ 50101, II

P Stiftsblick, Herberge Zum Göttlichen Erlöser, Abt-Karl-Str. 13, ✆ 52346

Jugendherberge, Abt-Karl-Str. 42, ✆ 52681, von 1. April-17. Okt.

⛺ Melker Fährhaus, ✆ 53291

⛺ Camping Kolomaniau

Emmersdorf L

Postal code: 3644; Telephone area code: 02752

ℹ Gemeindeamt, ✆ 71469.

H Donauhof, Nr. 40, ✆ 71777-0, V-VI

Gh Zum Schwarzen Bären, Nr. 7, ✆ 71249, IV-V

Gh Zu den drei Linden, Schallemmersdorf 10, ✆ 71893, II-III

Pz Frank, Hain 32, ✆ 71826, I

P Fleischmann, Nr. 92, ✆ 71972, II

P Hollerer, Birkeng. 9, ✆ 71608, II

P Kremser, Rote-Kreuz-Str. 9, ✆ 71878, II

P Sundl, Rote-Kreuz-Str. 18, ✆ 71419, I-II

Pz Lindenhofer, Hofamt 22, ✆ 71482, II

Bh Schwalbenhof, Grimsing 7, ✆ 72114, I-II

Bh Pemmer, Hofamt 24, ✆ 71291, II

Luberegg:

H Landhotel Wachau, Luberegg 20, ✆ 72572, V

St. Georgen:

Landhotel Wachau, Luberegg 20, ✆ 72572, IV

P Brunner, Hain 28, ✆ 71767, II

Gh Donaufelsen, Nr. 7, ✆ 71431, II

Pz Wintesperger, Nr. 4, ✆ 71726, II

Donaucamping, 71707, 71469

Schönbühel R

Postal code: 3392; Telephone area code: 02752

Gemeindeamt, 8619

Gh Stumpfer, Nr. 7, 8510, II

Pz Miedler, Nr. 81, 8421, I

Pz Handler, Nr. 120, 8580, II

Camping Stumpfer, Nr. 7, 8510

Berging:

Pz Krammel, Nr. 16, 8796, II

Aggsbach-Dorf R

Postal code: 3642; Telephone area code: 02753

Gemeindeamt, 8269 oder 8006

H Donauterrasse, Nr. 19, 8221, III

Gh Zur Kartause, Nr. 38, 8243, II-III

Gh Pension Domingo, Nr. 129, 8353, III

P Haidn, Nr. 100, 8277, II

Pz Reisinger, Nr. 20, 8372, II

Aggstein:

Bh Kienesberger, Nr. 8, 8455, II

Pz Ringseis, Nr. 21, 8428, II

Herberge Ruine Aggstein, (April-Okt), 8228,

Aggsbach-Markt L

Postal code: 3641; Telephone area code: 02712

Gemeindeamt, 214

Gh „Zum Kranz", Nr. 161, 210, II-III

P Angela, Nr.90, 541, I

P Smaragd, Nr. 86, 60440

P Franziska, Nr. 132, 371, I

P Donaublick, Nr. 139, 225, I-II

P Imme, Nr. 136, 548, I-II

P Mariandl, Nr. 128, 716, I-II

P Waldesruhe, Nr.118, 204, II

P Anna, Nr. 24, 253, I-II

P Loidol, Nr. 114, 387, I-II

Fw Haus Schleinkhof, Nr. 55, 349

Fw Alte Post, Nr. 9, 0664/1630861

Groisbach

Postal code: 3641; Telephone area code: 02712

Gemeindeamt Aggsbach, 214

P Prankl, Nr. 33, 552, I

P Rehberger, Nr. 22, 713, I

Pz Weingut Herlinde, Nr. 30, 551, I-II

P Wilhelm, Nr. 20, 557, II

Willendorf L

Postal code: 3641; Telephone area code: 02712

Gemeindeamt Aggsbach, 214

Gh Steinbrunner, Nr. 36, 290, II

P Schrutz, Nr. 63, 556, I-II

Fw Löwenhof, Nr. 30, 781 o. 01/4896431

Spitz a. d. Donau L

Postal code: 3620; Telephone area code: 02713

Zimmernachweis, 2363

H Mariandl, Kremser Str. 2, 2311, III-V

H Wachauerhof, Hauptstr. 15, 2303, III-IV

H Weinhotel Wachau, Ottenschlägerstr. 30, 2254, III-IV

H Goldenes Schiff, Mitterg. 5, 2326, III-IV

Gh Winzerkeller, Kirchenpl. 3, 2302, III

Gh Prankl, Hinterhaus 16, 2323, III-V

Gh Zur Ruine Hinterhaus, Hinterhaus 8, 2831, III-IV

Hg Winzerin, Am Hinterweg 11, 2938, III-IV

Hg Romantikhof Burkhardt, Kremser Str. 19, 2356, IV

Hg Ulrike, Rote Torg. 15, 2654, III

Hg Weinberghof, Am Hinterweg 17, 2939, IV-V

P Café Bruckner, Hauptstr. 9, 2329, II-III

P Donaublick, Schopperpl. 3, 2552, III

P „Haus Oestreicher", Hauptstr. 26, 2317, III

P 1000-Eimer-Berg, Marktstr. 3, 2334, III

Pz Gritsch, Kirchensteig 1, 2743, II

Pz Geppner, In der Spitz 1b, 2340, II-III

Pz Kausel, Am Hinterweg 10, 2514, II

Pz Leberzipf, Laaben-Heidg. 2, 2553, II

Pz Donaubaum, M. u. A., In der Spitz 3, 2644, II-III

Pz Donabaum Elfriede, In der Spitz 3, 72912, II

Pz Bracher, Marstal 7, 72939, II

Pz Datzinger, Rote Torg. 13a, 2493, II

Pz Donabaum J., Laaben 15, 2488, II

Pz Gritsch Ruinenblick, Kirchensteig 1, 2060, II

Pz Eibl, Mieslingtal 3, 2906, II

Pz Gebetsberger, Obere G. 12, 2660, II

Pz Gritsch R., Radlbach 11, 2208, II

Pz Hofstätter, Quitten 2, 2614, II

Pz Kobald, Mieslingtal 2, 2270, II

Pz König, Teichbach 3, 2135, I

Pz Kummer, In der Spitz 1a, 2154, I

Pz Machhörndl, Gärtnerweg 4, 2400, II

Pz Martin, Ottenschläger Str. 34, 2312, II

Pz Nothnagl, Radlbach 7, 2612, II

Pz Schütz, Schwallenbach 31, 2174, II

Pz Rixinger, Gut am Steg 8, 2304, II-III

Pz Stummvoll, Mieslingtal 26, 2582, II

Pz Will, Mieslingtal 26, 2919, II

Mühldorf L

Postal code: 3622; Telephone area code: 02713

Gemeindeamt, 8230

H Burg Oberranna, Oberranna 1, 8221, V-VI

Gh Schwarzer Adler, Nr. 15, 8203, II

Gh Weißes Rößl, Nr. 8, 8257, II-III

Gh Vorspannhof, Nr. 45, 8202, II

Gh Munk, Elsarn 12, 8206, I-II

Arnsdorf R

Postal code: 3621; Telephone area code: 02714

Gh Zur Wachau, Mitterarnsdorf 55, 8217, III

Gh Wurzberger, Oberarnsdorf 7, 8439, II

Pz Wessner, Oberarnsdorf 61, 8480, I-II

Pz Fuchsbauer, Hofarnsdorf 20, 8358, I-II

Pz Hick, Oberarnsdorf 58, 8214, II

P Hubmaier, Hofarnsdorf 26, 8448, II-III

P Pammer, Bacharnsdorf 18, 6545, II

Pz Wintner, Oberarnsdorf 66, 8364, I

Pz König, Oberarnsdorf 35, 8471, II

Pz Scharner, Bacharnsdorf 5, 6590, II

Wösendorf L

Postal code: 3610; Telephone area code: 02715

Pz Gruber, Nr. 50, ☎ 21634, II

Pz Lengsteiner, Nr. 53, ☎ 2224, II-III

Pz Machherndl, Nr. 105, ☎ 2402, II, III

Pz Wagner, Nr. 90, ☎ 2336, II

Pz Geith, Prof.-Gruberg. 35, ☎ 2356, I

Pz Fellner, Bachg. 5, ☎ 2698, II

Pz Wangler, Nr. 65, ☎ 2337, I, II

Weißenkirchen L

Postal code: 3610; Telephone area code: 02715

i Zimmernachweis, ☎ 2600

Hg Mandl, Nr. 298, ☎ 2353, IV-V

Gh Donauwirt, Wachaustr. 47, ☎ 2247, IV

Gh Zum Kirchenwirt, Kremser Str. 17, ☎ 2332, IV-V

Gh Achleitenstube, Weißenkirchen 5, ☎ 2540, II-III

Gh Weiße Rose, Weißenkirchen 24, ☎ 2371

P Raffelsbergerhof, Nr. 54, ☎ 2201, V-VI

P Heller, Nr. 14, ☎ 2221, II-III

P Schmelz, Nr. 151, ☎ 2272, II

P Meyer, Nr. 20, ☎ 2256, III

P Melitta, Kremser Str. 9, ☎ 2410, III

Pz Bernhard, Nr. 158, ☎ 2827, II

Pz Denk, Bachstr. 74, ☎ 2365, III

Pz Lehensteiner, Nr. 7, ☎ 2284, II-III

Pz Pomassl, Weißenkirchen 175, ☎ 02711/286, II

Pz Punz, Weißenkirchen 332, ☎ 2334, II

Pz Schmelz, Weißenkirchen 79, ☎ 2388, II-III

Pz Schneeweiß, Salzstadl 233, ☎ 2587

Pz Schwaiger, Wösendorf 22, ☎ 2222, II

Pz Mang O., Nr. 40, ☎ 2297, II

Pz Böck, Nr. 109, ☎ 2708, II

Pz Graßl, Nr. 98, ☎ 2822, II

Pz Meder, Nr. 37, ☎ 2266

Pz Leitner, Nr. 55, ☎ 2320, II

Pz Mang, Nr. 340, ☎ 2239, III

Pz Langmayr, Nr. 307, ☎ 2464, II

Pz Mang R., Nr. 299, ☎ 2236, n. V.

Pz Mandl, Nr. 31, ☎ 2345, II

St. Michael

Postal code: 3610; Telephone area code: 02713

Pz Bayer, St. Michael 4, ☎ 2364, II

Joching

Postal code: 3610; Telephone area code: 02715

Pz Ebner, Joching 23, ☎ 2379, II

Pz Jamek, Joching 33, ☎ 2596, I

Pz Brustbauer, Joching 35, ☎ 02732/87300, n. V.

Rossatz R

Postal code: 3602; Telephone area code: 02714

i **Gemeindeamt**, ☎ 6217

Gh Subenhof, Nr. 16, ☎ 6252, II

Gh Naumann, Rossatz 21, ☎ 6297, II

Pz Baumgartner, Nr. 16, ☎ 6261, II

Pz Graf, Rührsdorf 35, ☎ 6434, I

Pz Hofer, Rührsdorf 3, ☎ 6322, I-II

Pz Hofstetter, Kienstock 11, ☎ 6406

Pz Steinmetz, Rossatz 53, ☎ 6307, II

Pz Sigl, Rossatz 84, ☎ 6301

Pz Schlager, Rossatz 172, ☎ 6362

PZ Schubert, Rossatzbach 28, ☎ 6250

Pz Weidinger, Rossatzbach 38, ☎ 6247

Rossatzbach, ☎ 317

Dürnstein L

Postal code: 3601; Telephone area code: 02711

i Gemeindeamt, ☎ 219, Info 200

H Schlosshotel, Dürnstein 2, ☎ 212, VI

H Richard Löwenherz, Dürnstein 8, ☎ 222, VI

H Gartenhotel und Weinhof, Dürnstein 122, ☎ 206, IV-V

Gh Sänger Blondel, Dürnstein 64, ☎ 253, IV-V

Gh Zur Bahn, Dürnstein 96, ☎ 357

P Böhmer, Dürnstein 22, ☎ 239, II-III

P Altes Rathaus, Dürnstein 26, ☎ 252, II-III

Pz Pritz, Dürnstein 111, ☎ 302, II

Pz Weixelbaum, Dürnstein 52, ☎ 422, II

Pz Wagner, Dürnstein 29, ☎ 265, I, II

Pz Pölz, Dürnstein 95, ☎ 405, II

Pz Stöger, Dürnstein 57, ☎ 396, III

Ober-Loiben:

P Stockinger, Ober-Loiben 40, ☎ 384, III-IV

Pz Granner, Ober-Loiben 19, ☎ 02732/71754, II

Pz Böhmer A., Ober-Loiben 39, ☎ 237, II,

Pz Böhmer G., Ober-Loiben 44, ☎ 237, I

Pz Blieberger, Ober-Loiben 12, ☎ 02732/81781, II

Pz Doppler, Ober-Loiben 47, ☎ 02732/73711, II

Pz Scheibenpflug, Ober-Loiben 20, ☎ 02732/76152, II

Pz Elfriede, Oberloiben 50, ☎ 02732/73429, II

Unterloiben:

Pz Edlinger, Nr. 6, ☎ 02732/70600, II

Pz Schmelz, Nr. 87, ☎ 02732/78159, II

Pz Scheibenpflug, Unterloiben 58, ☎ 02732/72411, I-II

Pz Stierschneider, Unterloiben 8, ☎ 02732/71422, I-II

Stein a.d. Donau L

Postal code: 3500; Telephone area code: 02732

i Austropa Verkehrsbüro, ☎ 82676

Gourmet-Hotel „Am Förthof", Förthofer Donaulände 8, ☎ 83345, V-VI

P Einzinger, Steiner Landstr. 82, ☎ 82316, II-III

Pz Stasny, Steiner Landstr. 22, ☎ 82843, II-III

Pz Stasny Ferdinand, Reisperbachtalstr. 50, ☎ 76193

Pz Fiala, Reisperbachtalstr. 24, ☎ 77581, I

Pz Petz, Förthofstr. 7, ☎ 81466, II

Krems L

Postal code: 3500; Telephone area code: 02732

i Austropa Verkehrsbüro, Undstr. 6, ☎ 82676

H Donauhotel Krems, E. Hofbauerstr. 19, ☎ 87565-0, V

H Alte Post, Ob. Landstr. 32, ☎ 82276, III-IV

Gh „Zum goldenen Engel", Wiener Str. 41, ☎ 82067, IV

P Weingut-Heuriger Zöhrer, Sandgrube 1, ☎ 83191, III-IV

Gh-Weinkellerei Jell, Hoher Markt 8-9, ☎ 82345, III

Gh „Unter den Linden", Schillerstr. 5, ☎ 82115, III-IV

Gh Zur Wiener Brücke, Wiener Str. 2, ☎ 82143, III

P „Schwarzes Rößl", Langenloiser Str. 7, ☎ 82192, IV

Gh Kaiser, Landersdorfer Str. 34, ✆ 83265, II-III
P Kolping-Gästehaus, Ringstr. 46, ✆ 83541, III
Gh „Kremsleithenhof", Kraxenweg 15, ✆ 85671, II-III
P Hietzgern, Unt. Landstraße 53, ✆ 76184, II
Pz Andre, Ob. Landstr. 24, ✆ 78900, II
Pz Pauser, Kaiser-Friedrich-Str. 12, ✆ 82668, I-II
Jugendherberge Krems, Ringstr. 77, ✆ 83452 o. 02622/64210, 1. Apr. bis 31. Okt.
Campingplatz, Parz 1489-13, ✆ 84455

Rohrendorf

Campingplatz Ettenauer, ✆ 02732/57323

Mautern R

Postal code: 3512; Telephone area code: 02732
Gemeindeamt, ✆ 83151
H Landhaus Bacher, Südtirolerpl. 2, ✆ 82937, VI
H Zum Grünen Baum, Rathauspl. 2, ✆ 82909-0, II-IV
Gh Siedler, Mauternbach 2, ✆ 82859, II
Gh Nosko, Südtirolerpl. 3, ✆ 85824, III
P Winzerhof Eder, Hundsheim 7, ✆ 74949, II
P Weinhof am Römerw., Mauternbach 11, ✆ 72848, II
P Severinhof, Frauenhofg. 12, ✆ 84643, II
Pz Kaiser, Grüner Weg 45, ✆ 87429, II
Pz Redl, Hundsheim 10, ✆ 72948, II
Pz Schweigl, Hundsheim 20, ✆ 85750, I

Furth bei Göttweig R

Postal code: 3511; Telephone area code: 02732
Gemeindeamt, Untere Landstr. 17, ✆ 84622
Gh Zur Goldenen Krone, Unt. Landstr. 1, ✆ 84666, III
Gh Schickh-Salzer, Avastr.2, ✆ 7218, IV
P Brandl, Rudolf-Müllauer-Str. 455, ✆ 84882, II
P Parzer, Oberfucha 55, ✆ 2414, II
Pz Lipp, Unt. Landstr. 373, ✆ 70946, I, II
Pz Leitner, Herreng. 37, ✆ 87278, I
Pz Fischer, Hofwiesenstr. 60, ✆ 73092, I
Pz Rohrhofer, Holzstr. 44, ✆ 70002, I
Pz Schwarzhapl-Ramler, Landwidweg 394, ✆ 73763, II (Transfers for bicycles)

Aigen:

Pz Fischer, Hofwiesenstr. 60, ✆ 73092, I

Kleinwien:

Gh Schickh-Salzer, Kleinwien 2, ✆ 7218, IV

Steinaweg:

Pz Rohrhofer, Holzstr. 44, ✆ 70002, I

Oberfucha:

P Maier, Oberfucha 3, ✆ 02739/2259, II
P Parzer, Oberfucha 55, ✆ 02739/2414, II

Palt:

Pz Edlinger, Lindengasse 22, ✆ 77622, II

Angern

Postal code: 3506; Telephone area code: 02739
P „Rethallerhof", Angern 5, ✆ 2232, II
P „Weinhof" Aufreiter, Angern 7, ✆ 2205, IV-V
Pz Wolfsberghof, Fa. Koller, Wolfsbergstr. 5, ✆ 2919, II

Hollenburg R

Postal code: 3506; Telephone area code: 02739
P Fidelsberger, Hauptstr. 51, ✆ 2241, II

Wagram o.d. Traisen

Postal code: 3133; Telephone area code: 02783
Gh Zum Schwarzen Adler, Wachaustr. 43, ✆ 8481
Pz Neuhold, Bäckerg. 6, ✆ 394, II

Traismauer R

Postal code: 3133; Telephone area code: 02783
Informationsstelle, ✆ 8555
Gh Zur Weintraube, Wiener Str. 23, ✆ 6349, III-IV
Gh Zum Schwan, Wiener Str. 12, ✆ 6236-0, III-IV
Gh Venusberg, Venusberger Str. 65, ✆ 6357, III
Pz Schopper, Kremserstr. 84, ✆ 8885, II
Pz Raderer, Kremser Str. 82, ✆ 8903, II
Pz Stiegler, E-Werkg. 23, ✆ 6769, I
Pz Kaiblinger, Kriemhildstr. 6, ✆ 6391,II
Pz Maushammer, Am Nasenberg 8, ✆ 7184, I
Pz Troll, Kellerg. 6, ✆ 8572, I
Pz Schreiblehner, Unt. Siebenbrunneng. 15, ✆ 7471, II
Campingplatz Koller, Donaustr. 56, ✆ 7130, Open: March-Nov

Gemeinlebarn

Postal code: 3133; Telephone area code: 02276
Gh Zum Jägerwirt, Tullner Str. 24, ✆ 2289, II
Pz Schmid, Ortsstr. 13, ✆ 2388, II

Sitzenberg-Reidling R

Postal code: 3454; Telephone area code: 02276
Gemeindeamt, ✆ 2241
Gh Schmid, Schlossbergstr. 20, ✆ 2274, II
Pz Marschik, Weinbergg. 6, ✆ 2557, II
Pz Maier, Weinbergg. 11, ✆ 2762, II
Pz Scharl, Schlossbergstr. 28a, ✆ 6577, II
Pz Maier, ✆ 2762, II

Hasendorf R

Postal code: 3454; Telephone area code: 02276
Gemeindeamt Sitzenberg-Reidling, ✆ 2241
Bh Jilch, Hasendorf 40, ✆ 6733 o. 6724, II

Michelndorf

Postal code: 3451; Telephone area code: 02275
Marktgemeinde Michelhausen, ✆ 5241
H Messerer, Michelndorf 22, ✆ 5278, III

Mitterndorf R

Postal code: 3451; Telephone area code: 02275
Marktgemeinde Michelhausen, ✆ 5241
H Hütt, Mitterndorf 12, ✆ 5254, IV

Atzelsdorf R

Postal code: 3451; Telephone area code: 02275
Gh Zum Grünen Baum, Atzelsdorf 30, ✆ 6812, II
Gh Burchhart, Atzelsdorf 29, ✆ 6802

Asparn R

Postal code: 3442; Telephone area code: 02272
P Haus Silvia, Steinparzg. 5, ✆ 7401, II

Altenwörth L

Postal code: 3474; Telephone area code: 02279
Pz Weinbauernof Waltner, Sigmarstr. 23, ✆ 2851

Kirchberg (6 km abseits) L

Postal code: 3413; Telephone area code: 02242
H Marienhof, Unterkirchbacherstr 39, ✆ 6263 (pick up service)

Gh Bonka, Oberkirchbacherstr. 61, ☎ 6645, (pick up service)

Zwentendorf R

Postal code: 3435; Telephone area code: 02277

ℹ Gemeindeamt, ☎ 2209

P Langsteiner, Hauptstr. 12, ☎ 22213, II

P Keiblinger, Ing. Aug. Kaglstr. 21, ☎ 2271, I

Pz Jeschko, Barbarag. 13, ☎ 2263, II

Pz Zelenka, Mariahilferg. 16, ☎ 2960, II

Pz Zelenka, Moosbierbaumerstr. 7, ☎ 2931, II

Pischelsdorf

Postal code: 3435; Telephone area code: 02277

Gh Hinterwallner, Pischelsdorf 33, ☎ 2484, II

Pz Marschall, Pischelsdorf 16, ☎ 2480, II

Campingplatz, Pappelallee 1, ☎ 2444

Erpersdorf:

Pz Schreiblehner, Kalmanng. 11, ☎ 3283, II

Langenschönbichl R

Postal code: 3442; Telephone area code: 02272

P Bauer, Hauptstr. 33, ☎ 02272/7261, II

Tulln a. d. Donau R

Postal code: 3430; Telephone area code: 02272

ℹ Tourist Information, ☎ 65836

H Zur Rossmühle, Hauptpl. 12, ☎ 62411-0, IV-VI

H Römerhof, Langenlebarner Str. 66, ☎ 62954, IV

Gh Beim Salzturm, Donaulände 34, ☎ 62658, III

Gh Zum Schwarzen Adler, Rathauspl. 7, ☎ 626760, III

P Zum Springbrunnen, Hauptpl.14a, ☎ 63115, III

P Renate, Langenlebarner Str. 92, ☎ 65077, II

Pz Elisabeth, Nussalle 5, ☎ 64227, II

Pz Keindl, Wilhelmstr. 16, ☎ 63337, II

Pz Hirsch, Am Mittergwendt 33, ☎ 65496, II

Pz Erika, Schießstattgasse 25, ☎ 63692, II

Pz Kainz, Mauthausg. 4, ☎ 62237, II-III

Pz Sabo, A. Bruckner-Str. 9a, ☎ 82698, II

Pz Spieß, Siegmundg. 4, ☎ 64133, II

Pz Schwanzer, J.-Reither-Str. 14, ☎ 62950, III

H Schiff Stadt Wien, Donaulände, ☎ 68386-2, II-III

Alpenvereinsherberge, Donaulände, ☎ 62692, I

Marc Aurel-Park, ☎ 65165, 130 Betten

Donaupark Camping, Hafenstraße, ☎ 52000

Trübensee (L):

Pz Leisser, Trübensee 6, ☎ 64702, I-II

Staasdorf:

Gh Tullnerfelderhof, Tullnerfeldstr. 23, ☎ 66440, III

Nitzing:

Gh Zum Meilenstein, Teichstr. 5, ☎ 64104

Langenlebarn

Postal code: 3425; Telephone area code: 02272

Gh Zum Roten Wolf, Bahnstr. 58, ☎ 62567, III

Gh Buchinger, Wiener Str. 5, ☎ 62527, III

Gh Zum Grünen Baum, Wiener Str. 43, ☎ 62505, III

Pz Augustin, E.-Pollak-Str. 3, ☎ 81955, II

Pz Weidlinger, Tullnerstr. 48, ☎ 62568, II

Muckendorf

Postal code: 3424; Telephone area code: 02242

ℹ Gemeindeamt Muckendorf-Wipfing, ☎ 312300

Gh „Wolf in der Au", Tullner Str. 1, ☎ 32130-0, III

Pz Svoboda, Leopold-Bonengl-G. 13, ☎ 70636 od. ☎ 0664/7987370, I-II

Greifenstein

Postal code: 3422; Telephone area code: 02242

ℹ Gemeindeamt Greifenstein, Hauptstr. 43, ☎ 32231 od. Gemeindeamt St. Andrä-Wördern, ☎ 31300.

Gh Brauner Bär, Hauptstr. 10, ☎ 32349

P Villa Neuwirth, Hadersfelder Str. 11, ☎ 33589

Pz Sappert, Hadersfelder Str. 3, ☎ 32828, II

Höflein

Postal code: 3400; Telephone area code 02243

Gh Zum Goldenen Anker, Hauptstr. 134, ☎ 80134, II

Gh Zum Roten Hahn, Hauptstr. 117, ☎ 80180, III

Pz Pernitz, Silberseestr. 65, ☎ 80326, II, III

Stockerau

Postal code: 2000; Telephone area code: 02266

ℹ Stadtgemeinde, ☎ 695

Hg City-Hotel, Hauptstr. 49, ☎ 62930, III-V

H Kolpinghaus, Adolf Kolpingstr. 1, ☎ 62600, III

Hg Garni, Hauptstr. 49, ☎ 62930, III

Hg Lenaustuben, Wolfikstr. 10, ☎ 62812, II, III

Gh Drei-Königshof, Hauptstr. 29, ☎ 62788-1

P Pummer, Adolf. Kolpingstr. 8, ☎ 62477, I-II

P Neumayr, Hanuschg. 4, ☎ 62708

Korneuburg

Postal code: 2100; Telephone area code: 02262

ℹ Tourismusbüro, ☎ 770-700

H Zur Sonne, Laaer Str. 12, ☎ 72198, III

Gh Zur Kaiserkrone, Hauptpl. 5, ☎ 72331, III

Bisamberg:

H Ökotel, Kaiserallee, 31, ☎ 75002, II

Langenzersdorf

Postal code: 2103; Telephone area code: 02244

Gh Roderich, Wiener Str. 59, ☎ 2415, III

Kritzendorf

Postal code: 3420; Telephone area code 02243

Appartements Kritzendorf, Hauptstr. 90, ☎ 33884 od. 33885, III

P Zum Eisernen Mann, Hauptstr. 164, ☎ 34253,III

Pz Zuber, Schubertg. 22, ☎ 32914, III

Klosterneuburg

Postal code: 3400; Telephone area code 02243

ℹ Tourismusverein, ☎ 32038

H Schrannenhof, Niedermarkt 17-19, ☎ 32072-13, V

H Anker, Niedermarkt 5, ☎ 32134, IV

P Alte Mühle, Mühleng. 36, ☎ 37788, IV

P Strohmer, Kierlinger Str. 94b, ☎ 260900, III-IV

H Höhenstrasse, Kollersteig 6, ☎ 32191, IV

H Buschenreiter, Wiener Str. 188, ☎ 32385-0, IV

P Appartementhaus Andrea, Medekstr. 15, ☎ 25022, IV

Pz Bürgerhaus Salmeyer, Stadtpl. 17, ☎ 32146, III

Pz Kranister, Leopoldstr. 4, ☎ 32252, III-IV

Pz Appartement Kutschera, Josef-Brenner-Str. 15, ☎ 32644, III, IV

Pz Artmann, Kierlinger Str. 29, ☎ 32774, II

Pz Gaubitzer, Josef-Brenner-Str. 17, ✆ 34438, III
Pz Urbanek, Hölzlg. 4, ✆ 32373, III
Pz Fux, Doppelng. 55, ✆ 26942, II
Pz Bockmayer, Doppelng. 53, ✆ 25291, II
Pz Zich, Wiener Str. 54, ✆ 36949, II
Pz Tiefenbacher/Gottlieb, Schubertg. 20, ✆ 36712, III
CVJF-Ferienheim, Maria Gugging (5.5 km west), Hütersteig 8, ✆ 83501
Donaupark-Camping, near train station Klosterneuburg-Kierling, ✆25877
ÖCC-Österreichischer Camping-Club, Freizeitzentrum in der Au, ✆ 85877

Weidling:

Pz Weidlinger Krauthahn, Hauptstr. 42, ✆ 35737, III
Pz Auer, Hauptstr. 7, ✆ 22111, III
Pz Deschka, Dehmg. 33, ✆ 35903, III
Pz Kaiservilla, Dehmg. 32, ✆ 35244, III
Pz Scheiner, Klosterneuburger G. 20, ✆ 35672, III

Vienna

Postal code: 1xx0 (xx = Bezirk); Telephone area code: 01
Wien-Hotels & Info: ✆ 24555, Open: daily 9-19. Internet: www.wien.info.

1. Bezirk:

H De France, Schottenring 3, ✆ 313680, VI
H Vienna Marriott, Parkring 12a, ✆ 51518-0, VI
H Zur Wiener Staatsoper, Krugerstr. 11, ✆ 5131274, VI
H Römischer Kaiser, Annag. 16, ✆ 5127751-0, VI
H Kärtnerhof, Grashofg. 4, ✆ 5121923, V-VI
H Post, Fleischm. 24, ✆ 515830, V-VI
H Austria, Wolfeng. 3/ Fleischm. 20, ✆ 51523, VI
H Tigra, Tiefer Gr. 18, ✆ 5339641, V-VI
H König Ungarn, Schulerstr. 10, ✆ 515840, VI
P Schweizer Pension, Heinrichsg. 2, ✆ 5338156, V
P Dr. Geissler, Postg. 14, ✆ 5332803, III-V
P Residenz, Ebendorferstr. 10, ✆ 40647860, V
P Sacher Appartm., Rotenturmstr. 1, ✆ 5333238, V-VI
P Christina, Hafnerst. 7, ✆ 5332961, V-VI
P Aviano, Marco d'Àvianog. 1, ✆ 5128330, V-VI
P Riedl, Georg-Coch-Pl. 3/4/10, ✆ 5127919, V

2. Bezirk:

H Franzenshof, Gr. Stadtgutg. 19, ✆ 2166282, IV
H City-Central, Taborstr. 8a, ✆ 21105, VI
H Hol. Inn Crowne Plaza, Handelskai 269, ✆ 72777, VI
H Adlon, Hofenederg. 4, ✆ 2166788, V
H Lassalle, Engerthstr. 173-175, ✆ 213150, VI
H Capri, Praterstr. 44-46, ✆ 2148404, V-VI
H Stefanie, Taborstr. 12, ✆ 21150-0, VI
H Cristall, Franzensbrückenstr. 9, ✆ 2168142, V-VI
H Nordbahn, Praterstr. 72, ✆ 21130-0, V-VI
H Vienna, Gr. Stadtgutg. 31, ✆ 2143317, V-VI
H Stadt Brünn, Rotensterng. 7a, ✆ 2146322, V
H Praterstern, Mayerg. 6, ✆ 2140123, III
H Wilhelmshof, Kl. Stadtgutg. 4, ✆ 2145521, V-VI
P Vienna Appartm., Darwing. 8/18, ✆ 0699/19259421, V-VI

3. Bezirk:

H Im Palais Schwarzenberg, Schwarzenbergpl. 9, ✆ 7984515, VI
H Vienna Sporthotel, Baumgasse 83, ✆ 79882010, VI
H Biedermeier, Landstrasser Hauptstr. 28, ✆ 71671-0, VI
H Roter Hahn Tourotel, Landstrasser Hauptstr. 40, ✆ 7132568-0, V-VI
H Don Bosco, Hagenmüllerg. 33, ✆ 71184555, III
H Goldene Spinne, Linke Bahng. 1a, ✆ 7124486, V
H Urania, Obere Weissgerberstr. 7, ✆ 7131711, IV-VI
P Bosch, Keilg. 13 (Nähe Südbhf.), ✆ 7986179, IV-V
P Kirchbichler, Landstrasser Hauptstr. 33, ✆ 7121068, III-IV

4. Bezirk:

H Carlton Opera, Schikanederg. 4, ✆ 5875302, V-VI
H Beim Theresianum, Favoritenstr. 52, ✆ 5051606, V-VI
H Congress, Wiedner Gürtel 34, ✆ 5055506, V-VI
H Prinz Eugen, Wiedner Gürtel 14, ✆ 5051741, VI
H Hol. Inn Wien City, Margarethenstr. 53, ✆ 58850, VI
H Drei Kronen, Schleifmühlg. 25, ✆ 5873289, IV
H Margareten, Margaretenstr. 30, ✆ 588150, III-V

5. Bezirk:

H Art Hotel Vienna, Brandmayerg. 7-9, ✆ 54451080, V-VI
H Amarante, Matzleinsdorfer Platz 1, ✆ 5442743, VI
H Ananas, Rechte Wienzeile 93-95, ✆ 546200, VI

6. Bezirk:

H President, Wallg. 23, ✆ 59990, VI
H Schneider, Getreidemarkt 5, ✆ 588380, VI
H Füger, Fügerg. 3, ✆ 59767290, IV
Kolpinghaus-Wien Zentral, Gumpendorfer Str. 39, ✆ 5875631, IV-V
P Haydn, Mariahilferstr. 57-59, ✆ 58744140, V
P Corvinus, Mariahilferstr. 57-59, ✆ 5877239, IV-V
P Esterhazy, Nelkengasse 3, ✆ 5875159, II-III
P Spachta, Gfrornerg. 2, ✆ 5970305, IV

7. Bezirk:

H Fürstenhof, Neubaugürtel 4, ✆ 5233267, IV-VI
H Hospiz, Kenyong. 15, ✆ 5231304, III
H Kugel, Siebensterng. 43, ✆ 5233355, IV
H Am Brillantengrund, Bandg. 4, ✆ 5233662, VI
H Admiral, Karl-Schweigerhoferg. 7, ✆ 521410, V-VI
H K&K Maria Theres., Kirchbergg. 6-8, ✆ 52123, VI
P Alla Lenz, Halbg. 3-5, ✆ 52369890, IV-VI
P Atrium, Burgg. 118, ✆ 5233114, III-V
P Anna, Zieglerg. 18/1, ✆ 5230106, IV-V
P Carantania, Kandlg. 35, ✆ 5267340, V
P Minu 3, Neubaug. 11, ✆ 5264652, III-IV
Jugendherberge, 7, Myrtheng. / Neustiftg. 85, ✆ 5236316

8. Bezirk:

H Concordia, Schönborng. 6, ✆ 4011810, VI
H Graf Stadion, Buchfeldg. 5, ✆ 4055284, VI
H Rathaus, Langeg. 13, ✆ 4060123, IV-V
H Zipser, Langeg. 49, ✆ 404540, V-VI
P Andreas, Schlösselg. 11, ✆ 4053488, III-V
P Baronesse, Lange G. 61, ✆ 4051061, V-VI
P Columbia, Kochg. 9, ✆ 40567570, V-VI
P Felicitas, Josefsg. 7, ✆ 4057212, IV
P Baltic, Skodag. 15, ✆ 4056266, III-IV

9. Bezirk:

H Arkadenhof, Viriotg. 5, ✆ 3100837, VI

H Atlanta, Währingerstr. 33, ✆ 4051239, V-VI

H Albatros, Liechtensteinstr. 89, ✆ 3173508, VI

H Bellevue, Althanstr. 5, ✆ 313480, VI

H Harmonie, Harmonieg. 5-7, ✆ 3176604, VI

H Strudlhof, Pasteurg. 1, ✆ 3192522, VI

H Mozart, Nordbergstr. 4, ✆ 3171537, IV-VI

P Bleckmann, Währingerstr. 15, ✆ 4080899, V

P Appartm., Van-Swieteng.8, ✆ 40936800, V

P Samwald, Hörlg. 4, ✆ 3177407, III

P Franz, Währingerstr. 12, ✆ 31040400, V

P Auer, Lazarettg. 3, ✆ 4062121 oder 4067103, III

P Astra, Alserstr. 32, ✆ 4024354, IV-V

10. Bezirk:

H Bosei, Gutheil-Schoderg. 9, ✆ 66106, VI

H Schweizerhof, Bauernmarkt 22, ✆ 5331931, VI

H/P Cyrus, Laxenburgerstr. 14, ✆ 6022578, IV

P Am Kurpark, Burgenlandg. 72, ✆ 6884508, IV-V

P Puzwidu, Himbergerstr. 69, ✆ 6882168, IV-V

P Wildenauer, Quellenstr. 120, ✆ 6042153, IV

11. Bezirk:

H Weber, Kaiser-Ebersdorfer-Str. 283-285, ✆ 7696973, V

P Czeczil, Zinnerg. 42, ✆ 0664/1075969, V

12. Bezirk:

H Altmannsdorf, Hoffingerg. 26-28, ✆ 801230 , VI

H Cryston, Gaudenzdorfer Gürtel 63, ✆ 8135682, V-VI

H Bergwirt, Maxingstr. 76, ✆ 8773413, V-VI

Gh Riede, Niederhofstr. 18, ✆ 8138576, IV

Jugendgästehaus Kolpingfamilie, 12, Bendlg. 10-12, ✆ 8135487

13. Bezirk:

H Cortina, Hietzinger Hauptstr. 134, ✆ 87774060, VI

H Auhof, Auhofstr. 205, ✆ 8775289, II

Gh Schneider-Gössl, Firmiang. 9-11, ✆ 8776109, V

14. Bezirk:

H Kavalier, Linzerstr. 165, ✆ 910020, VI

H Matauschek, Breitenseerstr. 14, ✆ 9823532, IV

P Rosengarten, Underreing. 33-35, ✆ 91452800, V

P Pillmeier, Sofienalpenstr. 9, ✆ 9792183, III-IV

P Anzengruber, Anzengruberstr. 59, ✆ 9792214, III-IV

P Voggeneder, Josef-Palme-Pl. 3, ✆ 9791207, VI

Jugendgästehaus Hütteldorf-Hacking, 14, Schlossbergg. 8, ✆ 8771501

Wien-West I, Hüttelbergstr. 40 (U4 bis Hütteldorf), ✆ 941449, 15. Juli bis 28. Aug.

Wien-West II, Hüttelbergstr. 80, ✆ 942314

15. Bezirk:

H Zur Stadthalle, Hackeng. 20 (Westbhf.), ✆ 9824272, V-VI

H Reither, Graumanng. 16, ✆ 8936841, VI

H Lucia, Hütteldorferstr. 79, ✆ 78652720, V

H Westbahn, Pelzg. 1, ✆ 9821480, V-VI

H Altwienerhof, Herklotzg. 6, ✆ 8926000, V-VI

P Fünfhaus, Sperrg. 12, ✆ 8923545, III

P Mailberg, Holocherg. 17, ✆ 9835634, II

P Zur Stadthalle, Hackeng. 33, ✆ 9824272, IV-V

16. Bezirk:

H Gallitzinberg, Johann-Staudstr. 32, ✆ 4198770, V

H Hadrigan, Maroltingerg. 68, ✆ 4932062, IV-V

H Zur Schwalbe, Degeng. 45, ✆ 4861181, V-VI

H Thalia, Lindauerg. 2-6, ✆ 4054513, IV

P Moser, Maroltingerg. 73, ✆ 4939173, IV

Schlossherberge am Wilhelminenberg, 16, Savoyenstr. 2, ✆ 4858503-700

17. Bezirk:

H Maté, Ottakringerstr. 34-36, ✆ 40455, VI

H Maté-Dependance, Bergsteigg. 22, ✆ 40466, V-VI

H Jäger, Hernalser Hauptstr. 187, ✆ 48666200, VI

H Stalehner, Ranftlgasse 11, ✆ 4082505, III-IV

P Haus Neuwaldegg, Neuwaldeggerstr. 23, ✆ 4863396, III

P Appartm. Bernhofer, Haslingerg. 74, ✆ 4810441, III-V

18. Bezirk:

H Thüringer Hof, Jörgerstr. 4-8, ✆ 401790, VI

H Faist, Schulg. 9, ✆ 4062405, III-IV

19. Bezirk:

H Clima Villenhotel, Nussbergg. 2c, ✆ 371516, VI

H Schild, Neustift a. Walde 97-99, ✆ 44040 440, V-VI

H Park Villa, Hasenauerstr. 12, ✆ 3675700, VI

H Glanzing, Glanzingg. 23, ✆ 47042720, VI

Gh Zur Agnes, Sieveringerstr. 221, ✆ 4401424, IV-V

Haus Döbling, 19, Gymnasiumstr. 85, ✆ 347631-16, Juli bis Sept. , I-II

20. Bezirk:

H Ibis Wien, Lassallerstr. 7a, ✆ 217700, V

H Vienna, Grosse Stadtgutg. 31, ✆ 2143317, V-VI

H Laselle, Engerthstr. 173-175, ✆ 21315, VI

Jugendgästehaus Brigittenau, 20, Friedrich Engels-Pl. 24, ✆ 3328294-0

21. Bezirk:

H Karolinenhof, Jedleseer Str. 75, ✆ 2787801, V-VI

H Berger, Brünnerstr. 126, ✆ 2921665, V-VI

Gh Strebersdorferhof, Rußbergstr. 46 (linkes Donauufer), Strebersdorf, ✆ 2925722, IV

P Dreikellerhof, Strebersdorfer Str. 172, Strebersdorf ✆ 2925407

22. Bezirk:

H Hillinger Donaucity, Erzherzog-Karlstr. 105, ✆ 20446460, V-VI

H Donauzentrum, Wagramerstr. 83-85, ✆ 2035545, VI

H Forum Wien, Wagramerstr. 21, ✆ 260200, VI

H Alte Donau, Wagramerstr. 51, ✆ 2044094, V

H Asperner Löwe, Aspernstr. 96, ✆ 2882088, IV

Gh Müllner, Esslinger Hauptstr. 82, ✆ 7747484, IV

23. Bezirk:

H Stasta, Lehmanng. 11, ✆ 8659788, V

H Hoffinger, Schuppeng. 19-21, ✆ 661020, V

Gh Aschauer, Kirchenpl. 5, ✆ 8884163, III

P Altmann, Breitenfurter Str. 515, ✆ 8898882, IV

P Erlaa, Erlaaer Str. 148, ✆ 6671204, V

Schwimmbad-Camping Rodaun, An der Au 2 (S-Bahn bis Liesing), ✆ 884154, 25. März bis 20. Nov.

Index of Places

Page numbers printed in green refer to the list of accomodations.

German language titles, most of them have english map legend: